'More work! Less pay!'

Manchester University Press

'More work! Less pay!'

Rebellion and repression in Italy, 1972–7

Phil Edwards

Manchester University Press

Manchester and New York

distributed in the United States exclusively by Palgrave Macmillan

Copyright © Phil Edwards 2009

The right of Phil Edwards to be identified as the author of this work has been asserted
by him in accordance with the Copyright, Designs and Patents Act 1988.

Published by Manchester University Press
Oxford Road, Manchester M13 9NR, UK
and Room 400, 175 Fifth Avenue, New York, NY 10010, USA
www.manchesteruniversitypress.co.uk

Distributed in the United States exclusively by
Palgrave Macmillan, 175 Fifth Avenue, New York,
NY 10010, USA

Distributed in Canada exclusively by
UBC Press, University of British Columbia, 2029 West Mall,
Vancouver, BC, Canada V6T 1Z2

British Library Cataloguing-in-Publication Data
A catalogue record for this book is available from the British Library

Library of Congress Cataloging-in-Publication Data applied for

ISBN 978 0 7190 7873 6 *hardback*

First published 2009

18 17 16 15 14 13 12 11 10 09   10 9 8 7 6 5 4 3 2 1

The publisher has no responsibility for the persistence or accuracy of URLs for external
or any third-party internet websites referred to in this book, and does not guarantee that
any content on such websites is, or will remain, accurate or appropriate.

Typeset by SNP Best-set Typesetter Ltd., Hong Kong
Printed in Great Britain
by the MPG Books Group

I said to him I ask myself sometimes now it's all over I ask myself what did it all mean our whole story all the things we did what did we get from all the things we did he said I don't believe it matters that it's all over I believe what matters is that we did what we did and that we think it was the right thing to do that's the only thing that matters I believe

Contents

List of tables

List of figures

Preface

FARE FIGHT IN MILAN

Ever since Milan's Communist-Socialist government proposed a fare rise for
the city's bus and underground services a constant direct action campaign has
been waged against the public transport authorities . . . The campaign, which
has attracted support from *autonomia* groups, *Circoli Giovanili* (Youth Circles),
the *Indians* and also the highly opportunistic Leninist groups *Lotta Continua*
and *MLS*, has been organised by the recently formed *Lega Libertaria* (Libertarian League).

A tube occupation one Saturday in October went like this . . . On arrival one
comrade walked through the ticket barrier, to be stopped by the ticket controller.
Several others appeared to give support to the first, and this exchange took
place: 'This is a demonstration against the proposed fare increases. It is not a
violent demonstration so please stay calm.' 'All right, but I must go and report
it.' 'Look! we said a peaceful demonstration, but not a pacifist one, so just make
yourself comfortable and stay put.' By now other comrades had succeeded in
blocking all the ticket machines with bits of metal, plastic and generous help-
ings of glue. Others were giving out leaflets and others inviting people through
the barriers for free.

. . .

While the *Lega Libertaria* recognise many other areas of struggle that need to
be fought and won, Milan's anarchists and libertarians are determined to make
these liberatory actions a daily feature of the city's life until everyone rides for
free. ('Enne' 1977)

I first read this news story in December 1977, when it appeared in the 'anar-
chist/anarca-feminist monthly' *Zero*. Even in that context it seemed like a
bulletin from another planet. I was taken aback by the group's unapologetically forceful version of non-violent direct action, and by its goal, which
seemed at once surprisingly mundane and wildly utopian. At the same time
I was fascinated by the glimpse of a seething pool of competing radical

groups, from Leninists to the enigmatic 'Indians', all united in the cause of cutting the cost of living through wildcat sabotage.

Years later, studying Italian politics, I remembered the Milan tube action and wondered if the literature could tell me how things had turned out. I couldn't find much on the period in English, but my attention was caught by Sidney Tarrow's study of an earlier Italian 'protest cycle' (Tarrow 1989). Tarrow showed how, in the late 1960s and early 1970s, a wave of contentious and disorderly activism spread across the country before being neutralised and absorbed into the political mainstream. This book traces the progress of a second wave of activism, which was not absorbed and neutralised but excluded and defeated. Its two progenitors are Tarrow and *Zero*.

This book began life as a doctoral thesis; its existence consequently owes a great deal to the enthusiasm, dedication and patience of Martin Bull and Jim Newell at the University of Salford as well as the insightful feedback provided by Jocelyn Evans and Mark Donovan. My thanks are also due to Anna Beasley at the University of Reading, without whose assistance neither the thesis nor the book would have been possible. I'm grateful for comments and suggestions received from Aldo Agosti, Grant Amyot, Gennaro Barbarisi, Chiara Cretella, Donatella della Porta, Bill Gamson, Steve Hellman, Yannis Karamihas, Rudy Lewanski, Marlen Logotheti, David Moss, Yota Papageorgiou, Gianni Piazza, Sandro Portelli, Olivier Turquet, Steve Wright and two anonymous reviewers. None of these individuals bears any responsibility for my findings, arguments or conclusions.

All source material is quoted in translation (my own); the original text is reproduced in chapter endnotes, which are not used for any other purpose.

The book's epigraph is my rendering of a passage from Nanni Balestrini's novel *Gli invisibili* (Balestrini 1987: 258).[1] This book is dedicated to Balestrini and to the memory of his collaborator, Primo Moroni: *i migliori fabbri*.

My particular thanks go to Zoia, Lewis and Eleanor, who have lived with this book for some time. For their sake as well as my own, I promise never to write another doctoral thesis.

Note

1 'gli ho detto qualche volta mi chiedo adesso che tutto è finito mi chiedo che cosa ha voluto dire tutta questa nostra storia tutto quello che abbiamo fatto che cosa abbiamo ottenuto con tutto quello che abbiamo fatto lui ha detto non credo che è importante che tutto è finito ma credo che la cosa importante è che abbiamo fatto quello che abbiamo fatto e che pensiamo che è stato giusto farlo questa è l'unica cosa importante io credo'.

List of abbreviations

BC   Brigate Comuniste ('Communist Brigades')
BPEF   Brigata Proletaria Erminio Ferretto ('Erminio Ferretto
         Proletarian Brigade')
BR   Brigate Rosse ('Red Brigades')
BR-WA   Brigate Rosse-Walter Alasia ('Red Brigades – Walter Alasia')
CAO   Comitati autonomi operai di via dei Volsci ['i Volsci']
         ('Autonomous workers' committees')
CCPO   Comitati Comunisti per il Potere Operaio ('Communist
         Committees for Worker's Power')
CeL   Comunione e Liberazione ('Communion and Liberation')
CGIL   Confederazione Generale Italiana dei Lavoratori ('General
         Italian Workers' Confederation')
CISL   Confederazione Italiana dei Sindacati Liberi ('Italian
         Confederation of Free Trade Unions')
CLN   Comitati di liberazione nazionale ('Committees of National
         Liberation')
CoCoCe   Comitato Comunista di Centocelle ('Centocelle Communist
         Committee')
CoCoRi   Comitati Comunisti Rivoluzionari ('Revolutionary Communist
         Committees')
CoCoRo   Comitati Comunisti Romani ('Roman Communist
         Committees')
CPM   Collettivo Politico Metropolitano ('Metropolitan Political
         Collective')
CPO   Collettivi Politici Operai [*Rosso*] ('Workers' Political
         Collectives')
CPV   Collettivi politici veneti per il potere operaio ('Political
         collectives of the Veneto for worker's power')
CUB   Comitato Unitato di Base ('United Rank and File Committee')
DC   Democrazia Cristiana ('Christian Democracy')
ETA   Euzkadi Ta Azkatasuna ('Basque Homeland and Freedom')

FARO	Fronte Armato Rivoluzionario Operaio ('Revolutionary Armed Workers' Front')
FCA	Formazioni Comuniste Armate ('Armed Communist Formations')
FCC	Formazioni Comuniste Combattenti ('Communist Fighting Formations')
FGCI	Federazione Giovanile Comunista Italiano ('Italian Communist Youth Federation')
FLM	Federazione Lavoratori Metalmeccanici ('Metalworkers' Federation')
FLN	Front de Libération Nationale ('National Liberation Front')
FRAP	Frente Revolucionario Autifascista y Patriótico ('Revolutionary Anti-fascist Patriotic Front')
FUORI	Fronte Unitario Omosessuale Rivoluzionario Italiano ('Italian United Revolutionary Homosexual Front')
GAP	Gruppi di azione patriottica [1943–5] ('Patriotic action groups'); Gruppi d'Azione Partigiana [1970–3] ('Partisan Action Groups')
LAC	Lotta Armata per il Comunismo ('Armed Struggle for Communism')
MCR	Movimento Comunista Rivoluzionario (Revolutionary Communist Movement')
MLS	Movimento di lavoratori e studenti ('Movement of workers and students'); Movimento di lavoratori per il socialismo ('Movement of workers for socialism')
MPL	Movimento Popolare dei Lavoratori ('Popular Workers' Movement')
MS	Movimento Studentesco ('Student Movement')
MSI	Movimento Sociale Italiano ('Italian Social Movement')
NAP	Nuclei Armati Proletari ('Armed Proletarian Nuclei')
PAC	Proletari Armati per il Comunismo ('Armed Proletarians for Communism')
PAIL	Proletari Armati in Lotta ('Armed Proletarians in Struggle')
PCd'I	Partito Comunista d'Italia [1921–43] ('Communist Party of Italy')
PCI	Partito Comunista Italiano [1943–90] ('Italian Communist Party')
Pd'A	Partito d'Azione ('Action Party')
PdUP	Partito di Unità Proletaria ('Proletarian Unity Party')
PLI	Partito Liberale Italiano ('Italian Liberal Party')
POp	Potere Operaio pisano ('Worker's Power, Pisa')

POv-e	Potere Operaio veneto-emiliano ('Worker's Power of Veneto and Emilia')
PRI	Partito Repubblicano Italiano ('Italian Republican Party')
PSDI	Partito Socialista Democratico Italiano ('Italian Democratic Socialist Party')
PSI	Partito Socialista Italiano ('Italian Socialist Party')
PSIUP	Partito Socialista Italiano di Unità Proletaria ('Socialist Party of Proletarian Unity')
PSLI	Partito Socialista dei Lavoratori Italiani ('Italian Workers' Socialist Party')
RAF	Rote Armee Fraktion ('Red Army Fraction')
UCC	Unità Comuniste Combattenti ('Fighting Communist Units')
UIL	Unione Italiana dei Lavoratori ('Italian Union of Workers')

1

Introduction

A long wave of direct action spread across Italy between 1972 and 1977. Factory workers went on strike without union approval, walking out or occupying their workplaces; empty buildings were squatted and converted as 'social centres'; council tenants withheld the rent; groups of women went on 'can't pay? won't pay!' shoplifting trips. The streets were also busy, with marches and demonstrations running at around two per week throughout the period.

Sidney Tarrow has analysed an earlier wave of contentious activism in terms of a 'protest cycle' or 'cycle of contention' (Tarrow 1989). In cycles of contention, Tarrow argues, social movements introduce new forms of action to society as a whole: 'Cycles of contention are the crucibles within which new cultural constructs born among critical communities are created, tested and refined' (Tarrow 1998: 145). The rise and fall of a cycle of contention is the product of 'the interaction among mass mobilisation, movement organisers, and traditional associations' (Tarrow 1989: 18). The cycle peaks with widespread diffusion and emulation of the new protest tactics, then declines as existing organisations succeed in assimilating and neutralising them. The outcome is the demobilisation of the new movements and the absorption of most of their new repertoire of action into mainstream politics.

Tarrow described how, in the early 1970s, a wave of contentious and disorderly movements spread from the universities to the industrial north of Italy before being neutralised by the Partito Comunista Italiano (PCI; 'Italian Communist Party'). The PCI's qualified endorsement of the movement's tactics led to the demobilisation of the movement and the achievement, in modified form, of its principal goals, by way of an expansion of the political repertoire endorsed by the PCI. The PCI in this period occupied an ambivalent position, as a supposedly 'anti-system' party which nevertheless played a significant role in the Italian political system; this put it in a strong position as a political 'gatekeeper'. The outcome of the cycle was positive: under pressure from the movements, the PCI pushed back the boundaries of acceptable political activity. The activism of the mid- to late 1970s, for Tarrow, is an after-effect of this cycle. As the cycle declined, isolated activists adopted more and more extreme tactics in an attempt to regain the initiative, leading ultimately to the adoption of terrorist tactics: 'The extraparliamentary groups used mass mobilisation to outbid the unions and the PCI, while the terrorists used violence to outbid the extraparliamentary groups' (Tarrow 1989: 310).

In this book, I argue that the late 1970s wave should be given more attention; it should, in fact, be seen as a second cycle of contention. The movements of this second cycle include: the 'area of Autonomia', based in factories and working-class neighbourhoods and active between 1972 and 1977; a wave of activism among young people which gave rise to the 'proletarian youth movement' of 1975–6 and the 'movement of 1977'; and the left-wing terrorist or 'armed struggle' milieu, which can be considered as a social movement in its own right. Like Tarrow, I emphasise the role played by the PCI as a 'gatekeeper' to the political system. I argue that the outcome of the second cycle, like that of the first, was determined by the interaction between contentious social movements and the PCI. In this second cycle, however, the PCI operated as a hostile or exclusive gatekeeper. I suggest that the PCI's hostile engagement with the second cycle had lasting effects for the party, as well as for the movements of the cycle. The PCI committed itself to a narrower and more explicitly constitutional range of activities and values; the result was a lasting contraction of the party's ideological repertoire, and consequently of the repertoire of mainstream politics.

In Chapter 2 I review the events of the 1966–72 cycle of contention, revising Tarrow's account. I also trace the beginnings of the second cycle, showing that the 'early risers' of the cycle were active as early as 1970. Before turning to the second cycle, in Chapter 3 I follow the PCI's ideological development from the Fascist period to the party's assumption of a 'gatekeeper' role in the 1970s. I trace the development of the 'Italian road to socialism' and the repeated confrontations between left and right within the party, ending with Enrico Berlinguer's 'historic compromise' programme. I show how Berlinguer's leadership enabled the party to engage constructively with the first cycle, but made a hostile engagement with the second cycle inevitable.

I look at the second cycle of contention in Chapter 4, following the cycle through the phases of innovation (1972–3), diffusion (1974–6) and engagement (1976–7). I show how the spread and development of the movements was stymied by the hostility of mainstream political parties, the PCI above all. I also show how the armed groups profited from the disarray of the mass movements.

Chapter 5 focuses on the PCI's perception and presentation of the movements of the second cycle, from 1972 to 1977. I analyse the party's presentational or 'framing' strategies through analysis of material from the party's daily newspaper *l'Unità*. Key framings include 'adventurist', applied to radical groups in the early part of the cycle; 'disorganised lumpenproletariat', applied to the youth movement later in the cycle; 'anti-democratic extremist', applied to the armed groups at the close of the cycle; and, most prominently, 'provocateur', applied with different qualifications to mass movements, organised autonomists and armed groups, throughout the period. I argue that the weight given to different framings corresponds to the different stages of the PCI's interaction with the movements.

In Chapter 6 this analysis is validated against quantitative data on mass disorder and armed actions. I also use these data to support an account of the aftermath of the PCI's engagement with the mass movements. I show that armed actions rose sharply between 1977 and 1978 before declining more slowly, and that the proportion of armed actions involving personal violence rose as the frequency of actions increased, then rose again as the overall frequency declined. The closure of the cycle appears to have promoted armed activity, and its more violent forms in particular.

In Chapter 7 I review the effects of the PCI's negative engagement for the party itself, as well as the movements. I also look in depth at the key question of violence and ask whether the movements of the second cycle could have received a more inclusive engagement – or a better historical write-up. I conclude by drawing broader lessons about the interaction between social movements and 'gatekeeper' parties.

Chapter 8 is an appendix setting out the conceptual basis of this analysis in greater detail. Key concepts include the political opportunity structure, the process of framing, the tactical repertoire and the cycle of contention. I draw these together in a modified version of Tarrow's 'cycle of contention' model, focusing on the interaction between social movements and 'gatekeeper' organisations.

This is a book about social movements which were confrontational and thoughtful, creative and pugnacious, responsible for wild creativity and brutal violence. The autonomists' dissident Marxism combined unpredictably with the creativity of the youth movements and the broader resentment provoked by attacks on living standards, in a milieu defined by a restless enthusiasm for new ways to take political action and new ways to live together. The result, encapsulated in the slogan which gives this book its title, was a spirit of intransigent, rebellious mockery, directed as much against the institutions of the Left as against capitalism or the State.

This book is also about how, by the end of the 1970s, those movements had been defeated. The PCI had dealt constructively with opposition from the Left only a few years earlier, appropriating what the movements of the first cycle had to offer while marginalising their diehard loyalists. The party's failure to engage similarly with the later cycle was a tragic error. The PCI showed its greatest commitment to the Italian political system at the moment when that system was at its most blocked. By dooming the movements to a bitter and costly defeat, the party deprived both itself and the system of a potential source of renewal:

> at that point everything breaks everything is broken but to break everything it takes the all-party alliance it takes the armed forces it takes the judiciary it takes the whole of the mass media it's never been known in a modern state for it to take this whole array of forces to put a stop to what was defined as a minority (Balestrini 1989: 130)[1]

Note

1 'allora tutto si rompe tutto si è rotto però per rompere tutto occorre l'unione di tutti i partiti occorrono le forze armate occorre la magistratura occorrono tutti i mass media non è mai successo in uno stato moderno che ci voglia tutto questo spiegamento di forze per far fuori quella che viene definita una minoranza'.

2

The Hot Autumn and after: a cycle of contention reconsidered

The wave of contentious activism which spread across Italy in the late 1970s took many forms. Autonomist activism spread from the factories to working-class communities; youth groups demanded the 'right to luxury'; organised students brought entire campuses and city centres to a halt. Alongside these public events ran the gradual growth of armed actions by small, clandestine groups. As well as major groups such as the Brigate Rosse (BR; 'Red Brigades'), the late 1970s saw actions by dozens of smaller armed groups and hundreds of more ephemeral formations. By the end of the decade, obdurate political opposition and saturation policing had driven the mass movement from the streets and suppressed the armed milieu; the larger and more coherent armed groups, such as the BR, were all that remained.

To understand this cycle of contention, we need to go back a few years. The events of the late 1970s have been plausibly presented, notably by Tarrow (1989), as a morbid after-effect of an earlier cycle of contention. Following the 'Hot Autumn' of 1969, mainstream Italian political parties (primarily the PCI) succeeded in 'riding the tiger' of radical activism. In response, Tarrow argues, radical activists launched a succession of increasingly extreme, illegal and violent actions, 'outbidding' one another in an attempt to galvanise a working-class constituency which was now lost to them.

An alternative reading, which I shall be putting forward, is that the events of 1966–72 and 1972–7 are better seen as two separate cycles, whose different outcomes tell us something about the factors which govern the progress of cycles of contention. In particular, I shall be arguing that the PCI played a determining role in both these cycles: acting as 'gatekeeper' to the political system, the PCI endorsed and co-opted the first wave of activism, then rejected and denounced the second. Whichever interpretation we adopt, to understand the 1972–7 events we need to start six years earlier.

Innovation: 1966–8

The unrest of the cycle of 1966–72 began in the universities. The University of Trento in the north of Italy saw the first major protest. Trento's sociology degree, introduced in 1962, was the first ever offered in Italy (Lumley 1990: 58). In 1965 the university authorities proposed, with the approval of the official student body, to redesignate the five-year sociology degree as a three-year degree in 'social and political sciences'.

> The students are opposed. On the 24th of January 1966, meeting in a general assembly (a form of action almost unheard-of at the time) they decide to occupy the university. The occupation lasts eighteen days and ends with a victory . . . The struggle which ends in victory on the reformist objective of the degree . . . makes the students aware of their own power [and] validates a more or less new form of struggle (Silj 1977; quoted in Balestrini and Moroni 1997: 208)[1]

Activism at Trento continued and grew. In March 1967, students held a week of discussions in the town on imperialism and the Vietnam War, while calling a two-day strike at the university. Meanwhile, occupations had spread. 1967 saw a 55-day occupation of the Politecnico in Milan, with the participation of some lecturers and the submission of all decisions to a general assembly (Lumley 1990: 64). In February 1967, the occupation of the Sapienza building at the University of Pisa brought together students from several different universities. The Pisa occupation was highly politicised; a series of demands, later known as the Pisan Theses, looked beyond issues of university reform to question the role of the student within capitalist society. Meanwhile at Trento, student protest had brought the university to a halt by the autumn of 1967; many students, and some lecturers, set up a radical 'anti-university' or 'negative university'. The universities of Turin and Genoa, as well as the Cattolica ('Catholic University') in Milan, were occupied in November; by January 1968 half of Italy's 36 universities were occupied (Balestrini and Moroni 1997: 228).

The student movement set a precedent through its use of new and disruptive forms of protest and organisation: unofficial strikes, demonstrations, mass assemblies, the occupation of university buildings. These new tactics, together with innovative analysis, were brought to bear on local student grievances. The key innovations were the occupation and the assembly, both of which served political as well as tactical purposes:

> The occupation was only the framework within which the students arrayed a broader tactical repertoire, including public forms of protest like marches and public meetings, traffic blockages, forced entries into classrooms, department stores and art exhibits, and more routine forms – petitions, audiences and assemblies. . . . The 'wild' forms of action of the student

movement were part of a strategy designed to create new political space. (Tarrow 1989: 153–4)

The assembly was a particularly 'loaded' form, combining organisational, tactical and ideological innovation; an assembly was not simply a mass meeting but a body which made binding decisions and was open on an equal basis to all participants in an action. 'Lively and confrontationist, the new movement was notable not only for its size, but also for its efforts to redefine the very notion of politics, constructing forms of organisation – above all, the permanent "assembly" – which simply and brutally swept the traditional student bodies aside' (Wright 2002: 89).

Diffusion: 1968–9

'From the summer of 1968, the student movement in the universities ceased to concentrate on political activity within the educational institutions. ... The national conferences were dominated by discussion of worker–student unity, and the 'worker commissions' in the universities became the main locus of activity' (Lumley 1990: 112). This shift of focus was influenced by the *operaista* ('workerist') analysis which underlay the Pisan Theses. *Operaismo* in its developed form was a minority presence within the movement; old-school Communist, Maoist and anti-imperialist forms of radicalism dominated in many areas, notably at Trento and Milan's Statale ('State University'). However, the themes of the Theses were widely influential. The Theses followed the readings of Marx associated with Mario Tronti's journal *Classe Operaia* (1964–6) and its predecessor, Raniero Panzieri's *Quaderni Rossi* (1961–5); the authors were in contact with the networks established by Tronti and Panzieri, and would play a major role in the local group Potere Operaio pisano (POp; 'Worker's Power, Pisa') (Wright 2002: 94).

Panzieri held that a revolutionary challenge to Italian capitalism was possible and desirable, but could only come from a united working class; working-class unity was seen as a goal to be worked for, rather than a state which had been achieved within existing working-class organisations. Panzieri set this problematic of 'class composition' in the context of the capitalist restructuring associated with the Italian 'economic miracle', which appeared to have left the working class disunited, disengaged and politically passive. To address this situation, *Quaderni Rossi* printed sociological analyses (the so-called *inchiesta operaia* ('worker's inquiry')) as well as theoretical pieces.

Tronti broke with Panzieri in transposing the workerist stress on working-class action to the theoretical plane. The rationale of the break was set out in

Tronti's essay *'Lenin in Inghilterra'* ('Lenin in England'), published in the first issue of *Classe Operaia*.

> Capitalist society has its laws of development: they have been formulated by economists, applied by governments and endured by the workers. But who will discover the laws of development of the working class? Capital has its history and its historians to write it. But who will write the history of the working class? Capitalist exploitation has taken many forms of political rule. But how shall we achieve the next form of dictatorship, the dictatorship of the workers organised as ruling class? . . . We ourselves have put capitalist development first, workers' struggles second. This is wrong. We need to reverse the problem, change its sign, begin from first principles: and the first principle is the struggle of the working class. Where capital is developed on the social scale, capitalist development is subordinate to workers' struggles: it follows on from them and has to shape the political mechanisms of its own production accordingly. (Tronti 1964; quoted in Balestrini and Moroni 1988: 74 (omitted from 1997 revised edition))[2]

The title of the piece refers to Marx's work in the British Museum:

> The masterstroke of the Leninist strategy was to take Marx to St Petersburg: only the worker's point of view could be capable of this level of revolutionary audacity. We are attempting to make the journey in reverse, in the same adventurous scientific spirit of discovery. 'Lenin in England' means the search for a new Marxist practice for the workers' party (Tronti 1964; quoted in Balestrini and Moroni 1988: 79)[3]

Tronti's journal tended towards theory-driven abstraction while celebrating spontaneous working-class direct action; this combination, which would be faithfully reproduced by acolytes such as Toni Negri, contrasted with the caution and empiricism of Panzieri's journal. The *Classe Operaia* group itself harboured major differences over the question of organisation. Tronti, with allies such as Massimo Cacciari and Alberto Asor Rosa, believed that the group should work within the PCI. A second group, including Negri and Franco Piperno, rejected the PCI and believed that a new Leninist working-class organisation was needed. A third group, influenced by libertarian strands of Marxism, broke with the group in 1964 in reaction against the authoritarian Leninism of both these groups; members included Riccardo d'Este and Gianfranco Faina (Centro d'Iniziativa Luca Rossi 1998). In 1966, with the ascendancy of the Right within the PCI apparently assured, Tronti wound up the group, although his own heterodoxy soon saw him excluded from PCI membership (Grandi 2003: 24).

The Pisan Theses, influenced by both Panzieri and Tronti, analysed university education as a process of training the skilled workforce of the future. Education was 'the place of production of qualified labour-power'; students should be seen as labour-power 'in its process of qualification' (Wright 2002: 95). Tendencies such as these helped to shift the movement away from university-based issues and towards intervention in industrial struggles. Negri, based at the University of Padua, was a member of the workerist group Potere Operaio veneto-emiliano (POv-e; 'Worker's power of Veneto and Emilia'), which had a strong presence at the petro chemical plant of Porto Marghera in the Veneto. The summer of 1968 saw a series of strikes around the demand of a flat-rate pay rise. The strikes sidelined the Communist-affiliated Confederazione Generale Italiana dei Lavoratori (CGIL; 'General Italian Workers' Confederation'), which dominated the plant; mass meetings echoed the repertoire of the student movement. In Milan, Pirelli workers formed a 'United Rank and File Committee' (Comitato Unitato di Base; CUB), which operated outside union structures; meetings, held outside the factory, were open to student activists.

The right wing of the PCI viewed these new forms of activity with distrust. In 1968 PCI right-winger Giorgio Amendola wrote dismissively of 'the thesis, which tickles the vanity of certain groups of students, of a revolutionary initiative which would allegedly fall to the student movement, faced with the supposed opportunistic inertia and integration into the system of the working class, and with the bureaucratisation of its "traditional" bodies (unions and parties)' (quoted in Echaurren and Salaris 1999: 89).[4] The PCI-aligned film-maker Pier Paolo Pasolini went further. After students and police had clashed at Valle Giulia in Rome, Pasolini attacked the students in poetry:

> You have the faces of spoilt brats.
> Breeding will out.
> . . .
> Yesterday at Valle Giulia when you were fighting the cops
> I was on the side of the cops!
> Because the cops come from poor families.
> (quoted in Echaurren and Salaris 1999: 91)[5]

Throughout 1968, CUBs were set up at factories in Milan and elsewhere. New tactics continued to be developed and disseminated.

A whole new vocabulary of strike forms developed, from the *sciopero bianco* (go-slow) to the *sciopero a singhiozzo* (literally, hiccup strikes), the *sciopero a scacchiera* (chessboard strikes), the *corteo interno* (marches around the factory grounds to carry along undecided workers), and the *presidio al cancello* (blocking factory gates to prevent goods from entering or leaving the plant). These innovations were not 'wild'; their logic was to create the maximum amount of disruption with the minimum expenditure of resources. (Tarrow 1989: 188; emphases in original)

In April 1969 Mirafiori, Fiat's showcase factory in Turin, was hit by light-ning stoppages in support of rank-and-file demands for flat-rate pay rises. The growing unrest at Mirafiori was promoted by members of both POv-e and POp within the factory, publicised by a new workerist journal, *La Classe*, and supported by the Turin student movement. By June 1969 hundreds of Turin workers were attending 'worker/student assemblies'. A participant recalled: 'The worker/student assembly was a kind of spontaneous permanent political structure . . . but it was also direct democracy, a place where workers came to talk to other workers, giving first-hand accounts of the struggles they were carrying out in the factory' (quoted in Grandi 2003: 70).[6]

The workerists advocated organising in support of immediate demands, with the longer-term aim of decoupling wages from productivity. Their programme was encapsulated in the slogans *'È ora, è ora potere a chi lavora!'* ('Power to the workers!') and *'Più salario, meno lavoro!'* ('More pay, less work!'); these coherently workerist demands had considerable appeal on the factory floor, and would long outlast their immediate context. The slogan 'from the factory to society' gained currency; the movement demanded a flat-rate 'social wage' to be paid to all, in the factory or outside.

In July 1969 a strike was called in protest against high rents in the city; a demonstration in support of the strike, held outside the factory gates in Corso Traiano on 3 July, was attacked by the police. A running battle with the police developed, which spread to surrounding suburbs and continued through the night. Hailing the Corso Traiano 'insurrection', *La Classe* called a national conference of CUBs in Turin the same month. Ideological divisions were now becoming apparent, both between workerists and other leftists and within the workerist camp itself. A group around *La Classe*, which dominated POv-e, combined a tight focus on factory-based activism with a stress on centralised Leninist organisation. After the Turin CUB conference this group launched a new, national organisation under the name of Potere Operaio. A second organisation, Lotta Continua ('Continuous Struggle'), brought together students, former members of POp and POv-e dissidents from the *La Classe* line (Wright 2002: 124–6). From the outset Lotta Continua oriented itself towards working-class activity in society at large; *La Classe* charged that, for them, 'relating to the workers' struggle and relating to an old people's home are the same thing' (Bobbio 1988: 47).[7] Lotta Continua also challenged Potere Operaio organisationally, countering the latter's organisational rigidity with a stress on spontaneity. Meanwhile, student activists at the Statale in Milan, together with Pirelli CUB activists, had formed the Trotskyist-influenced Avanguardia Operaia; a rival, Maoist tendency based at the Statale took the name of Movimento Studentesco (MS; 'Student Movement'). The MS gave rise to the Movimento di lavoratori e studenti (MLS; 'Movement of workers and students'), later reorganised as the Movimento di lavoratori per il socialismo ('Movement of workers for socialism').

During 1968–9, tactical and ideological innovations spread from their origin into different geographical and social areas, both through diffusion by movement organisations and through spontaneous adoption. We can see this process at work in the interaction between student and worker activists, as well as both groups' encounter with the workerists.

Engagement: 1969–70

From 1969 onwards the increasing political salience of the new movements prompted a resurgence in activity by the unions. Wage levels across Italian industry were set through three-year contracts between unions and employers' organisations, which were due for renewal in 1969. CGIL organisers worked to integrate the more innovative forms of industrial action into contractual campaigns. As Franco Berardi of Potere Operaio recalled, 'again and again, autonomous organisations organised strikes in a single section of a factory, after which the union came in, asked all the workers what their demand was, and used it to regain control of a struggle which had completely got out of their hands' (quoted in Grandi 2003: 110).[8]

The contracts signed in December 1969 were highly favourable. Wage rises outstripped inflation; working hours were to be reduced in stages, with a 40-hour week promised within three years; parity between clerical and manual workers, a central workerist demand, was conceded in principle. December 1969 also saw the passage of the *Statuto dei Lavoratori* ('Workers' Statute'). This became law the following May, together with a general amnesty for those who had been charged with offences relating to industrial action: disorderly and violent acts committed by factory activists ceased to *have been* criminal offences. Feeling that the government and the employers had been forced to back down, some groups began campaigning on new or modified demands: abolition of piecework, mass regrading, an immediate 40-hour week (Lumley 1990: 250). However, many workers saw the contracts as a result with which they could be content. This view was encouraged by the unions, whose own position within the workplace had been greatly enhanced; for instance, the Statute entitled them to hold meetings in work time (Lumley 1990: 251).

The tension between these two positions resulted in a period in which the unions 'rode the tiger' of workplace militancy. Innovative and disruptive workplace activism continued and even spread, but it took place with union approval and was increasingly subordinated to union objectives. A typical example of this contradictory evolution was the delegates' movement, which emerged in 1968 and flourished after the settlement of 1969. This was a movement calling for factory councils outside the control of the unions: a type of organisation long advocated by 'council communists', a significant minority on the Italian far Left. However, the councils which emerged in 1969–70 showed enormous variation in both function and form. While some mounted a consistent challenge to the union hierarchy, others merely monitored the implementation of union agreements. In some cases delegates were elected from the workforce as a whole, as council communism would suggest; however, some were elected from union members and some directly appointed by union officials (Wright 2002: 128).

The workerist groups treated the councils with a mixture of disdain and suspicion. The councils were seen as a step backwards from earlier levels of worker participation; some workerists campaigned against them under the slogan 'we are all delegates' (Lumley 1990: 258). The workerists also feared, with some justification, that the councils would offer a back door through which the union hierarchy could re-establish itself. In December 1970 the CGIL endorsed workplace councils as 'the rank-and-file structure of the new unitary union': the plan was for a general merger of the trade union confederations to unite the CGIL with the centre-right Confederazione Italiana dei Sindacati Liberi (CISL; 'Italian Confederation of Free Trade Unions') and the centre-left Unione Italiana dei Lavoratori (UIL; 'Italian Union of Workers'), with workplace delegates replacing party-approved union officials (Wright 2002: 128). In the event unification was only achieved by the metalworkers' sections of the three main unions; these federated in 1972 as the Federazione Lavoratori Metalmeccanici (FLM; 'Metalworkers' Federation') under the leadership of Bruno Trentin, leading member of the CGIL. By this time, most workplace councils were under union control.

However, it would be wrong to associate the re-establishment of union control with a decline in activism, or to assume that the union hierarchy was working solely to combat and resist pressures from below. 'Tactical innovation developed in the strike wave only after it had peaked in the protest cycle as a whole, and continued . . . *after* the unions had re-established control' (Tarrow 1989: 187; emphasis in original). The unions embraced innovative forms of action while rejecting the political perspectives which had accompanied them. In doing so, the unions were not only protecting their own interests but responding to their members' demands – which in turn became more moderate as the unions re-established control. Lotta Continua, whose consistent opportunism made it something of a weathervane for the far left, abandoned its opposition to factory councils in October 1972.

According to Tarrow's account, this was the period in which the movement succeeded, to the benefit of society at large and the discomfiture of a hardline activist minority. A new tactical repertoire was adopted by a legitimate political actor 'in more diffuse and less militant form' (Tarrow 1998: 145); the organised groups which had grown from the movement were left beached by the loss of their constituency. However, the process of engagement appears rather more complex.

Firstly, the engagement was not a single interaction, in which the movement's challenge to the position of a gatekeeper was parried with a recognisable but neutralised version of the challenger's repertoire. Rather, the challenger asserted different elements of its repertoire, which the PCI and CGIL variously adopted, modified or rejected. This iterative process was mediated through *framing*: the presentation, interpretation and reinterpretation of the challenger's repertoire. A three-way filtering process resulted. New forms of industrial action such as the go-slow were sanctioned and adopted by the unions. Spontaneous mass meetings, delegate councils and the goal of flat-rate pay rises were given 'official' status after being modified to make them acceptable to both the movement and the union. Sabotage, worker–student assemblies and the 'social wage' were rejected outright by being framed as criminal or absurd, to be espoused only by marginalised minorities.

Secondly, tactical repertoires were not the only element at stake in the engagement phase. The movement brought a complex of interrelated practices, organisational forms and beliefs, all of which underwent processes of filtering and rejection. A typical example was the 'worker–student assembly': a form of organisation imbued with the movement's inclusive egalitarianism, and a radical alternative to union-approved forms. Little survived of the practice of open assemblies apart from sporadic provision for the election of council delegates by non-union members. The egalitarianism of the movement, meanwhile, survived only within the factory, with continuing and often successful campaigns against the rigidities of job classification.

Thirdly, the driving force of the engagement phase was not the union leaders' desire to broaden their appeal or even their need to overcome non-union opponents. The impetus for the adoption (and ultimate neutralisation) of new forms and repertoires came from below, both from activists who wanted to realise their goals through the union and from those who denounced union shortcomings. While Tarrow is right to note that the outcome was a genuine step forward, this outcome only became possible when the unions responded to their members' demands and criticisms. The CGIL's recognition of workplace councils, for instance, was a genuine (if heavily qualified) move towards rank-and-file control, and one which would not have been made without sustained pressure from its membership. It follows that the difference between the innovations which were absorbed by the union movement and those which were rejected was not inherent in the nature of the innovations. The line of demarcation was drawn by the historically contingent outcome of a conflictual and open-ended engagement, and could not have been drawn in advance.

The movement which created the Hot Autumn should thus be credited with ideological and organisational innovations as well as the introduction of new tactical repertoires. Moreover, the process by which some innovations were accepted and others rejected was an open-ended series of framing transactions between a contentious movement and an institutional 'gatekeeper', represented by the PCI and its union ally, the CGIL. Crucially, the choice of which innovations would be accepted and which rejected was decided not by an objective judgment of 'extremism' or disorderliness, but by this process of negotiation – a process strongly influenced by pressure from below. All these qualifications to Tarrow's account will be significant when we come to consider the later cycle of contention.

Aftermath: 1971–3

According to Tarrow's account of the first cycle of contention, the period from 1971 to 1980 can be understood as a long-drawn-out aftermath of the Hot Autumn of 1969–70. The modified model of the first cycle, by contrast, makes it possible to envisage a second cycle, beginning as the first cycle went into decline; in this perspective, the 'aftermath' phase of the first cycle ended in 1973 at the latest.

After the Hot Autumn, strike activity continued to rise; it peaked in 1971, before dropping back below the level of 1969 in the following year (Tarrow 1989: 190). Industrial action was now increasingly oriented towards union-approved goals. Some factories, particularly in Milan and the longtime workerist stronghold of the Veneto, continued to see levels of militancy sufficient to give both Lotta Continua and Potere Operaio a working-class base; at Porto Marghera, in particular, Potere Operaio members formed the nucleus of workerist agitation which continued into 1970 and beyond (Balestrini and Moroni 1997: 464). Even these redoubts grew less active over time, calling into question the organisations' capacity to respond to a future revival of factory-based activity.

In late 1970 Lotta Continua launched the slogan *'Prendiamoci la città!'* ('Let's take the city!'). The organisation attempted to take the class struggle out of the factory, organising and supporting housing occupations, rent strikes and projects to set up self-managed services such as food markets (*'mercatini rossi'*) and healthcare centres. The project had real but limited success, anticipating the spread of community-based activism later in the decade. Always alert to possible new sites of mobilisation, Lotta Continua began publishing spinoff journals, attempting to organise in the underdeveloped south (*Mo' che il tempo s'avvicina* ('The time's coming')) and in the armed forces

(*Proletari in divisa* ('Proletarians in uniform')). A third initiative, organising in the prison population under the name 'I dannati della terra' ('The wretched of the earth'), would have major and unexpected consequences in the changed context of the second cycle of contention. Their immediate effect was to create more areas on which the group could focus its dwindling resources, masking the decline of the group and the waning of the cycle of contention with voluntaristic activism.

Potere Operaio, meanwhile, had held its first national conference in January 1970, committing itself to the development of a centralised, Leninist party which could organise political interventions even in the absence of generalised industrial militancy. Berardi, who left the group later that year, recalled, 'Until the day before, Potere Operaio was thought to be, and was, a spontaneist group. The day after, it was a Leninist group' (Grandi 2003: 116).[9]

As the organisations which had grown out of the first cycle of contention lost their base, some groups and individuals began to experiment with organised violence. However, at this stage the 'armed struggle' was conceived almost entirely in defensive terms, in the context of an anticipated coup from the right. On 12 December 1969, a bomb had exploded in Milan, in the Banca Nazionale dell'Agricoltura in Piazza Fontana, causing 16 deaths. The initial investigation was led by the police officer in charge of monitoring the local radical Left, Luigi Calabresi; his investigation focused on a local anarchist group. While being interrogated, the anarchist Giuseppe Pinelli fell, or was pushed, from the fourth-floor window of Calabresi's office. On the Left, Piazza Fontana was immediately (and, as it turned out, correctly) labelled a *strage di stato* ('state massacre'); the bombing, the death of Pinelli and the subsequent repression were widely believed to form part of the Right's preparations for a coup (Balestrini and Moroni 1997: 340–6). Indeed, December 1970 saw a genuine coup attempt, launched by Prince Junio Valerio Borghese, who had held a high military rank in Mussolini's 'social-fascist' Republic of Salò. Borghese's troops briefly occupied the Ministry of the Interior, but were rapidly routed. The coup attempt was kept out of the news until the following March (Ginsborg 1990: 334).

By the middle of 1971, there was thus a widespread belief that the Left might soon need to resort to violence, up to and including armed struggle, in order to defend the gains made in previous years. Members of Lotta Continua contemplated an armed defence against repression and even prepared for the coming confrontation, as Adriano Sofri recalled in 1997:

Many of us in the organisation were considering the problem of violence and clandestinity, understood in terms of the ability to survive a potential *coup d'état* ... we were convinced, like others who later opted for terrorism, that violence was inevitable and that it was necessary to be prepared for the possibility of armed struggle against those who would repress popular and proletarian struggles: the State, the extreme right. . . . We thought these things, we carried out violent actions and some of us made preparations. (quoted in Biacchessi 1998)[10]

Within Potere Operaio, more drastic conclusions were drawn. The organisation was now divided between a minority of factory-oriented workerists, on one hand, and 'insurrectionists' such as Piperno on the other. Piperno argued that industrial activism could no longer achieve political results and advocated immediate preparation for a violent clash with the state; his position had strong support in Potere Operaio's *servizio d'ordine* ('order service'; the stewards' groups responsible for security on demonstrations and occupations). A third position, represented by Negri, called for the unification of industrial struggles through the construction of a Leninist party. An organisational conference in September 1971 ended with the marginalisation of the factory-based workerists by means of a compromise between Piperno and Negri: the group resolved to build 'the party of the insurrection' (Wright 2002: 143; Grandi 2003: 191–206, 331–4). Informal meetings during the conference led to the establishment of a sub-group dedicated to *lavoro illegale* ('illegal work'); the group was to prepare for insurrection and, more immediately, provide 'armed support' to demonstrations. At the end of 1971 this group disintegrated when members were arrested for possession of Molotov cocktails, prepared for the second anniversary of the Piazza Fontana bombing (Grandi 2003: 239–49). A group of Potere Operaio activists, using the name of Fronte Armato Rivoluzionario Operaio (FARO; 'Revolutionary Armed Workers' Front'), claimed responsibility for a brief series of bombings in March 1972 (Progetto Memoria 1994: 223).

Activism in the factories and elsewhere had fallen far below the high-water mark of 1969; understandably, groups which had grown out of the peak of the earlier cycle had difficulty adapting to the new conditions. However, this was not the whole story. Outside the purview of the established workerist groups, workplace activism was beginning to revive. In Rome, the Comitati autonomi operai (CAO; 'Autonomous workers' committees') was founded in 1972 (Monicelli 1978: 116). Known as 'i Volsci' after its base in the via dei Volsci, the group would be hugely influential within the 'area of Autonomia', whose first conference took place in November 1972 (Piazza 1987: 200).

New kinds of activity were also beginning elsewhere. In Milan, the magazine *Re Nudo* was launched in 1970 by Andrea Valcarenghi, veteran of the counter-cultural pacifist group Onda verde ('Green Wave') (Echaurren and Salaris 1999: 27, 167). The following year saw the launch of a second magazine, *L'erba voglio*, also based in Milan (Echaurren and Salaris 1999: 178). Both had a youthful audience, defined by *Re Nudo* in June 1971 as 'young proletarians'; both took their titles from fairy tales ('The emperor's new clothes' and *'L'erba voglio che non cresce nemmeno nel giardino del re'* ('I want the grass that doesn't even grow in the king's garden')). Both championed an intransigent but creative youthful rebellion, promoting an open-ended anti-authoritarian *decondizionamento* ('deconditioning') of their audience; *L'erba voglio* claimed to have *antenne rotanti in ogni direzione* ('antennae turning in all directions') (Echaurren and Salaris 1999: 179).

Issues of gender and sexuality had also begun to receive sustained attention. In 1966 a women's anti-authoritarian study group, Demau (short for *Demistificazione dell'autoritarismo*; 'Demystification of authoritarianism'), had been founded in Milan. The radical feminist group Rivolta Femminile ('Female Revolt') was founded in 1970; the following year saw the founding of Lotta Femminista ('Feminist Struggle'), which demanded wages for housework on the workerist grounds that women in the home were also proletarians, contributing as they did to the maintenance and reproduction of capitalist labour-power (Lumley 1990: 316–17). 1971 also saw the first meeting of the Fronte Unitario Omosessuale Rivoluzionario Italiano (FUORI; 'Italian United Revolutionary Homosexual Front'), whose acronym translates as 'Outside' (Echaurren and Salaris 1999: 163).

Tarrow's model of the aftermath of the cycle is supported by the voluntaristic activism adopted by both Lotta Continua and Potere Operaio in the face of declining mobilisation, and in particular by the latter's 'insurrectionist' turn; one Potere Operaio activist, Valerio Morucci, was urging the organisation to devote more resources to violent activity as early as 1970 (Morucci 1994: 21). Indeed, the FARO experience is perhaps the single strongest piece of evidence for the thesis of violent 'outbidding', with activists moving from mass agitation to small-group violence and thence to terrorism. However, if activists in Lotta Continua and Potere Operaio were suffering from the decline of mobilisation, the social movement sector as a whole was clearly characterised by beginnings as well as endings. Moreover, FARO itself was an insignificant and ephemeral organisation, both marginal and atypical within the early 'armed struggle' milieu. The impetus to the widespread adoption of the 'armed struggle' in the late 1970s would come from three groups whose roots lay outside the mainstream of the first cycle of contention: the Gruppi d'Azione Partigiana (GAP; 'Partisan Action Groups'); the Gruppo XXII ottobre ('22 October Group'); and the BR.

Towards a new repertoire: from defence to attack, 1969–72

The Brigate Rosse group identification, or 'signature', was first used in early 1970 by a Milan-based group, Sinistra Proletaria ('Proletarian Left'). Sinistra Proletaria brought together a group of former members of the PCI's youth wing, the Federazione Giovanile Comunista Italiano (FGCI; Italian Communist Youth Federation) with a split from the Collettivo Politico Metropolitano (CPM; 'Metropolitan Political Collective'); the CPM was a Maoist-influenced group which had grown out of the 1967–8 wave of student activism in Trento. Sinistra Proletaria was committed to *doppia militanza* ('double militancy'), in which clandestine violence would be rooted in overt activism. The group maintained a double identity: as Sinistra Proletaria, members participated in occupations and published two issues of a newspaper (*Sinistra Proletaria* appeared in July and September 1970); as the Brigate Rosse, they produced leaflets and carried out at least one arson attack. At the end of 1970 Sinistra Proletaria announced its own dissolution and the formation of the first true Brigata Rossa, still in Milan. The reorganised group produced its own newspaper (*Nuova Resistenza* ('New Resistance'), published in April and May 1971) while carrying out and publicising a series of low-level clandestine actions; these were primarily arson attacks on the cars of factory bosses and members of the neo-fascist Movimento Sociale Italiano (MSI; 'Italian Social Movement') (Caselli and della Porta 1991: 72–3; Progetto Memoria 1994: 48; Centro di Documentazione 'Fausto e Jaio' 1995).

Sinistra Proletaria's perspectives were broadly Maoist: while claiming fidelity to the work of Marx and Lenin, they championed Third World resistance to Western imperialism and dismissed the PCI's 'social-democratic' programme. Following the dissolution of Sinistra Proletaria, the BR adopted a more militaristic stance, influenced by de Gaulle's coup in France and the early successes of the Rote Armee Fraktion (RAF; 'Red Army Fraction') in Germany (Balestrini and Moroni 1997: 412). In September 1971 the group called, not for insurrection, but for counter-attack: 'The armed confrontation has already begun, and its aim is to destroy the working class's capacity for resistance. X-hour for the insurrection will never come' (Progetto Memoria 1996: 37).[11] To situate this counter-attack within an overall revolutionary strategy, the guiding hand of an armed Leninist party would be required. Even at this early stage, the BR aspired to constitute itself as the sole revolutionary party capable of representing the working class in the period of armed struggle. 'The Red Brigades are the first organisational points for the formation of the Armed Party of the Proletariat. This is the source of our profound connection with the revolutionary and communist tradition of the workers' movement' (Progetto Memoria 1996: 38).[12]

Like the early BR, the Gruppo XXII ottobre was based in a single city, in this case Genoa. The Circolo XXII ottobre, a militant Maoist group, was formed on 22 October 1969; it became an active armed struggle group the following year. Between April 1970 and February 1971 the group carried out a series of arson and sabotage attacks, as well as holding the son of a local industrialist to ransom. The group also made several radio broadcasts which interrupted television news programmes; the first, on 16 April 1970, called for mobilisation against a forthcoming neo-fascist meeting in Genoa (Progetto Memoria 1994: 41). The Gruppo XXII ottobre's outlook combined an anti-imperialist worldview of Maoist origin with perspectives and concepts derived from the Resistance: the group aimed to constitute a 'partisan vanguard' which would unleash 'revolutionary partisan war'. In March 1971 two Gruppo XXII ottobre members attempted to rob the IACP (council housing) office in Genoa and shot dead an IACP clerk, Alessandro Floris; as they made their escape one was caught and the other identified. Subsequently, the group's members were either arrested or joined the GAP (Progetto Memoria 1994: 41). While the group's roots were its own, its career as an 'armed struggle' group began and ended within Giangiacomo Feltrinelli's GAP network; its radio transmitters were obtained through the GAP, while the first broadcast was announced as 'Radio GAP' and may even have been read by Feltrinelli (Feltrinelli 2001: 403). Organisationally, the group can reasonably be regarded as the GAP's Genoa 'column'.

The history of the GAP itself began in the late 1960s, when Feltrinelli, radical publisher and hereditary millionaire, built a network of contacts who shared his political perspectives, including former Partisans such as Communist senator Pietro Secchia. According to former partisan leader Giovanbattista Lazagna, himself arrested in 1970 on suspicion of GAP involvement, Feltrinelli used '*gruppi d'azione partigiana*' as a generic label for the groups with which he was in contact (Feltrinelli 2001: 400); the name recalls the *Gruppi di azione patriottica* ('Patriotic action groups'), Communist-aligned Resistance groups which had been active in the north of Italy. Born in 1926, Feltrinelli had joined the Resistance and the Communist Party in his teens (Feltrinelli 2001: 33–4). After leaving the Communist Party in 1958 he committed himself and the publishing house to anti-imperialist causes (Feltrinelli 2001: 178); in particular, he actively supported the guerrilla war then being waged by the Algerian Front de Libération Nationale (FLN; 'National Liberation Front') (Feltrinelli 2001: 242). In Italy, Feltrinelli endorsed the proto-hippie 'Beat' movement. In 1967, writing in the magazine *Mondo Beat* under the transparent pseudonym of 'Gigi Effe', he hailed the movement as a new and more effective form of strike action: 'they are going on strike against the very essence of capitalism, against the consumer society' (quoted in Echaurren and Salaris 1999: 61).[13]

Feltrinelli's publications in the 1960s included translations of works by Fidel Castro and the memoirs of a commander of the original GAP, Giovanni Pesce's *Senza Tregua: la guerra dei GAP* ('No Quarter: the GAP's war'). Writing in 1967, Pesce characterised the GAP as 'groups of patriots who never gave the enemy quarter: they struck him at all times, in all circumstances, day and night, in the streets of the city and in the heart of his fortresses' (quoted in Massari 1979: 191).[14] Feltrinelli also published writings by contemporary exponents of armed struggle, including the Brazilian Carlos Marighella's *Handbook of the Urban Guerrilla* and an anthology on the Tupamaros of Uruguay, a group which had considerable influence on the BR; according to one member the group's structures were 'borrowed, broadly speaking, from the Tupamaros and the Algerian FLN' (Piccioni 1997: 128).[15]

In the summer of 1969 Feltrinelli wrote a brief text warning of the imminence of a coup in Italy: 'To resort to a coup d'état, or a radical authoritarian shift to the right, would be entirely in keeping with the requirements of the system'.[16] The Left must prepare for combat: 'confrontation can't be avoided by choosing to agree to or abstain from a battle – a battle which now seems inevitable; the only result would be to come to the battle unprepared' (quoted in Balestrini and Moroni 1997: 411).[17] His judgment of the contemporary revolutionary Left was scathing. As Oreste Scalzone recalled in 1988: 'As revolutionaries, Feltrinelli considered us in Potere Operaio to be sincere but deluded and obsessed with the long term, because we didn't think about counter-revolution and we didn't give adequate attention to the military question' (Biacchessi 1998).[18] Those members who were involved in the Lavoro Illegale/FARO experience were more enthusiastic. For Morucci, Feltrinelli 'had seen revolutions around the world at first hand, much more so than we who only experienced their epic effects. He knew that revolution wasn't a laughing matter, it was a matter of risking your life. He'd adopted the organisational techniques of Carlos Marighella and the Tupamaros to the letter. And this, while for others it raised a smile, fascinated me' (Morucci 1994: 22).[19]

Feltrinelli was travelling at the time of Piazza Fontana. Hearing that his office had been searched and his home was being watched by police, he went underground and devoted himself to the 'reconstitution' of the GAP network (Feltrinelli 2001: 384–7). This claim to continuity with the Resistance was largely an ideological manoeuvre, assimilating the contemporary authoritarian danger to the experience of Fascism. However, the network did involve some former Partisans; many others, including Secchia, Pesce and Lazagna, were sympathisers. 'An entire political tendency of militants and ex-partisans had never ceased . . . to nurture a political position strongly critical of the outcome of the Resistance, which was to have proceeded to a generalised class confrontation and ultimately to the establishment of a socialist state' (Balestrini and Moroni 1997: 400).[20]

However, Feltrinelli went beyond the Resistance template, proposing an incremental development of armed counter-power. Urban guerrilla warfare would lead to the construction of a 'proletarian army' capable of engaging the capitalist state in battle: 'to inflict an irreversible defeat on the enemy requires an army which is able to take on its adversary in many battles before we reach the decisive battle which, if it's won, will open the way to the mass revolutionary insurrection' (Progetto Memoria 1996: 20).[21] This model drew on the Cuban and Uruguayan experiences, and in particular on Régis Debray's analysis of Latin American guerrilla warfare. Debray's analysis centred on the concept of the guerrilla *foco* ('focus'), a cohesive group which undertook both military and political activity. In Debray's model, known as *foquismo*, guerrilla war effectively took the place of Leninist revolution. 'Under certain conditions the military and the political are not separate but form one organic whole, consisting of the people's army, whose nucleus is the guerrilla army. The vanguard party can exist in the form of the guerrilla *foco* itself' (Debray 1967: 105). Developing a *foco* was the first priority, from which all else would follow: 'It is not a front which will create this nucleus, but rather the nucleus which, as it develops, will permit the creation of a national revolutionary front. . . . It is the "small motor" that sets the "big motor" of the masses in motion and precipitates the formation of a front, as the victories won by the small motor increase' (Debray 1967: 82–3).

While the 'small motor'/'big motor' image was coined by the Cuban guerrilla leader Raúl Castro, in its broad outlines this analysis was shared by the BR, many of whose Maoist reference points Debray shared. That said, Feltrinelli's project must be classed as idiosyncratic even by comparison with the BR; around 1967, for example, he had spoken of using Sardinia as a base from which to begin the liberation of Italy. (A Sardinian contact recalled: 'He left us all somewhat puzzled, if not downright flabbergasted: "Sardinia as the Cuba of the Mediterranean"?' (Feltrinelli 2001: 350)). Feltrinelli met members of the BR after going underground, but agreed with them on little. 'He inundated us with speeches on revolutionary strategy, on the structure of the proletarian army, the Soviet Union and its guiding role,' recalled Alberto Franceschini of the BR. 'We didn't want to build a proletarian army but an armed party.' (Biacchessi 1998).[22] Nor did Franceschini sympathise with Feltrinelli's tactical objectives: 'his idea of blowing up high-tension pylons in the mountains . . . struck us as rather eccentric' (Biacchessi 1998).[23] Contacts between Feltrinelli and Morucci, Scalzone and Piperno of Potere Operaio were no more productive. Despite Morucci's sympathies for the GAP project, Feltrinelli's proposals for 'a process of integration and co-ordination on the operational level as well as the logistical and political levels' (quoted in Grandi 2003: 224) fell on deaf ears.[24] The only perspective Potere Operaio could offer Feltrinelli was 'the possibility of creating armed structures within a legal organisation working in mass movements' (Morucci 1994: 22);[25] in other words, a bigger and better FARO. Feltrinelli's commitment to the armed struggle, proved by his death in 1972, was widely perceived on the Left as both shocking and exemplary. However, this does not diminish the eccentricity and marginality of the GAP project itself.

A fourth group should also be mentioned briefly. In Turin, the libertarian workerist Riccardo d'Este was active from 1969 onward in a series of radical organisations: 'Ludd', a network of autonomous workers' councils founded in 1969; the 'Organizzazione consiliare' ('Council organisation'), formed in 1970 and dissolved the following year; and 'Comontismo', an untranslatable coinage signifying 'existence in common'. Drawing on situationist and council communist sources, the Comontisti set themselves against contemporary capitalist society in all its forms (work, money, the family, the law), and attempted to live out this theoretical stance in practice. During 1972 the Comontisti embarked on an 'armed phase', successfully kidnapping the son of the Turinese industrialist Antonio Carello and releasing him in exchange for a ransom. After the arrest of those responsible, the group disintegrated. In the late 1970s, some former Comontisti were active in later armed groups, including Gianfranco Faina's Azione Rivoluzionaria (Progetto Memoria 1994: 255).

Both the GAP and the BR drew on ideological and tactical vocabularies which lay far outside the first cycle of contention. The Resistance was a shared reference point for all the early armed struggle groups. As we have seen, the Gruppo XXII ottobre had referred to itself as a 'partisan vanguard'; in 1973 the BR would commit itself to 'the *war against fascism* which is not only the fascism of Almirante's blackshirts but the fascism of Giulio Andreotti and the Christian Democrat white shirts [and] the *resistance inside the factories*' (quoted in Manconi 1991: 122; emphasis in original). Like the use of '*Nuova Resistenza*' by the nascent BR as the title of its newspaper, this formulation both subsumes contemporary anti-fascism into a broader struggle against capitalism, and validates the BR's conception of that struggle by tying it to images of Resistance anti-fascism. Like Feltrinelli, in other words, the BR exploited the emotional appeal of the Resistance even as they reconceptualised it.

Significantly, the cerebral workerists of Potere Operaio were critical of invocations of the Resistance, writing in 1972: 'We want nothing to do with that bourgeois tradition of the "right to resistance" codified in some constitutions. Resistance is a form of rebellion which aims to conserve or restore a pre-existing order. This was true also of the Italian Resistance: of the latter, we recognise only the contribution of revolutionary communist workers' (quoted in Wright 1998). The group specifically rejected the conflation of factory-based struggles and anti-fascism, exemplified by the BR's June 1973 kidnapping of Alfa Romeo director and Christian Democrat Michele Mincuzzi. In a judgment which summed up the distance between the workerists and the 'militant anti-fascism' of the early armed struggle groups, Potere Operaio commented: 'It would have been right to strike Mincuzzi even if he were a sincere democrat, instead of the fascist that he is. It is certainly useful to personalise the enemy, but it becomes damaging and confusing to define ideologically or – even worse – morally, positions of command that are per se abstract and interchangeable' (quoted in Manconi 1991: 124).

As well as referring back to the achievements of the Communist-led Resistance, the GAP and the BR both invoked Communism in older and more straightforward forms, uncontaminated by the social-democratic opportunism of the PCI – or the theoretical elaborations of the workerists. Both groups argued that the class struggle needed to be fought with weapons and straight away; each presented itself as the nucleus of the future armed revolutionary party. In short, in the context of the first cycle of contention, both groups were idiosyncratic to the point of lunacy.

As well as their lack of connection with the mass organisations of the first cycle of contention, the armed groups of the early 1970s are remarkable for their relatively limited size and levels of activity. Fewer than 100 people were ever investigated by the police for membership of either the GAP or the Gruppo XXII ottobre; for comparison, 911 people were investigated in connection with the BR, whose total membership is estimated to have been under 500 (Progetto Memoria 1994: 36, 43, 60; Moss 1989: 67). The BR itself had made only 32 new recruits by the end of 1971 (Moss 1989: 67). The armed struggle groups of the late 1970s flourished against the background of the second cycle of contention. While the earlier groups were an influence on this cycle, in the circumstances of the early 1970s they could achieve little in their own right.

Analysing the aftermath: 'outbidding' and beyond

As we have seen, the Italian social movement sector in 1972 presented a mixed picture. Industrial activism had come under the tutelage of the PCI and was now beginning to ebb. Lotta Continua was in search of new social subjects to mobilise; Potere Operaio was grinding to a halt amid internal dissension, while some members experimented with 'armed struggle' tactics. Meanwhile, the women's liberation movement was beginning to make itself heard; the first 'autonomist' groups were forming; and teenagers in Milan were starting to recognise themselves as 'proletarian youth'.

At this point it is worth engaging with Sidney Tarrow's model of the aftermath in more detail. Following the institutionalisation of a new repertoire of contention, Tarrow argues, the draining of the pool of mass protest leaves few outlets for those attracted by the movement's radicalism, other than the violence of direct action:

once worker mobilisation declined, there was little real possibility of employing the energies of these young people in a serious project of industrial conflict.

> Many were instead inducted into increasingly militaristic *servizi d'ordine* . . . the
> extraparliamentary groups left them with a rejection of reformism, with the
> tools of violence, but with little else. (Tarrow 1989: 308)

Some believed that 'the tools of violence' would get better results than the
tools of reformism: 'The extraparliamentary groups used mass mobilisation
to outbid the unions and the PCI, while the terrorists used violence to outbid
the extraparliamentary groups' (Tarrow 1989: 310). However, violence
brought repression, leading to clandestinity; clandestinity brought isolation,
leaving the groups no alternative to further violence. 'The more radical [a
group's] forms of action, the greater the risk of violence and the higher the
level of repression. Once repression is triggered, the group has no alternative
but to go underground, where the only tactical alternatives left to it are
violent' (Tarrow 1991: 58). Radicalism led to violence; violence led to terrorism; terrorism led to clandestinity; clandestinity closed the vicious circle,
which could end only with the isolation of the groups, their ultimate disinte-
gration and the return of social peace.

There are a number of problems with Tarrow's 'outbidding' model. The
concept is imprecise: it is applied both to repertoire innovation in the rising
phase of the cycle and to a rearguard action by organised minorities during
the aftermath. A more parsimonious approach might be simply to regard the
introduction of violent tactics as a form of repertoire innovation. Tarrow's
model also makes the organisational motivation for escalating levels of violence something of a mystery, given that this tends to cut off violent groups
from their supporters and make it harder for them to realise their goals. The
gap is covered by vague terms such as 'radical' and 'extreme'. The term
'violence' itself is loaded but imprecise. References to militants 'using
violence' could refer to factory bosses being assaulted, machinery being
sabotaged or *servizio d'ordine* members brandishing staves, all of which are
forms of action which characterised the first cycle as well as the second.

More to the point, it is not clear how the 'outbidding' model applies to the
Italian experience. This is not to deny any continuity between armed struggle
groups and the organisations of the first cycle of contention. The formation of
the group Prima Linea in 1976 owed a great deal to Lotta Continua's *servizi
d'ordine* (Novaro 1991); former Potere Operaio members played a key role in
the Red Brigades in the late 1970s ('If those of us from Potere Operaio hadn't
entered the Red Brigades, they probably wouldn't even have been able to
organise the Moro kidnap' (Maccari 2000)).[26] However, Tarrow's timescale
is unsatisfactory. Referring to 1973, Tarrow writes: 'the beginning of organised terrorism coincided with the definitive decline of mass violence and with
the period in which small-group violence peaked' (Tarrow 1989: 307). In fact,
Italian left-wing terrorism began, as we have seen, in the spring of 1970; even

the emergence of left-wing terrorism as a national phenomenon can be dated at the latest to the death of Feltrinelli in March 1972.

If we focus on the peak period of left-wing terrorist activity, on the other hand, Tarrow's model is unsatisfactory for the opposite reason. The immediate aftermath of the first cycle saw no more than experimentation with terrorist tactics by small and scattered groups; the 'armed struggle' milieu grew, suddenly and rapidly, between 1976 and 1979. If there was any kind of spiral of outbidding, with rival 'armed parties' adopting ever more violent tactics, it cannot have begun until 1976 at the earliest. Thirdly, Tarrow's account of the 'area of Autonomia' is unpersuasive. He writes:

> At the high point of the cycle, in 1967–9, autonomy was exhilarating and liberating; but it could also mean sectarianism and isolation . . . This meaning was predominant in the tragic history of the term in the mid-1970s, when a collection of miscellaneous clandestine and semi-clandestine groups formed what came to be called the 'area of autonomy'. For these groups, autonomy meant separation from the state, from the institutional Left, from the unions, and eventually from reality. (Tarrow 1989: 132)

The sketchy and dismissive quality of this account is obvious. Tarrow also associates Autonomia explicitly with the trio of terrorism, clandestinity and isolation: '[from 1974 on] the banner of autonomy, first raised by the students in 1966–8 to call for grassroots democracy, was used to wrap a faction of the extreme Left in clandestinity and mask its acts of terror in a rhetoric that – however hard they tried – could not cloak its members' detachment from the masses' (Tarrow 1989: 133). Elsewhere, dating the birth of Autonomia to the still later period of 1975–6, Tarrow writes:

> United only by opposition to the institutional left and by the desire to contest the 'leap into politics' that the 'old' extraparliamentary left was taking, these groups were practically *born* in clandestinity. With the decline of mass mobilisation of the early and mid-1970s, the only way for them to gain the attention of the workers was through violence. (Tarrow 1991: 60; emphasis in original)

Again, the time frame is inconsistent with the 'outbidding' model; as a depiction of the area of Autonomia in the mid-1970s, this is also highly unsatisfactory. This is not to say that there were no groups which were 'practically *born* in clandestinity', using heightened levels of violence as their first and only means of communicating with their constituency. In the words of the narrator of Balestrini's 1987 novel, himself in prison awaiting trial for association with terrorists,

> many of the new arrivals had ridiculous stories they were the last generation of fighters all extremely young and they all had a similar story they hadn't had

any movement experience partly because by now the movement had been swept
away their only experience was reading some document the clandestine distribution of some leaflet writing on the walls a banner across a flyover and then
perhaps a murder straight away among the first actions and then arrest on the
word of some informant (Balestrini 1987: 270)[27]

However, the time frame here is 1980 at the earliest: after 'the movement
had been swept away' by the wide-ranging arrests of 1979. As we shall see
below, conditions in the mid-1970s were far less repressive, and the repertoires brought into play less restricted.

Finally, while Tarrow's model is inexact or misleading with regard to the
left-wing armed struggle milieu and the area of Autonomia, other areas are
omitted completely. Three have been touched on already: the women's liberation movement, the gay radicalism of FUORI and the 'proletarian youth
movement' heralded by *Re Nudo* and *L'erba voglio*. The last of these, in
particular, was closely linked with the fortunes of Autonomia and the left-
wing terrorist milieu, particularly in the 1976–8 period.

The 'outbidding' model seems to be underpinned by an *a priori* dismissal
of violent repertoire innovation; this assumption leads the formation of the
'armed struggle' milieu and the area of Autonomia to be seen as endings
rather than beginnings. This in turn leads Tarrow to telescope these movements' own history, reading their eventual defeat in terms of deviant tendencies immanent from their formation. Political violence becomes both a
symptom of social movement decline and a contagion which taints any group
using it; the history of the 1970s becomes the story of the inexorable degeneration of the movements of the first cycle. This framing distorts the record
of the late 1970s in several ways. The 'terrorist' model is stretched to fit
contentious social movements such as the 'area of Autonomia', whose activities, while confrontational and often violent, were carried out openly and on
a large scale. Social movements which cannot be made to fit this framework,
such as the proletarian youth movement, are omitted altogether; external
influences on the formation of the armed struggle milieu itself, such as the
distinctive ideological heritage of the BR and the GAP, are ignored.

A second cycle?

I suggest that we can get a better picture of radical activism between 1972
and 1977 if we start from the assumption that there was a second cycle of
contention, driven, like the first, by the emergence of new and innovative
tactical repertoires. These tactics, with associated organisational and ideological innovations, were pioneered both by the area of Autonomia and, in
more complex and qualified ways, by the 'armed struggle' groups. The tactics
in question were frequently illegal, violent or both, but this did not prevent

their diffusion and emulation. Like the first cycle, I shall argue, the second progressed from a phase of innovation through a period of diffusion, culminating in a phase of engagement with a 'gatekeeper' of political legitimacy: a role taken in both cycles by the PCI. As in the first phase, the process of engagement was an extended series of interactions, and involved the winnowing, selection and rejection of organisational and ideological forms as well as purely tactical repertoires. The process was driven (once again) from below, by demands for top-down reform and integration of radical movements – or, rather, for the kinds of movement success which could be delivered by reform and integration. Also as in the first phase, the outcome of the engagement process was determined, not by an inherent dynamic towards expansion of the repertoire of political participation, but by political choices made by the PCI in its role as gatekeeper.

The course of the two cycles is represented schematically in table 2.1 below (events after 1972 are discussed in chapter 4). The 'one-cycle' model is the model put forward by Tarrow; the 'two-cycle' model is the one for which I argue in this book.

Table 2.1 Comparison of one-cycle and two-cycle models of key social movement events, 1966–77

Year	Event	One cycle	Two cycles
1966	Trento protests	I	I (1)
1967	Pisa occupations	I	I (1)
1968	Widespread university occupations	I	I (1)
	Factory committees set up	D	D (1)
1969	Wildcat strikes	D	D (1)
	Contract negotiation	E	E (1)
1970	Workplace councils	A	A (1)
1971	'Lavoro illegale' group set up within Potere Operaio	A	I (2)
	First actions by Brigate Rosse	A	I (2)
1972	First autonomous committees	A	I (2)
1973	First national meetings of Autonomia	A	D (2)
1974	Housing occupations, rent strikes	A	D (2)
1975	Organised shoplifting	A	D (2)
1976	Emergence of proletarian youth movement	A	D (2)
	Formation of Prima Linea	A	D (2)
1977	Widespread adoption of 'armed struggle' tactics	A	D (2)
	Confrontation between PCI and 'movement of 1977'	A	E (2)

I = Innovation, D = Diffusion, E = Engagement, A = Aftermath

The movements of the second cycle have generally been presented, by Tarrow and other writers, in terms of violence, hooliganism and terrorism. It is true that the tactical innovations associated with the second cycle were generally confrontational and often involved violence; however, much the same could be said of the first cycle, particularly at its peak (in the period immediately preceding the December 1969 contract agreement). The key difference between the two cycles derived not from the nature of their innovations but from the course of the 'engagement' phase of the cycle. Unlike the 1969–70 experience, the second cycle's engagement phase was uniformly hostile, barring the movements' innovations from the mainstream and stigmatising the movements themselves as deviant or criminal. Subsequently, there was an unquiet and drawn-out aftermath, with the choice between complete demobilisation and outright criminality posed ever more insistently. Given the hostility of the engagement phase, this cycle did not lead to an 'expansion of the repertoire of democratic participation' (Tarrow 1989: 67). Rather, it led to the narrowing of mainstream repertoires, as the PCI in its gatekeeper role differentiated itself from the stigmatised movements.

The theoretical framework used here to analyse the second cycle of contention has three interrelated elements. The first is the cycle itself: a model of how waves of contentious activism arise, spread to different political and geographical areas and rise to a peak of intensity before a settling of accounts with the sphere of institutional politics. The second key element is the structural role of 'gatekeeper' within relatively closed political systems. In such a system, I argue, pressure from would-be political actors outside the system tends to be absorbed and neutralised by a political actor representing the extreme limit of acceptability. In the Italian First Republic, most external pressure came from the Left, and was neutralised by the PCI in its role as gatekeeper. The third key element, finally, is the concept of framing: the use of discursive and rhetorical devices to present social forces and issues in ways which mobilise support or opposition. I argue that framing transactions are a constitutive part of interaction between political actors, used in particular to identify social groups as legitimate or deviant, and to set the political agenda accordingly.

Although interrelated, these three elements of the model have different theoretical ancestries and require distinct analytical approaches. For simplicity, a separate chapter has been given to each one. In the fourth chapter, the sociological model of the cycle of contention is brought to bear on a detailed account of the 1972–7 period. The fifth chapter uses content analysis methods to trace successive framing strategies in PCI publications over the period. Both of these depend on a historical understanding of the third element of the model, the role of the PCI as gatekeeper: this is the subject of the next chapter.

The PCI was a major but deeply contradictory presence in twentieth-century Italian politics; its internal contradictions were never more apparent than in its dealings with the two cycles of contention. If we see the PCI as a revolutionary party, it is hard to explain its late 1970s position of entrenched hostility to radical movements. Equally, if we see the party as thoroughly integrated into the Italian political system, its openness to the first cycle of contention becomes a mystery. In either case, the party's rapid transition from one stance to the other calls for explanation. The next chapter sets the PCI's changing orientations in the context of the factional debates which dominated the party in this period, which in turn are situated within the 70-year history of the party.

Notes

1 'Gli studenti si oppongono. Il 24 gennaio 1966 riunitisi in assemblea generale (istanza quasi inedita per quei tempi) decidono l'occupazione dell'università. L'occupazione durerà diciotto giorni e si conclude con una vittoria . . . La lotta conclusasi con una vittoria sull'obiettivo corporativo della laurea . . . dà agli studenti la coscienza della propria forza, valorizza una forma di lotta quasi nuova'.

2 'La società capitalistica ha le sue leggi di sviluppo: gli economisti le hanno inventate, i governanti le hanno applicate e gli operai le hanno subite. Ma le leggi di sviluppo della classe operaia, chi le scoprirà? Il capitale ha la sua storia e i suoi storici la scrivono. Ma la storia della classe operaia, chi la scriverà? Tante sono state le forme di dominio politico dello sfruttamento capitalista. Ma come si arriverà alla prossima forma di dittatura degli operai, organizzati in classe dominante? . . . Abbiamo visto anche noi prima lo sviluppo capitalistico, poi le lotte operaie. È un errore. Occorre rovesciare il problema, cambiare il segno, ripartire dal principio: e il principio è la lotta di classe operaia. A livello di capitale socialmente sviluppato, lo sviluppo capitalistico è subordinato alle lotte operaie, viene dopo di esse e ad esse deve far corrispondere il meccanismo politico della propria produzione.'

3 'La strategia leninista, con un colpo magistrale, portò Marx a Pietroburgo: solo il punto di vista operaio poteva essere capace di una simile audacia rivoluzionaria. Proviamo a fare il cammino inverso, con lo stesso spirito scientifico di avventurosa scoperta politica. Lenin in Inghilterra è la ricerca di una nuova pratica marxista del partito operaio'.

4 'la tesi, che solletica la vanità di certi strati studenteschi, di una pretesa iniziativa rivoluzionaria che spetterebbe al movimento studentesco, di fronte alla presunta inerzia opportunistica e integrazione nel sistema della classe operaia, e alla burocratizzazione dei suoi strumenti "tradizionali" (sindacati e partiti)'.

5 'Avete faccie di figli di papà. / Buona razza non mente. /. . . / Quando ieri a Valle Giulia avete fatto a botte / coi poliziotti, / io simpatizzavo coi poliziotti! / Perché i poliziotti sono figli di poveri.'

6 'L'assemblea studenti-operai era una specie di struttura politica spontanea permanente . . . ma era anche la democrazia diretta, un luogo dove gli operai arrivavano e parlavano con altri operai raccontando in diretta le lotte che conducevano in fabbrica'.

7 'il rapporto con la lotta operaia e il rapporto con i vecchi dell'ospizio sono la stessa cosa'.

8 'le organizzazioni autonomie avevano ripetutamente organizzato gli scioperi di reparto dopodiché intervenne il sindacato, raccolse un'esigenza di tutti gli operai, e ne fece la condizione per riprendere in mano la gestione di una lotta che gli era, invece, completamente sfuggita'.

9 'Fino a quel giorno Potere Operaio era considerato ed era . . . un gruppo spontaneista. Il giorno dopo era divenuto un gruppo leninista.'

10 'Nell'organizzazione in molti si posero il problema della violenza e della clandestinità, intesa come capacità di sopravvivere ad un eventuale colpo di Stato . . . noi eravamo convinti, come altri che poi scelsero il terrorismo, dell'inevitabilità della violenza, della necessità di prepararsi all'eventualità di una lotta armata contro chi reprimeva le lotte proletarie e popolari: lo Stato, l'estrema destra. . . . Noi abbiamo pensato queste cose, praticato azioni violente, qualcuno di noi si è preparato.'

11 'Lo scontro armato è già iniziato e mira a liquidare la capacità di resistenza della classe operaia. L'ora x dell'insurrezione non arriverà.'

12 'Le Br sono i primi punti di aggregazione per la formazione del Partito Armato del Proletariato. In questo sta il nostro collegamento profondo con la tradizione rivoluzionaria e comunista del movimento operaio.'

13 'Essi scioperano contro l'essenza stessa del capitalismo, contro la società dei consumi'.

14 'gruppi di patrioti che non diedero mai "tregua" al nemico: lo colpirono sempre, in ogni circostanza, di giorno e di notte, nelle strade delle città e nel cuore dei suoi fortilizi'.

15 'i nostri moduli organizzativi – grosso modo mutuati dai Tupamaros e dall'FLN algerino'.

16 'Il ricorso al colpo di stato oppure una radicale autoritaria svolta a destra sarebbe quindi del tutto conforme alle esigenze del sistema'.

17 'non è con l'acquiescenza o col sottrarsi a una lotta, che appare ormai inevitabile, che si evita lo scontro: lo unico risultato è che ci si giunge impreparati'.

18 'Feltrinelli ci considerava a noi di Potere Operaio, dei rivoluzionari sinceri, ma illusi e avveniristi perché non pensavamo alla controrivoluzione e non ci ponevamo adeguatamente la questione militare.'

19 'aveva conosciuto da vicino, molto più di noi che ne vivevamo solo il riflesso epico, le rivoluzioni di tutto il mondo. Sapeva che non c'era da scherzare, semmai da rischiare la pelle. Aveva adottato alla lettera le tecniche organizzative dei Tupamaros, di Carlos Marighella. E questo, mentre induceva gli altri al sorriso, affascinava me.'

20 'tutta una corrente politica di ex partigiani e di militanti non aveva mai smesso . . . di coltivare una posizione politica fortemente critica sugli esiti della

Resistenza, che avrebbe proseguire con uno scontro di classe generalizzato fino all'instaurazione di uno stato socialista'.

21 'per sconfiggere in modo irreversibile il nemico occorre un esercito capace di confrontarsi con l'avversario in molte battaglie prima che si giunge alla battaglia decisiva che, se vinta, apre la strada alla insurrezione rivoluzionaria di massa'.

22 'Ci sommergeva di discorsi sulla strategia rivoluzionaria, la struttura dell'esercito proletario, l'Unione Sovietica e il suo ruolo guida . . . Non volevamo costruire un esercito bensì un partito armato.'

23 'la sua idea di far saltare i tralicci dell'alta tensione in montagna . . . ci sembrava quantomeno stravagante'.

24 'un processo . . . di integrazione e di coordinamento tanto sul piano operativo, quanto su quello e politico'.

25 'la possibilità di creare strutture armate pur in un'organizzazione legale interna ai movimenti di massa'.

26 'Probabilmente se noi di Potere operaio non fossimo entrati nelle Brigate rosse queste ultime non sarebbero riuscite nemmeno ad organizzare il sequestro Moro.'

27 'molti di questi nuovi venuti avevano storie assurde erano l'ultima generazione di combattenti tutti giovanissimi e avevano tutti una biografia simile non avevano avuto nessun percorso di movimento anche perché ormai il movimento era stato spazzato via per cui il percorso era stato la lettura di qualche documento la distribuzione clandestina di qualche volantino scritte sul muri uno striscione su un cavalcavia e poi magari un omicidio subito tra le prime azioni e poi l'arresto su dichiarazioni di qualche pentito'.

3

From Resistance to Historic Compromise: the politics of the PCI

The PCI from Fascism to Liberation

The roots of the PCI lay in the Partito Comunista d'Italia (PCd'I; 'Communist Party of Italy'), founded in 1921. The PCd'I's early membership was battle-hardened from street fighting with Fascist *squadre* ('squads'), particularly in the near-insurrectional conditions of 1919. Following the Fascist takeover in 1924 and the banning of non-Fascist political parties the following year, around a third of the PCd'I's membership was imprisoned; the party's leader Antonio Gramsci was arrested in 1926 and died in prison eleven years later. Most party members who were left at liberty fled the country (Sassoon 2003: 38). The party's early identity was thus formed in clandestinity and in exile.

One significant episode in this early history was the 1928 discussion of guerrilla warfare against Fascism. Ottavio Pastore's proposal of what was effectively a *foquista* strategy, using armed attacks to encourage a broader rebellion, was endorsed by Pietro Secchia, a senior member of the party, but rejected by the party leadership (Massari 1979: 171–3). Secchia later returned to the topic, rejecting the *foquista* line but arguing that 'when the working masses are already on strike it is not hard to get them out on the streets . . . And it is at these moments that bombings . . . can be both useful and necessary' (quoted in Massari 1979: 177).[1] Specifically, Secchia urged attacks on power stations, telephone lines and railway lines, as a means of precipitating and then consolidating a general strike (Massari 1979: 178).

Secchia's proposals were broadly in line with the contemporary direction of Communist Party policy: in 1930, a handbook for urban guerrilla warfare was produced in Moscow (Massari 1979: 174). The Communist Party programme was dominated in this period by the 'Third Period' analysis, according to which the collapse of capitalism was imminent. 'The economic crisis was thought to be the crisis of the "system" . . . From this a set of simplistic equations followed: capitalism equals fascism; economic crisis equals political crisis; political crisis equals revolutionary crisis. The struggle was essentially one of class against class with no intermediate goals and no tactical and strategic alliances' (Sassoon 1981: 9). This 'class against class' line implied a rigid division of society: any social force not allied to the Communist Party was an ally of the ruling class, and would be an enemy in the coming revolutionary struggle. As well as preparing for insurrection, Communist parties around the world were called to give unconditional support to industrial militancy and to polemicise with political forces to the right of the party, such as the Partito Socialista Italiano (PSI; 'Italian Socialist Party').

The rise to power of Hitler's National Socialists in 1933 led to a revision of Communist Party thinking. The Popular Front line, promulgated in 1935, argued for 'an alliance between the working class and elements of the petty bourgeoisie and the bourgeoisie proper' (Amyot 1981: 25). The Popular Front programme was based on a two-stage model of revolution.

> In the first phase, a democratic, anti-fascist coalition government, the Popular Front, would come to power. This stage was later named 'progressive democracy'. This government would control or nationalise only the large monopolies, while non-monopolistic capital would be protected and even encouraged. This progressive democratic government would somehow lay the basis for the second stage, the socialist revolution and the dictatorship of the proletariat. (Amyot 1981: 37)

Popular Front Communism required trade union activity to be reined in if it threatened to inflict more damage on capitalism than the working class could exploit. Only once democracy had been secured could the party, conceivably, change gear and work for the construction of socialism.

Palmiro Togliatti, leader in exile of the PCd'I, contributed to the Popular Front programme and formulated an Italian variant. In 1928 Togliatti argued that 'the petty bourgeoisie . . . was always politically subordinate to some other class. The outcome of the class struggle between the proletariat and the bourgeoisie, he went on, depended on which of the two contending classes secured an alliance with this intermediate stratum' (Amyot 1981: 41). Fascism, Togliatti argued, had come to power by mobilising the petty bourgeoisie, alarmed both by the Italian economic situation and by the activities of the Communists, particularly their violence against Fascist *squadre*. It followed that '[i]nstead of waiting for the economic breakdown of capitalism, or, worse, accelerating it, the party had to advance positive political proposals that would offer a solution to the country's problems and consolidate a broad alliance, including the petty bourgeoisie and part of the bourgeoisie' (Amyot 1981: 43). The advent of Fascism had demonstrated that the PCd'I line was mistaken: henceforth *squadrismo* and *diciannovismo* ('1919ism') would be pejorative terms. To exacerbate the contradictions of capitalism was to aid Fascism, deliberately or not. Communists should be particularly vigilant against 'provocateurs', undercover Fascists who attempted to divide and weaken the Left by advancing ostensibly radical positions.

While Togliatti's stress on long-term cross-class alliances could be seen as conservative, his reading of the relationship between progressive democracy and socialism was more radical. Rather than postponing the construction of socialism to a later stage, Togliatti proposed 'structural reforms'; these could be carried out by a democratic government, formed through an alliance of the Communist Party with progressive elements of the bourgeoisie. Agrarian reform would distribute land to landless peasants, whose specific interests the Left had hitherto ignored; industrial reform would nationalise the leading monopolies. Structural reforms would erode the potential constituency of Fascism, enhance that of the Left and create a base from which further reforms could be carried out.

Togliatti's *via italiana al socialismo* ('Italian road to socialism') was a significant departure from the two-stage Popular Front programme. Mobilisation for intermediate goals would obviate the need for a perilous and divisive frontal struggle for socialism; it would also enable Communists to extend their presence within society, serving as a bulwark against a revival of Fascism. At the same time, the goal of far-reaching structural reforms would keep the party leadership from proposing a reformed capitalist democracy as an end in itself: pressure from below would drive Communists in government to integrate reforms into a programme for social transformation. As Togliatti wrote in 1956:

> On its own a nationalisation may not mean very much . . . But things change when this or other measures taken against monopoly capital are an integral part of a continuous action, of a constant struggle . . . by big political mass organisations with the support of a large section of public opinion in order to impose . . . an economic policy which would be to the advantage of the workers and of the middle strata (quoted in Sassoon 1981: 142)

The result would be a party which was 'institutionally pro-system – the champion of the new democratic republic – and yet anti-system – antagonistic to capitalism' (Sassoon 2003: 41).

This policy began to be put into action in March 1943, albeit in a superficially contradictory form. Broadcasting from exile, Togliatti greeted a wave of strike action in the north of Italy by calling for sabotage and guerrilla warfare, in terms which would seemingly have gratified Pastore:

> We want someone to derail these trains . . . These factories must not be allowed to work any longer. We need some groups of fearless men to think about blowing them up . . . When these squaddist thugs make the acquaintance of Partisan bombs and revolvers, we can be sure that their numbers will go down. So we need some fearless groups, groups of Partisans who will take up arms

and place themselves in the vanguard of the struggle to save the whole nation. (quoted in Massari 1979: 184)[2]

In July 1943 the Western Allies landed in Sicily. On 25 July King Victor Emmanuel dismissed Mussolini and appointed Marshal Badoglio in his place; Badoglio announced Italy's surrender to the Allies on 8 September. While Badoglio and the King set up a 'kingdom of the South', with British and US support, the north and centre of the country came under German occupation. The PCd'I, like sister parties elsewhere, was now committed to a war of national liberation against Fascism; in 1943 it was renamed the Partito Comunista Italiano (PCI), emphasising its national roots. Following Togliatti's broadcast the party began organising Gruppi di azione patriottica (GAP; 'Patriotic action groups'). In November Secchia issued a call for action:

> We need to act at once and on a wide scale against the Germans and the Fascists, against their property and against them in person; we need to fight with all means, from sabotage of production, machinery and means of transport, to the interruption and destruction of telegraph, telephone and electrical lines, to arson attacks on depots, warehouses, supplies, to the storming of German positions and headquarters, etc. (quoted in Massari 1979: 187–8)[3]

The GAP carried out numerous attacks on German and Fascist troops and commanders. Comitati di liberazione nazionale (CLN; 'Committees of National Liberation') and irregular Partisan forces became established across the north of the country; by mid-1944 liberated areas were being established. In the latter half of 1944, the initial phase of informal GAPist activity gave way to outright guerrilla warfare and formal paramilitary organisation, with Secchia appointed commander of the 'Garibaldi Brigades'. While the GAP's membership was 80–90 per cent Communist (Massari 1979: 186), the later Resistance was more heterogeneous. In particular, the Communists worked alongside the Partito d'Azione (Pd'A; 'Action Party'): a secular left-wing party founded in 1942 as a successor organisation to the pre-war anti-Fascist group Giustizia e Libertà ('Justice and Freedom'). The Pd'A collapsed shortly after Liberation (Ginsborg 1990: 89); many members went on to be active in the PCI, PSI and the centre-left Partito Repubblicano Italiano (PRI; 'Italian Republican Party'). Prominent former *azionisti* included Ugo La Malfa, Ernesto De Martino, Norberto Bobbio, Riccardo Lombardi, Vittorio Foa and FLM leader Bruno Trentin.

The PCI's reversion to Secchia's 1928 positions was more apparent than real. It is worth noting that Togliatti's call to arms came in response to a wave of strikes: Communists were urged, not to spread the strikes or occupy the factories, but to take paramilitary action for patriotic objectives, up to and including the destruction of the factories themselves. The alternatives were clearly stated by Secchia in June 1944: 'The supreme duty of Communists and patriots is now to leave the factory, the office and the fields, to pick up a rifle against the German invader' (quoted in Massari 1979: 195).[4] For Massari, 'GAPism represented a political line which substituted for the mobilisation of the proletariat in the workplace, oriented towards the bourgeois-democratic programme around which the Resistance developed. . . . The propaganda of GAPism justified it in terms of morality and national patriotism' (Massari 1979: 195–6).[5] Thus Pesce could idealise the GAP as 'groups of patriots who never gave quarter to the enemy'; similarly, in 1974 Luigi Longo characterised GAPists as 'moved by a fierce refusal to compromise . . . the necessity of reacting against the destruction of every human value' (quoted in Massari 1979: 191).[6] Massari sums up: 'This is the myth of the terrorist, substituting for political description and above all isolating GAPist acts from the broader context of the anti-fascist struggle, making the GAPist in one sense the "hero" of the struggle against Fascism, but also the "exception"' (Massari 1979: 191).[7]

In March 1944 Togliatti returned to Italy, landing at Salerno; the continuing transformation of party policy became known as the *svolta di Salerno* ('Salerno turn'). The *svolta* had two immediate implications. Firstly, Togliatti's emphasis on continuing popular mobilisation and diffuse anti-fascism required the PCI to establish a deep-rooted presence within Italian society. The resulting *partito nuovo* ('new party') has been described as 'a blend of elements taken from the Bolshevik Party and the Catholic Church' (Shore 1990: 71), with party sections vying with parish churches to be 'the focus and sponsor of all local public events' (Shore 1990: 71). An open-door recruitment policy led to massive expansion. From around 6,000 in 1943, party membership grew to 400,000 by the end of 1944, then to three or four times that number by the end of 1945; official membership figures peaked in 1947 at a little over 2,250,000 (Shore 1990: 34; Istituto Carlo Cattaneo 2005).

Secondly, in order to achieve structural reforms the PCI had to be in government. However, the party's alliance policy ruled out the election of a Communist government, let alone the seizure of power: the goal was a cross-class coalition. In the short term, the parties of the CLN should suspend their republicanism and enter Badoglio's government. The PCI's progressive patriotism thus brought it to the point of endorsing a monarchist government which had continuities with Fascism; a step the Pd'A refused to take. In the north, the Resistance was presented in terms of a united front against German invaders, whose patriotic unity was increasingly elevated from a fact on the ground to a historic achievement.

After Liberation, the Communists were represented in a series of interim governments. The party received 19 per cent of the vote in the 1946 election to the Constituent Assembly, compared with 35.2 per cent for Democrazia

Cristiana (DC; 'Christian Democracy') and 20.7 per cent for the PSI, reconstituted after Liberation under the name of Partito Socialista Italiano di Unità Proletaria (PSIUP; 'Socialist Party of Proletarian Unity'). The Assembly had the task of drawing up a Constitution for the new republic (the Italian monarchy had been abolished by a referendum held on the same day as the elections).

The PCI played a doubly influential role in the Assembly, affecting both its outcome and the approach by which it was achieved. The Constitution has an unusually 'progressive' slant; it defines Italy as a republic 'based on labour', while articles guarantee the right to work and the right of employees to participate in the running of their workplaces. While working to secure these constitutional guarantees, Togliatti sedulously avoided confrontation with the Catholic Church, or its key political ally, the DC. Formed in 1942, the DC had taken little part in the Resistance. It had, however, gained Vatican endorsement and constructed a broad cross-class Catholic coalition. The party matched Togliatti's analysis of society only too well: it clearly represented broad social currents which the PCI would have to engage with.

In 1944 Togliatti characterised the fledgling DC as including 'a mass of workers, peasants, intellectuals and young people, who basically share our aspirations because like us they want a democratic and progressive Italy' (quoted in Ginsborg 1990: 43). There was some truth in this: prominent DC left-winger Giuseppe Dossetti wrote in 1945 that 'between the ideology and experience of liberal capitalism on one hand, and the experience, if not the ideology, of the mass anti-capitalist movements on the other, it is the first, not the second, which is more radically anti-Christian' (Ginsborg 1990: 472). However, Togliatti's goal was to ally the PCI, not with radical elements of the DC bloc, but with the DC as a whole, even at the cost of the PCI's own policies. The limits of this stance rapidly became visible. In January 1947 the Partito Socialista dei Lavoratori Italiani (PSLI; 'Italian Workers' Socialist Party') formed as a centre-left split from the PSIUP, which readopted the historic name of PSI in response. During the debate on the Concordat, the PSLI's Giovanni Grilli proposed an amendment which prevented the Constitution from declaring marriage indissoluble. The amendment passed with PCI support, but against Togliatti's instructions: Communist members had been under instruction not to raise the issue. In March 1947 the PCI even voted to endorse the incorporation of the Vatican's 1929 Concordat into the Constitution, to the astonishment of other left-wing parties; Italy continued to be defined, in law, as a Catholic country (Ginsborg 1990: 101).

Togliatti's concessions to the DC were not reciprocated. In May 1947 the DC ejected the PCI and PSI from government. In 1948, in the first elections to the Chamber of Deputies, an alliance of the PCI and PSI received 31 per cent of the vote: this was a drop of nearly 9 per cent relative to 1946, although the vote for PCI candidates appears to have held or even risen. The DC, buoyed by US intervention 'breathtaking in its size, its ingenuity and its fla-grant contempt for any principle of non-interference in the internal affairs of another country' (Ginsborg 1990: 115), received 48.5 per cent of the vote. Dossetti, the leading representative of radical Christian reformism, dissolved his faction and retired from politics in 1951, frustrated at the DC's rightward drift (Ginsborg 1990: 142). The PSLI, which had effectively outflanked the PCI to the Left on the question of divorce, merged with other centre-left groups to form the Partito Socialista Democratico Italiano (PSDI; 'Italian Democratic Socialist Party'), which would be a governing partner of the DC for 25 out of the next 40 years.

The *partito nuovo* and the *via italiana* were significant and powerful elaborations on the Popular Front programme; together, they gave the PCI social roots and a political presence unrivalled by any Communist Party operating in a capitalist democracy. That said, the principle of mass recruit-ment was inherently problematic. The PCI could not have gained a mass membership if it had insisted that new recruits were versed in the complexi-ties of the *via italiana*; however, this meant that the pre-war hardcore mem-bership, and even the substantial wartime Party, were vastly outnumbered by post-war members who had their own, often very different, understanding of Communism. 'For them the Communist Party was the Party of the Resis-tance, but they were also attracted to Communism by the example of the Soviet Union in the war and by Stalin. . . . "Ha' da veni' Baffone" ["Big Moustaches is coming"] was the rallying cry of the southern workers' (Sassoon 1981: 33).

Given the prevalence of attitudes like these, the party's professed modera-tion was widely seen – among the party's opponents and its members alike – as a facade hiding more radical designs. Occasionally there were attempts to put the party's supposed 'hidden agenda' into practice, notably in the near-insurrectional disturbances which erupted in July 1948 after an assassination attempt on Togliatti. More consistently, the effect of this perspective was to downgrade the importance of the PCI's overt (and genuine) agenda, and hence to discourage day-to-day activism. Thus in 1956, Togliatti attacked the 'maximalist sectarianism' which was 'withdrawn within itself waiting for the "great day"' (quoted in Sassoon 1981: 194). Of the Turin PCI federation in the early 1960s, Amyot writes, 'Having lost the perspective of an "X-hour", [older members] had become discouraged and ceased to devote their energies to day-to-day struggles. . . . There were workers who were in favour of an eventual armed seizure of power, but refused to take part in strikes' (Amyot 1981: 123).

The PCI's structures effectively insulated the leadership from these ten-dencies. As a democratic centralist organisation, the PCI had a pyramidal structure, in which elected bodies at each level elected delegates to the next level up; once a policy decision is made at the apex of such a structure, it is binding on every lower level. The limited accountability offered by this structure allowed a fundamental divergence between party policies and the beliefs of party members to remain, undermining that linkage between top-down structural reform and a mass anti-fascist party which was central to the *via italiana*.

Problems were also created both by the PCI's belief in cross-class coalitions and by its belief that such a coalition had been achieved, in the Resistance and after. For orthodox Communists, the Resistance and the post-war coalition represented an unfinished project, combining patriotic anti-fascism with democratic structural reform. The Constitution was at once a proof of the validity of the Communists' strategy, that strategy's crowning achievement, and a resource which could be drawn on in the future. As late as 1975, PCI right-winger Giorgio Napolitano declared that '[t]he patrimony of anti-fascist unity remained as a political fact capable of revival'; the Constitution '[held] open the possibilities of a relaunching of the anti-fascist revolution' (Napolitano 1977: 17, 15).

Clearly, this account of the post-war period is highly idealised – and this idealism could be disabling in a confrontation with less high-minded opponents. The PCI saw the coalition forged in the Resistance as a historic achievement; it followed that it was too valuable to be disrupted by calculations of short-term political advantage. Regrettably, the Communists' allies were less scrupulous: '[w]hile the Communists postponed in the honourable name of national unity, their opponents acted, decided, manoeuvred and, not surprisingly, triumphed' (Ginsborg 1990: 47). Even the achievements of the Constitution were circumscribed. The implementation of many constitutional provisions was subject to inordinate delay; a regional tier of government was introduced in 1970, 22 years late. Other provisions were defined in a 1948 legal decision as 'programmatic norms', which would determine future legislation but could not strike down existing laws (including those passed under Fascism). The Constitution could thus prompt a critical as well as a supportive reading: Piperno dates his political awakening to 'my criticism of the idea – the hypocrisy – of claiming that our nation was "based on labour"' (Grandi 2003: 38).[8] Moreover, the party's strategy offered no guidelines for situations in which it was out of government. If excluded from power, the PCI could not coherently call for their opponents to be excluded in turn; instead, the party was reduced to repeatedly offering itself as a potential member of a patriotic coalition, reproaching its opponents for being so unprincipled as to exclude it.

The equivocal results of the Resistance period also betray a weakness in the underlying strategy: '[The Communists'] two-stage strategy – liberation first, social and political reform second – caused them to dissipate the strength of the Resistance and of worker and peasant agitation' (Ginsborg 1990: 47). The reference to a 'two-stage strategy' here is telling, given that the *via itali-ana* was predicated on a single stage of progressive mobilisation and reform. The problem for the PCI after Liberation was that the enduring cross-class alliance on which the *via italiana* depended could not be taken for granted. The fear of fracturing the anti-fascist alliance could be aroused by any issue liable to divide the Communists from their allies. This threat was clearly overstated: while the alliance between PCI and DC evidently was breakable, the episode of the constitutional provision for divorce, and the subsequent history of Grilli's party, suggest that it was not Communist radicalism that broke it. The threat was very real in its effects on the PCI, however: by making any meaningful structural reforms conditional on the consent of the DC, the party effectively re-imposed a rigid 'two-stage' model on the *via italiana*.

Lastly, the PCI explicitly evoked the Resistance political coalition as the model for the peacetime cross-class coalition it hoped to build. This was an inherently problematic approach, requiring the party to identify its main political opponent as an ally while identifying some other political force as the Fascist enemy. Amyot notes:

> The cult of the Resistance, in which the *unity* achieved by all the anti-fascist forces is constantly stressed, has been assiduously cultivated by the PCI. An extensive round of commemorative activities associated with the Resistance provide many opportunities for returning to the theme; the Party attempts to make these events as 'unitary' as possible, with the participation of Christian Democrats, Republicans and even Liberals. It also tries to recreate the unity of the armed Resistance in the present, by urging unity of the anti-fascist forces against the threat to democracy represented by the MSI, other neo-fascist organisations and their terrorist arms. (Amyot 1981: 26; emphasis in original)

The length to which the party would take this policy was illustrated in 1973, when the Milan edition of *l'Unità* printed a picture of a local assembly in support of the metalworkers' campaign for a pay deal. The caption merits quoting in all its considerable length:

> MILAN – Tens of thousands of metalworkers yesterday continued to participate in assemblies, open to social and political forces and organised by the Milan branch of the Metalworkers' Federation [FLM], in 30 large factories in and around the city. Representatives of the PCI, the PSI and the DC, district, pro-vincial and regional councillors, MPs, trades council representatives, delega-tions from youth and student associations and members of the clergy brought their public solidarity and their support to the contractual battle which involves more than 300,000 eligible workers in our area. At the Falck factory in Sesto

San Giovanni, where workers from all the firms in the area gathered, the open assembly was also the occasion for celebration of the anti-fascist strikes which began precisely on 23 March 1943. The celebration was joined by the entire membership of Sesto's democratic district council, bearing the banner [*gonfalone*] of the city. (Anon. 1973a)[9]

MPs, DC representatives, priests, assembled under the banner of the medieval city of Milan: this array of 'social and political forces' takes the PCI's commitment to cross-class alliance to almost self-parodic extremes. The broadest possible alliance is sanctified by the evocation of the Resistance; nobody and nothing is excluded, apart from the extreme right – and any extreme left forces opposed to the PCI's hegemony over the Left. In fact, groups to the left of the PCI and opposed to the Communists' coalition policy had existed in Italy as early as the Liberation; the party's anti-fascist ideology left it few resources for dealing with these. In the 1970s this approach became especially problematic: ' "defence of the Republic born in the Resistance" was a classically anti-fascist rallying cry . . . To the extent that the Party was successful in employing this line against the extreme left . . . it seemed to imply that the real enemy was still on the Right and that the Red Brigades were a right-wing phenomenon' (Hellman 1988: 84).

The PCI Left from Secchia to Ingrao

In the early 1950s, the PCI seemed to have been permanently excluded from government, a situation exacerbated by a sustained attack on the CGIL's presence in industry (Hellman 1988: 45). At this stage Secchia was the party's vice-secretary, with responsibility for party organisation. Secchia advocated selective recruitment and a tight-knit organisation, rooted in workplace-based cells as well as, or in preference to, community-based sections. This was a strategic as well as an organisational position: 'Whereas the section is an organ for absorbing, recruiting and "wooing" the wider public, the cell is an instrument of attack . . . Whereas the cell is by tradition semi-clandestine and barely visible, the section vaunts its legitimacy and proudly displays its presence' (Shore 1990: 93). Meanwhile, Giorgio Amendola was promoting the 'Movement for the Rebirth of the South' – a region with few industrial workplaces and a minimal Communist presence. Amendola's movement included 'many people who were neither Communists nor Socialists, but generically progressive' (Amyot 1981: 47). In 1953 Togliatti came down in favour of Amendola's open-door approach (Amyot 1981: 53): henceforth PCI organisation would be based on sections rather than cells and on broad alliances rather than ideological purity. In 1954 Togliatti instructed Secchia to write an article on the PCI's organisation; the article should stress the PCI's nature as a 'mass party' and 'explain the novelty of what we are doing' (quoted in Sassoon 1981: 86). The contrast with Secchia's own positions must have been obvious to all concerned. Later the same year, a bizarre political and financial scandal led to (or facilitated) Secchia's removal from the party leadership; his place was taken by Amendola (Ginsborg 1990: 200).

Secchia was a leading representative of what was widely seen as the Stalinist element of the PCI: believers in socialist revolution, disciplined organisation and the leading role of the USSR. The orthodoxy of this current can be both under- and overstated. Despite his later association with Feltrinelli, during the Resistance and afterwards Secchia had not departed from the party's 'patriotic' line; indeed, he played a major role in defusing the incipient insurrection of July 1948. On the other hand, the Secchian current's vocal allegiance to the Soviet Union and the figure of Stalin did not bespeak Communist orthodoxy. There had never been any prospect of *Baffone* coming to Italy; Secchia's lingering belief in socialist revolution was rather more heretical than the *via italiana*.

Perhaps the most significant aspect of Secchia's 'Stalinism' was the stress it placed on party unity, to be enforced through democratic centralism. Ironically, this made it extremely difficult for Secchia's current to make its presence felt. Writing of a later period, Shore observes: 'the pro-Soviet tendency could not form an organised current without risking expulsion for "factionalism"; therefore they had not organised' (Shore 1990: 134). The ideology of the group coincided with the maintenance of the cohesion of the leadership coalition, even when this coalition excluded the group itself. The leadership could, in effect, use the Secchian current against itself; the price was that it would remain an element of silent or passive dissent within the party.

Following the removal of Secchia in 1954, Khrushchev's 1956 speech to the Twentieth Congress of the Communist Party of the Soviet Union heralded a larger 'renovation' of the party apparatus. While the 'secret' section of the speech, initially distributed only to Communist Parties, denounced the excesses of Stalin's rule, the 'open' section broke new ground by admitting the possibility of different roads to socialism (Sassoon 1981: 98–9). This removed Togliatti's remaining ideological inhibitions in dealing with opponents of the *via italiana*. Following the PCI's Eighth Congress of 1956, the middle and junior ranks of the leadership were purged and a layer of 'renovators' introduced throughout the party (Hellman 1988: 168). The 'renovators' were members of the generation which had flocked to the PCI after Liberation, and had undergone intensive training in the Togliattian party line. United by social and ideological ties, the *rinnovatori* formed 'a strongly homogeneous, hegemonic leadership' (Hellman 1988: 150) which would remain in place until the end of the 1960s.

Both the PCI's and the PSI's votes rose at elections during the 1950s, with the PSI vote remaining the smaller of the two. At the 1963 election the two parties took 39.1 per cent of the vote: only slightly below the 39.7 per cent the two parties had taken at the Constituent Assembly election of 1946, but with the PCI taking nearly two-thirds of the total (25.3 per cent) rather than less than half (19 per cent). At the end of 1963, the PSI entered a governmental alliance with the DC as part of a 'centre-left' coalition embracing the PSDI and the PRI. The 'centre-left' coalition, the PSI's first entry to government since 1947, endured until June 1968. In the longer term, it marked a decisive shift in Italian politics, beginning a period in which the DC looked for allies primarily to its left: the small right-wing Partito Liberale Italiano (PLI; 'Italian Liberal Party'), a governmental partner of the DC for six of the sixteen years since the exclusion of the Left, was a formal member of government for less than two years out of the next seventeen, as opposed to the PSI's eight (Ginsborg 1990: 6–7). This second period, moreover, would be followed by the *pentapartito* ('five-party') governments of the 1980s, with the DC joined by PLI, PRI, PSDI and PSI alike.

For the PCI, the 'centre-left' coalition was devastating; it was seen as marking the incorporation into the DC 'system' of a party with a significant claim to represent the Left. On one hand this would broaden the DC's appeal and reinforce its hold on power; on the other, it threatened to polarise Italian politics between the DC bloc and the Communists, marginalising the latter. The danger was that a cross-class coalition was about to be formed, without or against the PCI. As Napolitano recalled, 'This complex of developments – the capitalist boom and in Italy the end of the socialist–Communist alliance and the centre–left alignment – weighed heavily on us until 1968. It caused a sense of uncertainty and preoccupations about the future' (Napolitano 1977: 34).

Togliatti died in 1964, aged 71. His death triggered a fresh round of debate within the party. The leading Right and Left candidates for the leadership were Amendola and Pietro Ingrao, a member of the PCI Executive and former editor of the party's paper *l'Unità*; in the event the veteran Partisan Longo, Togliatti's preferred candidate, was elected instead of either. Longo's election had the effect of turning the contest between Amendola and Ingrao into an ideological dispute. In the Ingraian analysis, while capitalist modernisation might ward off fascism, this was not in itself a progressive process: 'the Party's aim had to be not an acceptable quantitative level of economic growth, but rather a qualitatively different type of economy' (Amyot 1981: 58). The threat of bringing capitalism into crisis could be averted by foregrounding structural reform within an 'alternative model of development'. As well as providing a road map for the construction of socialism, this would furnish goals for industrial struggles, ensuring that these had a constructive outcome and integrating Communist political leadership with the industrial base. The *via italiana* had followed its Popular Front precursor in advocating a cross-class governing alliance, built under the sign of progressive and patriotic anti-fascist unity; more innovatively, it had proposed continuous two-way communication between leadership and mass party, integrating strategic political reform with activism from below. The Ingraian re-reading of the *via italiana* emphasised the second element while downplaying the first.

The Ingraians also took issue with the centralising tendencies of the Secchian Left and the institutional focus of the Amendolan right, arguing that 'it was necessary to decentralise power by creating a network of centres of local power and direct democracy' (Amyot 1981: 59). The extension of working-class power within society would complement top-down reform; specifically, the Ingraians proposed to build influence in local government and the trade unions rather than focusing solely on a DC-dominated parliament. A '"new historic bloc" of social forces' was to be formed, 'primarily in civil society rather than at the political level' (Amyot 1981: 61). This 'historic bloc' (an allusion to Gramsci) would embrace working-class DC voters, and perhaps a left-wing Catholic party created by a future split in the DC, while excluding the 'bourgeois' centre parties. In the short term the PCI should align itself only with Foa's PSIUP (a new party whose MPs had left the PSI rather than participate in the alliance with the DC), and perhaps with the left-wing faction in the PSI led by Lombardi. These positions represented a coherent and far-reaching development of the *via italiana*, which might have rallied support outside as well as within the PCI: Lombardi had proposed a '"revolutionary reformism", a process that continually destroys the equilibrium of the system and creates a series of counter-powers' (quoted in Ginsborg 1990: 266).

The Ingraian proposals were characterised by urgency, reflecting an underlying pessimism. The Ingraians 'believed that capitalism was capable of integrating the working-class movement, and saw the centre-left as an attempt to do so which had good chances of succeeding' (Amyot 1981: 64): should the project of an 'alternative model of development' fail, the PCI might never have another chance. Moreover, 'the capitalists' reaction to any left-wing victories would be sharp and rapid, and would soon precipitate a crisis' (Amyot 1981: 62); progress towards socialism would be made quickly or not at all. By contrast, Amendola and the right wing of the party 'were more sanguine about the margins for reformism within Italian capitalism; this was in part because they contemplated less radical reforms' (Amyot 1981: 62). On the questions of structural reform and extra-parliamentary activity Amendola's own reading of the *via italiana* effectively rejoined Popular Front orthodoxy. Industrial militancy should not be harnessed but controlled; political activity should focus on the maintenance of cross-class alliances. The PCI had nothing to fear from the centre-left: 'the centre-left would, in the long run, bring new votes to the PCI as disillusionment set in and at the same time prepare the way for the Communists' entry into government as the only party capable of ensuring the success of a reform programme' (Amyot 1981: 64). Organisationally, Amendola proposed a merger of the PCI and the PSI; this would be the core of an alliance of all the parties of the secular Left and centre, including the staunchly anti-Communist PSDI.

Ingrao sealed the fate of his embryonic faction by calling for an extension of open debate and democratic decision-making within the PCI. This second-ary issue, and the even more secondary issue of whether Ingrao had acted within his rights in openly stating his dissent from the Executive's majority line on the subject, led in 1966 to a purge of Ingraians from positions of influence throughout the Party. The PCI Right's defeat of Ingrao was facili-tated by the party's democratic centralist structures, and more fundamentally by party members' belief in the importance of unity. Ironically, as we have seen, this belief was particularly strong on the Secchian left. 'One of the strongest attacks [on Ingrao] came from the traditionalist leader Arturo Colombi who stated that the Party rank and file was "perplexed" by the appearance of divisions in the leadership' (Amyot 1981: 69). (As Hellman notes, 'in the PCI vocabulary . . . "perplexity" has very negative connota-tions' (Hellman 1988: 159).)

By the end of 1966, PCI policy had been redrawn along Amendolan lines; the prevailing reading of the *via italiana* erred on the side of Popular Front orthodoxy, elevating the re-establishment of a cross-class governing alliance over the achievement of short-term political goals. The Ingraian left remained a dissenting presence within the party; so too did the smaller Secchian left. Secchia himself remained a PCI Senator until his death in 1973. In the late 1960s he was in contact with Feltrinelli, whose catastrophist outlook he shared (Feltrinelli 2001: 407). However, Feltrinelli remained isolated, not only because the PCI leadership did not share Secchia's nostalgia for partisan warfare, but because the Partisan war itself had had very different goals. Secchia himself, between 1943 and 1948, had been just as committed to a 'democratic or anti-fascist revolution' as Togliatti or Amendola; Feltrinelli's revolutionary GAP were founded on myth rather than memory.

The PCI and the first cycle

Then came 1968. . . . The new militant thrust that then came from the working class put the problem of the unity of the workers' movement and of a change in social relations firmly on the agenda. In 1969, the Socialist Party recovered its autonomy and began to review its political line. A gradual reconciliation between socialists and Communists began. (Napolitano 1977: 34)

For Napolitano, in 1977 a rising star of the Amendolan right, the revolu-tionary years of 1968–9 should be celebrated primarily for prompting the PSI

to 'review its political line' and making the party available as a potential partner to the PCI. While this perspective might now seem eccentric,
Napolitano's account offers testimony, from an unimpeachably hostile source,
to the benefits which contentious movements could offer the PCI. Having
ignored the cycle of contention while new tactics were innovated and diffused, around 1969 the PCI and CGIL engaged with the cycle constructively,
adopting or endorsing elements of the new repertoire. At the same time, the
PCI worked to detach the new repertoire from its associated ideological and
organisational forms. Movement innovations could thus take their place
within the PCI's own repertoire, while persistent activist minorities could
safely be dismissed as adventurists and hooligans. The result was a larger,
more active and more influential PCI, and hence a shift in the balance of the
party's relations with the PSI.

The process, and in particular the disjuncture between the earlier phases
and the phases of engagement, is visible in Napolitano's analysis of the
period. On one hand, there was the student movement, seen essentially as a
symptom of a breakdown of communications between the PCI and its
constituency:

> Between the end of 1967 and the beginning of 1968, we went through a
> critical period: we were acutely aware of the danger of a break with new
> forces – especially but not only students – that were moving in a revolutionary
> direction, even if in confused and often unacceptable forms, and did not
> identify with our Party, with its political and ideological heritage (Napolitano
> 1977: 35–6)

Although a similar communications breakdown occurred between the CGIL
and parts of its constituency, this was under control by the time of the 1969
strike wave, which can thus be sharply dissociated from the unruly spontaneity of the 'young people's protest' of 1967–8:

> In 1968 and 1969 the unions had serious difficulties and had to carry out a
> major effort at renewal, but they fully affirmed their leadership in shaping the
> struggles of 1969, precisely because they understood the lesson and the thrust
> which had come from the young people's protest . . . So the protest touched
> only the fringes and did not penetrate deeply into the working class. (Napolitano
> 1977: 36–7)

What remained in the aftermath of the cycle was a reinvigorated PCI and a
scattering of misguided minorities, insignificant and, in the last analysis,
hostile to the party:

> What has been called the extra-parliamentary left arose not from a criticism but
> from a radical denial of the leadership capabilities of the parties and other 'tra-
> ditional' organisations of the working class.

... the glorification of the spontaneity of the movement and the radical negation of the strategy and of the role of the 'traditional' institutions of the working class ... led the 'Manifesto' group to break with our party. But the facts have demonstrated the inconsistency of those positions: many vague aspirations or expectations of that group, and of other formations of the extra-parliamentary left, fell and gave way to rather different modes of behaviour. The line of founding new political and union tools as an alternative to the 'traditional' institutions of the workers' movement has had to be abandoned. (Napolitano 1977: 35, 37)

Napolitano sums up both the PCI Right's hostility to contentious social movements and its ultimate willingness to profit from their 'new militant thrust'. As he himself had written in 1972, referring to the workerist groups, 'Our judgment on them is deep-seated and decisive. We believe it is to our credit that we have been able to detach from them a large proportion of the young people who had fallen under their influence' (Napolitano 1972).[10]

The immediate effect of the first cycle, however, had been to exacerbate the PCI's left–right divisions. In June 1968 Amendola argued that 'the PCI had to carry out a struggle against the "extremist and anarchist positions that have appeared in the student movement"; he even called for "revolutionary vigilance" because of the possibility of "provocateurs" in the movement' (Amyot 1981: 175). Against this position, which risked generalising the PCI's institutional focus into outright opposition to new social movements, the left-winger Rossana Rossanda proposed to integrate the student movement into the Ingraian project of a new 'historic bloc'. The debate was resolved at the Twelfth PCI Congress in January 1969, where Enrico Berlinguer displayed his aptitude for preserving party unity by evoking both left- and right-wing versions of PCI orthodoxy:

Berlinguer proposed that the autonomy of the various mass movements be recognised. Furthermore, they were to be an integral part of the Party's strategy for the conquest of power, as they formed part of the 'historic bloc' the PCI was seeking to form ... in practice Berlinguer proposed to insert the new mass movements into the PCI's struggle for a new parliamentary equilibrium, and to use them eventually as a means of bringing pressure to bear on the DC and other potential coalition partners. (Amyot 1981: 177–8)

At this stage, Berlinguer – like Napolitano and Rossanda – was in his mid-forties: the three were rising stars in a party whose leading figures were older by ten years (Ingrao) or twenty (Amendola, Secchia, Longo). Berlinguer, uniquely, offered to unite the party around a version of the PCI Right's institutional approach, but articulated in terms which evoked the Ingraian project for long-term social transformation. The strategy paid off in 1972, with his appointment as Secretary of the party. By then, Rossanda was outside the party. In November 1969 she was one of a group of Ingraian leftists, associated with the paper *Il manifesto*, who were 'struck off' from party membership (*radiati*): a measure short of outright expulsion, leaving open the possibility of readmission.

Berlinguer's synthesis, with differences of emphasis, would dominate the party at least until his death in 1984. Like Amendola, Berlinguer believed that a fascist revival was a real and present danger, and that capitalist democracy could save itself through an alliance with the PCI. Both prioritised alliance-building over reforms; in 1971, Berlinguer argued that '[i]f tension arises between a given reform and the maintenance of the broadest possible alliance front, the alliance should be favoured' (quoted in Hellman 1988: 202). Both, moreover, mistrusted industrial militancy, fearing an irresoluble crisis of capitalism; as early as 1970, Berlinguer intervened during a strike at Fiat to call for a 'qualified' revival of productivity – '"qualified" in the sense that it had to favour the truly productive forces in the country' – so as to forestall attempts to 'use the economic difficulties and disorder as a pretext to attempt reactionary, adventurist, rightist political operations' (Amyot 1981: 200).

Two factors set Berlinguer apart. Firstly, he was prepared to think the hitherto unthinkable, bypassing the secular left and centre so as to approach the DC directly. As well as the secularist Amendolan right, this differentiated Berlinguer from the Ingraians' openness to the Catholic left, which was predicated on a convergence between Christian and secular leftists. Berlinguer appeared sympathetic to Christianity as such: he aligned himself with 'Catholic Communists' such as Antonio Tatò and Franco Rodano, who argued that both Marxism and Catholicism involved 'a critique of liberal individualism . . . and an emphasis on discipline and social, collective goals' (Amyot 1981: 205).

Secondly, Berlinguer was careful to avoid polarising the party. If the Left would have found Amendola's leadership hard to accept, they would have had little more patience with a cynical attempt to dress up Amendolan policies in Ingraian rhetoric. Instead, Berlinguer consistently set his policies within the perspective of a broader programme of social transformation. In its early stages, at least, Berlinguer's opening to the left was real as well as rhetorical. By presenting a version of Communist orthodoxy which evoked the Ingraian Left, Berlinguer gave the Left and its positions qualified 'orthodox' endorsement. While this opening was the product of Berlinguer's tactical need for allies, it allowed (among other things) for a constructive engagement.

The PCI could now adopt the role of inclusive gatekeeper and engage constructively with the first cycle of contention. The PCI's engagement with the first cycle was a great success for the party, not least in terms of membership. Even when party membership was at its height, year-on-year changes were as likely to be negative as positive. 1969 and 1970 were the first two successive years of membership growth since 1954, and six more years of growth followed (Istituto Carlo Cattaneo 2005).

Under Berlinguer the party seemed to have the best of both worlds: while appealing to former activists on the basis of its adoption of the innovations of the first cycle, the party was embarking on an 'institutional' strategy based on a claim to political legitimacy. With the ascent of the Berlinguerian cadre coinciding with the decline of the first cycle, the new institutional project was seen as a constructive exit from the disorderly radicalism of the Hot Autumn. The activism of the Hot Autumn could thus be legitimated and simultaneously consigned to history.

However, this double success was conjunctural, springing from the tactical needs of a new PCI leader who had yet to impose himself fully on the party. It was also, by definition, unrepeatable. Once the Berlinguerian reorientation was complete, the post-Ingraian left would no longer be required. Moreover, there was no serious contender within the party whose interests would have been served by a second opening to the left. A hostile engagement with the second cycle of contention, narrowing the party's own tactical and ideological ground, was the inevitable result. The outcome was negative both for the movements and for the party. 1977, the year of engagement, was the first year since 1968 when membership fell rather than grew; thereafter it fell steadily year by year from 1978 to 1989, and more steeply thereafter (Istituto Carlo Cattaneo 2005).

The strange success of the Historic Compromise (1972–6)

The Thirteenth Congress of the PCI opened in Milan on 13 March 1972; the following day, Feltrinelli's abortive attempt to black out the city would cost him his life. Addressing the Congress, Berlinguer argued that 'a new perspective can be realised only by collaboration between the great movements of the people: communist, socialist and Catholic'. This broad alliance was necessitated by 'the pressing nature of great social questions which are also political and ideological' and by 'the depth of the roots of fascism' (quoted in Amyot 1981: 202).

Eighteen months later, in September 1973, Pinochet's military coup in Chile overthrew Allende's democratically elected socialist government. The following month Berlinguer returned to his theme in the PCI journal *Rinascita*. He argued that Allende's defeat showed that the Left must prevent the formation of 'a broad front of the clerico-fascist type' by developing an alliance with 'popular forces of Catholic inspiration' (quoted in Amyot 1981: 203–4). In 1964 Amendola had speculated about uniting 'the 48% of Italians to the left of the DC' (quoted in Amyot 1981: 198); 48.5 per cent was the

DC's share of the vote in its landslide victory of 1948. Berlinguer now dismissed even a victory of this magnitude: 'it would be illusory to think that, even if the left-wing parties and forces succeeded in gaining 51% of the vote and seats in Parliament . . . this fact would guarantee the survival and work of a government representing this 51%' (quoted in Sassoon 1981: 224). He advocated, not an Amendolan 'left alternative', but a 'democratic alternative', beginning with an 'emergency government' including the DC, the PCI and other democratic parties. The success of this coalition would later make possible a 'historic compromise' between Left and Right: in Napolitano's formulation, 'this experience of several years of government in common . . . [might] open the way – if all agreed – to a more clear and certain choice directed towards what we have called the "historic compromise"' (Napolitano 1977: 105).

The proposal of an 'historic compromise' (*compromesso storico*) could be seen as orthodoxy: a revival of the post-war coalition project. In 1977 Tatò went further, presenting the policy in terms of a Hegelian vision of historical progress: 'The days of [bourgeois] hegemony are over. . . . The historic compromise will provide the transition period to the new hegemony . . . alternatives to the historic compromise . . . cannot work as they have no conceptually valid base in history' (quoted in Ruscoe 1982: 114–15). However, the DC which broke with the PCI in 1947 had had a substantial left-wing element: in 1949 Dossetti's faction accounted for as much as a third of the party (Ginsborg 1990: 130). In 1972, two decades after Dossetti's retirement, a left-wing split from the DC contested national elections. Livio Labor's Movimento Popolare dei Lavoratori (MPL; 'Popular Workers' Movement') gained no seats and split soon afterwards; many members joined the PSI or the newly formed Partito di Unità Proletaria (PdUP; 'Proletarian Unity Party'), which had incorporated the Manifesto group.

The failure of the MPL made Berlinguer's task easier in the short term, discrediting the Ingraian left's longstanding goal of alliance with a left-wing Catholic party, but also called his chances of success into question. The DC which Berlinguer approached was, by definition, not the DC of Labor, let alone Dossetti. Whatever common ground Berlinguer might be able to find with Rodano and Tatò's austere Catholic social reformism, to ally the PCI with the actually existing DC represented a significant move to the right.

The PCI leadership had some reason for caution. The 'Hot Autumn' had been followed by an economic recession; this lent credence to the Amendolan belief that union activism risked destabilising capitalism. An atmosphere of impending crisis was heightened by a wave of right-wing bombings and by the first actions of left-wing armed struggle groups. The PCI understood these groups' actions in terms of right-wing provocation; stories of fascist infiltration of anarchist and far-left groups abounded. The legal far right was also on the rise: in the May 1972 elections the MSI, which had recently absorbed the Monarchist Party, took 8.7 per cent of the vote, compared to a combined vote of 5.7 per cent for the two parties in the election of 1968. The dissolution of Emilio Colombo's centre-left government in January 1972, followed by the formation of a centre-right government excluding the PSI, added to the impression of a political balance shifting to the right. Moreover, the PCI leadership was predisposed to a pessimistic judgment of these developments: 'we are so marked by the historical experience of the defeat of the workers' movement by fascism that we believe in never underestimating the possibilities of right-wing solutions' (Napolitano 1977: 41).

However, this pessimistic outlook rapidly proved to be out of tune with the times. Local elections were held in parts of Italy in November 1973 and June 1974; on each occasion the vote for both the DC and the MSI fell. Even more telling was the outcome of the May 1974 referendum on repealing the 1970 law legalising divorce, requested by conservative Catholic groups. The DC leadership campaigned vigorously for repeal, hoping to gain popular support by mobilising Catholic family values. Believing that the referendum was bound to be won, and that campaigning against it would only polarise the country, the PCI proposed to forestall the referendum by tabling an amended version of the divorce law, to be drafted in terms more acceptable to the religious right. (Under Italy's referendum legislation, a referendum can only call for the repeal of a specific law; a rewritten divorce law would have pre-empted the referendum.) The strategy was both ill-judged and counterproductive. The referendum was heavily defeated; 40 per cent voted in favour, compared with the 47 per cent who had voted in 1972 for the DC and the MSI, the two parties which supported repeal of the law. '[The religious right], convinced that they had the PCI and the left on the ropes, were not mollified. And the secular left began to wonder about the lengths to which the Communists would go to strike a deal with the DC' (Hellman 1988: 30).

By now the radical left was growing in strength as the second cycle of contention began. The PCI held its course. Early signs appeared to vindicate this strategy. In the country-wide local elections of June 1975, the party took 33 per cent of the votes: a rise of 6.5 per cent relative to the local elections of 1970. The results gave the PCI its strongest ever position in local and regional politics throughout Italy, with advances in the south and the industrial northwest as well as the central 'Red belt'. PCI–PSI coalitions governed several cities and regions. However, the party still held to the goal of an all-embracing cross-class alliance: 'numerous concessions were offered to the Christian Democrats . . . in all areas of the country, including parts of the South where the local DC often was linked to the Mafia' (Hellman 1988: 34). The party's new-found civic responsibilities also accentuated the leadership's commitment to 'responsible' economic policies, putting it at loggerheads with the activists of the second cycle of contention. The party took control of Turin city council in 1975; four years later a third of council tenants either paid no rent or set their own figure. Efforts to combat this phenomenon seriously eroded the PCI's popularity among council tenants: in the Turin wards dominated by council tenancy, the PCI vote dropped from 50 per cent to 41.4 per cent between the general elections of 1976 and 1979 (Hellman 1988: 234, 55).

In the general election of June 1976, the party's 34.4 per cent vote represented a rise of 7.2 per cent since 1972. The shift to the left which had been apparent in previous years was still more evident in elections in which, paradoxically, both the DC's and the PSI's share of the votes were unchanged (38.7 per cent and 9.6 per cent respectively). The large rise in the PCI's vote was matched by lower votes for the PSDI, the PLI and the MSI. Assuming that few supporters of these firmly anti-Communist parties switched directly to voting PCI, it would appear that both the DC and the PSI lost votes to the major parties to their left and gained votes from the minor parties to their right. The Italian political situation was becoming more rather than less polarised, with the DC and the PCI sharing an unprecedented 73.1 per cent of the total vote. The gap between the DC's and the PCI's share of the vote, moreover, had narrowed from 11.6 per cent in 1972 to 4.3 per cent; 'overtaking' the DC for the first time began to seem a possibility (figures from Ginsborg 1990: 442).

The enhanced electoral credibility of the PCI under Berlinguer had disturbed the social and cultural unity of the DC bloc; reformist Catholic voters were starting to look further afield. Moreover, the aftermath of the Hot Autumn had favoured moderate left-wing forces which could institutionalise protest; the PCI's successes in this area since 1970 could now be repaid in electoral terms. What was potentially a new PCI vote was emerging, uniting the majority of the PCI's existing constituency with moderate left-wingers from other traditions. To capitalise on these developments, the party needed to consolidate its position as a 'respectable' reformist party, capable of managing industrial activism, while maintaining the core progressive values which had attracted these new voters and as far as possible retaining its traditional constituency. The party's response to this complex conjuncture was complicated still further – and ultimately vitiated – by two additional constraints.

The first of these was the 'historic compromise' strategy itself. While this certainly helped the party gain votes from some quarters, it also set it at odds with many party members and supporters, including supporters who had been attracted by the party's apparent radicalism following the first cycle of contention. Worse, the strategy was predicated on the willingness of the DC to make concessions, meaning that the party's fate was out of its own hands. The party's refusal to consider the possibility of the exclusion of the DC from power by a PCI-led left-wing alliance was symptomatic.

> [The DC] was portrayed as a party with a powerful progressive component that was held back by retrograde leaders. If they were replaced by a less self-serving, more realistic lot, serious collaboration and long-awaited reforms would be on the nation's agenda. . . . Had these been tactical moves, they would have been brilliant . . . Yet it was obvious that the Communists were not simply manoeuvring tactically; their pronouncements had suggested, and their behaviour rapidly proved, that they were very much committed to collaborating with the DC. And they did this with such conviction that they quickly dissipated much of the new support they had gained. (Hellman 1988: 31–2)

By 1976, the PCI risked missing an opportunity to broaden and deepen its support. What turned this risk into a certainty was the party's response to a second external constraint: the return of the contentious activism of the first cycle, in new and more confrontational forms. The history of the first cycle might have suggested an inclusive engagement with the new movements; however, this would have required a new and more problematic opening to the left. By 1976, the conditions for such an opening by the PCI had dissipated – beginning with the ability to imagine it.

The Historic Compromise hits the rocks (1976–8)

In August 1976 Andreotti formed a DC-only government, sustained by a pledge by the PCI not to move a vote of no confidence. After the establishment of this 'government of abstention', the PCI redoubled its alliance-building efforts. The concept of the *arco costituzionale* ('constitutional arc'), frequently cited by the PCI in this period, demonstrated the sincerity (and growing desperation) of the party leadership's desire to enter the political mainstream. The 'arc' included all those parties which had contributed to and were committed to the Italian Constitution, from the DC and the PLI on the Right to the PCI on the Left. Right-wing journalist Vittorio Feltri's acerbic comments are suggestive: 'the constitutional arc [was] a reanimated photocopy of the CLN. . . . And here we are again with a single-party government, that system which Italians have always looked back on nostalgically. . . . Anti-fascism is powerful: it's a glue which can hold together a crowd of over fifty million people. Nothing else has ever been this powerful, apart from Fascism' (Feltri 1994: 81, 85).[11]

However, in practice the PCI could not turn itself easily or unhindered into a partner of the DC, either alone or as part of a broad coalition. The left-leaning De Martino, who had led the PSI for most of the 'centre-left' period, had recently been replaced by Bettino Craxi, whose insistence on the independence of the PSI made any alliance with the PCI conditional on parity of status between the two parties – effectively deferring it indefinitely. Craxi would ultimately steer the PSI firmly into the centre ground, facilitating the reconstruction of the centre-left (Ginsborg 1990: 377). Meanwhile, despite the influx of new members, PCI strategy was increasingly at odds with the demands and assumptions of the party's base. In December 1976 the party adopted the slogan 'A party of government and a party of struggle' (Hellman 1988: 33); in practice the former took precedence over the latter.

The contradictions inherent in the 'historic compromise', exacerbated by the rise of the second cycle of contention, came to a head with the policy of 'austerity'. Expounded first by CGIL leader Luciano Lama and then by Berlinguer on 29 and 30 January 1977, this represented the PCI leadership's endorsement of the deflationary measures being proposed by liberal economists, whose costs would be borne in large part by the party's own constituency. The rhetoric of 'austerity' gave this right-wing policy the distinctive Berlinguerian twist, couching the call for sacrifices in idealistic, 'Catholic Communist' terms while attempting to placate the Left by demanding that sacrifices should be imposed equitably. In the words of Berlinguer:

> certain sectors of the Christian Democrats and the employing class [attempt] to unload new sacrifices to be borne exclusively by the working class . . . we have struggled instead to see that sacrifices . . . should be imposed in an appropriate way on those classes of people best able to bear them . . .
>
> Austerity, by definition, means restrictions on certain availabilities to which we have become accustomed . . . But we are deeply convinced that to replace certain habits of life with others that are more exacting and not extravagant, can lead not to a worsening in the quality of life, but to substantial improvement, to growth in the 'humanity' of life. A more austere society can be – indeed ought to be – a society that is more just, better ordered, with less inequality, in reality more free and democratic, certainly more humane. (quoted in Sassoon 1978: 133, 135)

The PCI had reined in its supporters and suspended its reforming ambitions in order to build an alliance with its former DC opponent; it now adopted a DC diagnosis of the economic situation and endorsed DC demands on the PCI's supporters. Partial local elections in April 1977 saw a drop in the PCI vote. Meanwhile, the second cycle of contention was peaking with the emergence of the 'movement of 1977', which was explicitly opposed to the PCI. Worse, the FLM demonstration of 2 December 1977 served notice that the PCI could no longer depend on its trade union constituency. A remark current at the grass roots in Turin summed up the party's double-bind: 'As a party of government, we lose to the left. As a party of struggle, we lose to the right' (Hellman 1988: 66). If the PCI leadership was not to lose contact with its base altogether, it needed to show that the alliance policy had delivered reforms. However, this required the co-operation of the DC, which was conditional on the PCI leadership moving to the right – and each move to the right put more distance between leadership and party members, increasing the pressure for results. Negotiations in the early months of 1978, with the PCI demanding inclusion in the cabinet, led only to the renomination of the existing, DC-only cabinet (Hellman 1988: 35). Aldo Moro, leader of the DC, proposed to accept the PCI as a member of the 'government area' without cabinet representation; this arrangement could be reviewed after nine months of co-operation between the parties (Amyot 1981: 225). The 'historic compromise' reached its nadir with the PCI's acceptance of this nebulous and subordinate position.

Faced with the activism of the second cycle of contention, and subsequently with widespread left-wing armed activity, the PCI supported repressive police measures and refused to countenance a political interpretation of events. Rather than a principled loyalty to the constitution on which the Italian state had been founded, the party now appeared to stand for unconditional loyalty to the state as it was. The Amendolan reading of the *via italiana* predisposed the PCI to associate the Right with progressive cross-class alliances and the Left with disruptive activism. The PCI's strategic choices during the 'historic compromise' period, and in particular its engagement with the second cycle of contention, suggested that the party leadership was strongly committed to maintaining these associations, defying all evidence that this was a losing strategy both for the party and for its constituency.

The Historic Compromise and the second cycle

In its aspiration to bridge Right and Left within the party, delivering sustainable reform while keeping open the prospect of radical change, the 'historic compromise' echoed Togliatti's *via italiana*. Its failure similarly echoed the problems Togliatti had faced: the gap between leadership and membership created by the mass party strategy; the tendency to view politics in terms of high principle rather than short-term advantage; the associated tendency to subordinate policy goals to the maintenance of political alliances, tacitly reintroducing a 'two-stage' strategy; and the inability to recognise the possibility of opposition to an anti-fascist coalition from sources which were not themselves fascist.

Each of these problems was accentuated and exacerbated by new elements of the 'historic compromise', which in some cases broke with the Togliattian model altogether. Within the party, Berlinguer's leadership provoked divergences between the base and the leadership just as surely as Togliatti's. In one late 1970s survey, one in three full-time PCI officials disagreed with

Berlinguer's dictum 'If tension arises between a given reform and the maintenance of the broadest possible alliance front, the alliance should be favoured' (printed without attribution) (Hellman 1988: 202). Like Togliatti, Berlinguer believed that the party's culture and democratic centralist structures would override personal reservations. However, there was a crucial difference. Imperfect though its realisation was, the Togliattian concept of the mass party rested on a double level of activity: activists would be guided by the policies of the leadership, but would also put pressure on them to implement radical reforms. Under Berlinguer, the party leadership ceased even to pay lip service to its base. Increasingly, both PCI and CGIL campaigns were driven by the centre and centred on rallying support for party initiatives, while local and economic benefits receded; indeed, as of 1977 party and union members were effectively under instruction to accept attacks on their living standards. Berlinguer's insistence that 'The war on waste must be fought even where it appears most complex and least popular . . . [including] those forms of waste . . . caused by laxity in work and study and pathological levels of absenteeism' (Berlinguer 1976)[12] – suggested that, having suspended its opposition to the DC, the PCI would turn against 'parasitic' elements of the working class. Under the circumstances, democratic centralism could not be relied on to secure even passive acquiescence.

Secondly, the party's pursuit of reform by way of an alliance with the DC was inherently contradictory. The experience of the centre-left governments between 1963 and 1972, to say nothing of Togliatti's own experience in 1945–7, suggested that the DC was not only a 'great movement of the people' but also an efficient machine for holding power and distributing its spoils. The PCI's commitment to evoking the DC's hidden reforming tendencies precluded any sustained critique of the DC as it was; the party's unconditional defence of the state prevented any acknowledgment of the DC's 'interpenetration with and occupation of all aspects of the Italian state machinery' (Hellman 1988: 25). In effect, Berlinguer aimed not only to separate the elements of the DC bloc but to set them against one another: the PCI would uphold the Christian principles of the DC movement and the republican virtues of the state, while rationalising the DC machine and attacking 'parasitic' vested interests. The strategy was little better than quixotic. Sciascia sums up:

> Neither Moro nor the party he presided over had ever had a 'sense of the State'. The idea of the State, as it had first been threateningly bandied about by some representatives of the Italian Communist Party the previous May [1977] – an idea which seemed to derive . . . from Hegel, and the Right rather than the Left of Hegel – had probably only crossed Aldo Moro's mind in his youth [i.e. under Fascism] . . . what has attracted and continues to attract at least a third of the Italian electorate to the party of Christian Democracy is precisely the absence

in that party – an attractive and reassuring absence – of an idea of the State (Sciascia 1987: 29; translation modified)

Sciascia's reference to the 'Right . . . of Hegel' evokes Hegel himself, for whom Napoleon represented the culmination of the dialectic of history, as opposed to the Left-Hegelian Marx. The implication is that the Communist Party had become a force for stability rather than revolution.

Thirdly, the difficulties of building a reforming cross-class alliance with the DC remained: never more so than in the 1970s, when Berlinguer's principled commitment to compromise came up against Moro's mastery of delaying tactics. The PCI successively called its industrial base to a halt; suspended its own political programme; adopted what were, in effect, DC policies; and accepted a subordinate and dependent position, permanently in the penumbra of government. Unfortunately for Berlinguer, Moro had his own agenda throughout this period:

> While for the PCI the alliance with the DC depended on the eventual transformation of this party into a progressive force, then for the DC alliance with the PCI depended on the eventual transformation of the PCI into a mildly reforming machine, whose task would be to bring its supporters and the masses it inspired under the political hegemony of a new governing system led by the Christian Democrats. Thus the DC's strategy was also a strategy of 'historic compromise' (Sassoon 1981: 229)

Moreover, the PCI's bargaining position in this period was significantly weaker than it had been under Togliatti. Instead of 'structural reforms', Berlinguer advocated nebulous 'elements of socialism'; these would be introduced by an 'emergency government', which might or might not lead to the 'historic compromise' itself. In effect, the Popular Front programme had returned, now ' "enriched" by the addition of a third stage' (Amyot 1981: 198). In 1978 the PCI even accepted a DC veto on the composition of the 'emergency government' stage and the point at which it would begin.

Lastly, the PCI's longstanding deafness to criticism of the policy of antifascist unity was exacerbated both by the ideological closure accompanying Berlinguer's ascent, and by Berlinguer's distinctive ideological approach. Since Togliatti, the party had believed that social crisis could foster fascism, so that progress depended on social order. This viewpoint was further accentuated by Berlinguer's adoption of a Catholic-influenced critique of individualism, libertarianism and materialism. This made it difficult for the party to assign any positive value to the libertarianism of the second cycle of contention: 'the Communists looked on various actions and manifestations of autonomy emanating from the social sphere – from students, young people in general, feminists, ecologists, civil libertarians – with incomprehension and even open hostility . . . behind the PCI's hostility was also a deeply negative reaction to what it considered episodes of degeneration and social breakdown, which the *compromesso* would remedy by recomposing a system in crisis' (Hellman 1988: 218). At worst, the new movements were seen as quasi-fascist. In June 1978 Berlinguer characterised the PdUP and MSI's shared opposition to the draconian Legge Reale as 'an alliance neither accidental nor temporary' (Hellman 1988: 237); more bluntly, in September 1977 he characterised the area of Autonomia as 'the new fascists' (Berlinguer 1977a).

A sleeping gatekeeper?

From its birth in 1948, the political system of the First Republic was closed to new entrants; the PCI, itself permanently excluded from government, represented the left-most extreme of the system. This liminal position gave the party two linked imperatives: to represent itself as a worthy participant in the system; and to neutralise any organisational challenger on the Left. The PCI was structurally a 'gatekeeper' party: these two imperatives necessarily dominated its response to any left-wing challenger. What was not preordained was how the party's gatekeeper position would be articulated. The two cycles of contention show the party taking two diametrically opposed responses, for reasons both ideological and conjunctural.

The PCI was ill-equipped to draw any benefit from interactions with disorderly rivals. The party built by Togliatti was designed to contain social conflicts while seeking a broad institutional consensus for progressive policies. It had an inbuilt tendency to take its members' support for granted; its commitment to the politics of the broad coalition made it liable to dismiss external hostility as irresponsible or worse. In the first cycle of contention, however, these tendencies were temporarily outweighed by the internal upheaval following the 'centre-left' experiment and the death of Togliatti. The new movements were a destabilising factor for the PCI and a key point of reference for the new Left of the party; Berlinguer's centrism enabled the PCI and the CGIL to profit from the movements' decline, integrating their potentially disruptive innovations into an overall institutional strategy.

The movements of the second cycle, by contrast, faced a PCI with no obvious alternative to Berlinguer; the new Left had been removed from the picture when the Manifesto group was 'struck off'. The first cycle, moreover, had ended with the marginalisation of the radical groups which survived it; this created a tendency to interpret the new cycle as a revival of these groups in new forms. Even a Togliattian PCI would have had little incentive to moderate its focus on institutional alliances, its selective deafness to the grass roots or its mistrust of political opponents. Under Berlinguer, the PCI leadership's enthusiasm for alliances with the Right and its disregard for party members reached new heights, while its suspicion of external critics took on a moralistic colouring which was peculiarly ill-suited to dealing with the second cycle.

A hostile engagement was the result: a period in which the PCI developed a comprehensively negative judgment on the new movements and their repertoires, which were consequently denied any form of political reabsorption. In the long term, this cut off the PCI from sources of renewal and constricted the party's own repertoires, leading it (and its successors) into the dead end of a cautious and subordinate right-wing politics. In the medium term, the main result was the suppression – political, cultural and eventually physical – of the movements of the second cycle, with the loss of all the cultural and political innovations they might have been able to offer. But perhaps the most dramatic effects were seen in the short term, when the enforced decline of the mass movements gave the 'armed struggle' groups a temporary boost in support: the peak years for mass and armed activity were 1977 and 1978 respectively.

Notes

1 'Quando invece la massa operaia è già in sciopero non è difficile trascinarla nelle strade . . . Ed è in questi momenti che . . . gli attentati . . . possono essere utili e necessari.'

2 'Questi treni ci vuole qualcuno che li faccia deragliare . . . Queste fabbriche bisogna non lasciarle più funzionare. Ci vuole dei gruppi di uomini arditi che pensino a farle andare in aria . . . Quando questi sgherri squadristi incominceranno a far conoscenza con la bomba e con la rivoltella partigiana, non c'è dubbio che il loro numero diminuerà. Anche da noi dunque occorre il gruppo ardito, il gruppo di partigiani che impugna le armi e si pone all'avanguardia della lotta per la salvezza di tutta la nazione.'

3 'È necessario agire subito e ampiamente contro i tedeschi e contro i fascisti, contro le loro cose e le loro persone; è necessario lottare con tutti i mezzi, dal sabotaggio della produzione e delle macchine, dei mezzi di trasporto, all'interruzione e devastazione delle linee telegrafiche, telefoniche, elettriche, all'incendio di depositi, magazzini, rifornimenti, ai colpi di mano su posti e comandi tedeschi, ecc.'

4 'Oggi è dovero supremo dei comunisti e dei patrioti, abbandonare la fabbrica, l'ufficio, i campi, per imbracciare un fucile contro l'invasore tedesco'.

5 'Il gappismo rappresentò, quindi, una linea politica sostituiva alla mobilitazione del proletariato sui luoghi di lavoro, finalizzata al programma democratico-borghese su cui la Resistenza si svolse. . . . Fu piuttosto propagandato con un linguaggio che lo giustificava in termini morali, di patriottismo'.

6 'Li muoveva una aguerrita volontà di non transigere . . . la necessità di reagire contro l'annullamento di tutti i valori umani'.

7 'È la mitologia del terrorista, che sostituisce la descrizione politica e soprattutto isola il gesto gappista dal contesto generale della lotta antifascista, facendone in un certo senso l' "eroe", ma anche l' "eccezione" '.

8 'la mia critica all'idea e all'ipocrisia che il nostro Paese fosse fondato sul lavoro.'

9 'MILANO – Decine di migliaia di metalmeccanici hanno partecipato anche nella giornata di ieri alle assemblee aperte alle forze politiche e sociali e organizzate dalla Federazione lavoratori metalmeccanici milanesi in una trentina di grandi fabbriche della città e della provincia. Rappresentanti del PCI, del PSI, della DC, amministratori comunali, provinciali e regionali, parlamentari, rappresentanti delle giunte, delegazioni di associazioni giovanili, studentesche, esponenti del clero hanno portato la loro aperta solidarietà e il loro appoggio alla battaglia contrattuale che impegna, nella nostra provincia, più di trecentomila lavoratori della categoria. Alla FALCK di Sesto, dove sono confluiti i lavoratori di tutti gli stabilimenti della zona, l'assemblea aperta è stata anche l'occasione per la celebrazione degli scioperi antifascisti, iniziati proprio il 23 marzo del '43. Alla celebrazione ha partecipato l'intera Giunta dell'amministrazione comunale democratica di Sesto, con il gonfalone della città.'

10 'La nostra condanna nei loro confronti è netta e profonda. Ascriviamo a nostro merito avere operato in modo da staccare da essi una grande parte dei giovani che erano caduti sotto la loro influenza.'

11 'l'arco costituzionale. Cioè la fotocopia ravvivata del Cln. . . . E rieccoci al partito unico al quale gli italiani hanno guardato e guardano sempre con nostalgia. . . . Potenza dell'antifascismo, un collante capace di tenere insieme una folla di oltre cinquanta milioni di individui. Una potenza simile, prima dell'antifascismo, l'ebbe solo il fascismo.'

12 'La battaglia contro gli sprechi va affrontata anche dove essa appare più complessa e meno popolare. . . . questi particolare "sprechi" . . . costituiti dal lassismo nel lavoro e nello studio e da fenomeni patologici di assenteismo.'

4

From Feltrinelli to Moro: a second cycle of contention

Autonomy, youth, armed struggle

The 1972–7 cycle of contention centred on four interrelated movements: the 'area of Autonomia'; the 'proletarian youth movement' of 1975–6; the closely related 'movement of 1977'; and the 'armed struggle' milieu. The 'area of Autonomia' was a country-wide social movement; beginning in the factories, where it was associated with innovative and confrontational forms of industrial action, groups associated with Autonomia subsequently practised such 'direct action' tactics as squatting, 'self-reduction' of bills and 'proletarian shopping' (i.e. organised shoplifting). Autonomia first appeared in 1972 and peaked in the mid-1970s. The 'proletarian youth movement' appeared in 1975 in Milan and flourished over the next two years, sparking off similar forms of activism elsewhere in the country and feeding into the youth-based 'movement of 1977', which centred on Rome and Bologna. Local groups set up 'social centres' in squatted buildings and organised 'proletarian patrols' to impose themselves on the neighbourhood, assaulting known heroin dealers and vandalising sweatshops. The two youth movements were strongly associated with 'self-reduction', but their targets were generally cinemas and restaurants rather than electricity bills; the proletarian youth movement in particular openly proclaimed 'the right to luxury'. All three movements were met with political exclusion and repressive policing; 1977, the year of peak movement activity, was also the last year in which they posed a challenge to the political status quo.

One effect of a hostile engagement is that the history of the cycle itself is likely to be difficult to recover. Following a constructive engagement, a movement will tend to appear as a progressive phenomenon with a criminal or deviant fringe. A movement rejected in total, by contrast, will bear the marks of the framing operations through which it was rejected. As we have seen, even the key questions of violence and illegality are subject to this type of renegotation: the May 1970 amnesty for activists in the Hot Autumn contrasts starkly with the arrests of 1979, which effectively criminalised the area of Autonomia. The question is whether the second cycle can be afforded the same analytical respect as the first, recognising it as a cycle of contention whose defeat ensured that its innovations remained crimes.

This question is particularly acute with regard to the fourth movement cited above: the milieu of left-wing 'armed struggle' groups, with which the three mass movements had close but problematic relations. While the term 'terrorist' cannot entirely be avoided in discussing these groups, a sharp distinction must be drawn between their actions and terrorist acts such as the Piazza Fontana bomb: indiscriminately lethal attacks on apolitical targets, calculated to produce maximum alarm. The actions of the 'armed struggle' groups were mainly directed against property rather than people; all violence against the person was directed against individuals, and most was non-lethal; and targets were invariably selected for political or strategic reasons, albeit with varying degrees of accuracy. Interviewed by a former member of the BR in 1997, former Minister of the Interior Francesco Cossiga went so far as to deny that the BR had been terrorists: 'Terrorists plant bombs in cinemas. This was something else: your forms of action were precisely those of the partisan war' (Cossiga 1997: 80).[1]

In most cases, the covert violence of the armed groups was 'sectoral', applying paramilitary methods to open confrontations already taking place: industrial conflict, political street battles, internationalist protest and conflict with the police. Two extremes departed from this pattern. As Cossiga suggests, the BR harked back to the Partisans; they also drew on Maoism, *foquismo* and the organisational practices of the Uruguayan Tupamaros and the Algerian FLN. In a 1971 'self-interview', the BR describes itself as 'the first rallying-points for the formation of the Armed Party of the Proletariat' (Progetto Memoria 1996: 38).[2] The 1974 statement of intent to '*portare l'attacco al cuore dello Stato*' ('take the attack to the heart of the state') registered the BR's perception of itself as a revolutionary alternative to the state; a similar impression is given by the 1974 internal discussion paper proposing to authorise the BR leadership to 'issue and apply revolutionary laws and regulations' (Progetto Memoria 1996: 43).[3]

The broader 'armed struggle' milieu interested the BR only as a source of supporters and recruits. ('The BR don't believe in the "hundred flowers" of armed struggle. One flower is plenty' (Monicelli 1978: 211).[4]) However, the BR were a constant reference point within the armed struggle milieu: their ability, not only to survive 'underground', but to strike ever more prominent targets, made them both the envy and the inspiration of the smaller groups. One participant recalled how, when his group disintegrated, some members fell victim to 'the fascination of the Red Brigades . . . it really is just that, because no one really knows what the Red Brigades are . . . you think about an extremely compact and organised body and so on'

(Catanzaro 1991b: 197). Within the area of Autonomia, the BR were a subject of constant debate: some autonomists regarded them as *compagni che sbagliano* ('mistaken comrades'), others as *compagni e basta* ('just plain comrades').

At the other extreme from the 'revolutionary laws' of the BR, 'armed struggle' could also stand for a diffuse and spontaneous attack on a class enemy. Cossiga's image recalls the historic association of indiscriminate violence with anarchism, exemplified by the anarchist bombing of the Teatro Diana in Milan in March 1921 (Massari 1979: 166). Writing in 1978, the anarchist Alfredo Bonanno celebrated this type of violence. 'We cannot say: attacking commodity capitalism is legitimate but it is not legitimate to attack the man who puts exploitation into practice; similarly, we cannot say that it is legitimate to attack a single exploiter but not to attack ten of them. What would be the sense of that?' (Bonanno 1979: 19).[5] Such an action could not be described as terrorism, Bonanno argued: 'What if we don't want to wait for the "big day", and we begin to do something, here and now, to stop defending ourselves and begin to attack power? . . . What would doing this make us – would it make us terrorists?' (Bonanno 1979: 31).[6]

The 'violent class struggle' model advanced by Bonanno gained currency towards the end of the 1970s, as violent activism spread from its sectoral roots to become the common currency of the new movements. In 1978, Toni Negri celebrated the violence of the autonomists as one of the movement's key achievements: 'Violence is the *rational thread* which connects proletarian valorisation to the destructuration of the system and the latter to the destabilisation of the regime' (Negri 1978: 67–8; emphasis in original).[7] For Negri, proletarian justice began not with the decisions of an 'armed party' but with spontaneous violence. Similarly, 'proletarian community' began with the isolation of the masked commando: 'I immediately feel the warmth of working-class and proletarian community every time I put on my ski-mask. This solitude of mine is creative; this separateness is the only real collectivity I know' (Negri 1978: 43).[8]

Like the mass movements, the armed milieu grew dramatically between 1975 and 1977. However, the armed groups were not immediately affected by the repressive measures applied to the mass movements, from whose difficulties they even benefited in the short term. After 1977 the armed struggle milieu follows a different trajectory from the movements which it had hitherto shadowed. So as to maintain the primary focus on the interlinked mass movements of the cycle, the post-1977 period will not be addressed in detail here.

One other movement must also be mentioned, if only briefly. The relations between the Italian women's liberation movement and the other movements mentioned here were significant but complex and relatively distant. The women's liberation movement contributed to the rising phase of the cycle; thereafter, the movement's stress on culture, ideology and personal relationships, together with its suspicion of violence and hierarchical organisation, promoted a withdrawal from the political sphere which helped it to weather the repression and demobilisation of the late 1970s.

Innovation and disintegration: Lotta Continua, Potere Operaio and the armed struggle groups

The immediate aftermath of the first cycle of contention, between 1972 and 1973, was dominated by the complex relationship between the surviving groups of the first cycle and the nascent armed struggle milieu. March 1972 saw the beginning and end of Potere Operaio's FARO experiment, as well as the BR's first kidnapping: Sit Siemens manager Idalgo Macchiarini was kidnapped on 3 March and released after a few hours, bruised but otherwise unharmed. Potere Operaio welcomed the Macchiarini kidnap, downplaying the BR's isolation: 'These are actions with a class-based, proletarian and communist quality, actions which express a will to subversion and a need for revolution which belongs to the exploited masses and not to some small minority.'[9] Lotta Continua struck a similar note: 'We hold that this action can be seen as a consistent element of the masses' general willingness to pursue class war, even on the terrain of violence and illegality'[10] (both quoted in Mieli 1984).

Eleven days after Macchiarini's kidnap, Feltrinelli died under an electricity pylon at Segrate, outside Milan, when a bomb he was planting exploded prematurely. The plan was to black out the city; other members of GAP had planted a second bomb, which failed to explode, under a pylon on the other side of Milan (Feltrinelli 2001: 458). The thirteenth Congress of the PCI, which elected Berlinguer party secretary, had opened in Milan on 10 March. The shock of Feltrinelli's death was such as to make it imperative for the Left to take a position on 'armed struggle'. The unpunctuated prose of Balestrini's 1989 novel vividly depicts the impact of the news on a group of friends:

> they could not stop arguing because they felt that the violence of that death created and imposed on everyone irreversible situations that were different contradictory conflictual but irreversible . . . there are double meanings that blow up ambiguities that blow up a series of positions which weren't fully clarified but which could coexist now can no longer coexist in ambiguity . . . everyone is faced by this death as if it were a litmus paper a watershed and they know it (Balestrini 1989: 73)[11]

The point is clarified by 'the bookseller', a character Balestrini based on the bookshop proprietor and movement historian Primo Moroni (personal communication):

> this is where the transition takes place from a form of resistance against counter-revolution against a *coup d'état* a form which is no longer enough for the young people for the movement we pass to the desire to transform society radically and violently in other words revolution and so we see all this coming dramatically to light after the death of the publisher under the pylon (Balestrini 1989: 107) [12]

More acerbically, Morucci noted, 'For the red intelligentsia, who for years had been playing at being radicals in the newspapers and the lounges of Milan, his death was bad news. But perhaps not so much bad as embarrassing' (Morucci 1994: 23).[13]

Potere Operaio hailed Feltrinelli as a fallen comrade. While Feltrinelli's 'underestimation of workers' struggles' might have been open to criticism, his personal commitment to revolution was decisive: 'Feltrinelli betrayed the bosses and the reformists. Thanks to this betrayal, to us he is a comrade. . . . A revolutionary has fallen' (Potere Operaio 1972a).[14] Lotta Continua, more circumspect, criticised Feltrinelli's lack of any connection with radical movements: 'a link which makes revolutionaries into a conscious instrument of the needs of the masses, and which was missing for Feltrinelli and others who made a choice like his'[15] (quoted in Bobbio 1988: 106). Shortly afterwards, however, Lotta Continua underwent a 'militarist turn', rejecting the '*Prendiamoci la città!*' line in favour of 'a political programme which has the state for its adversary and uses as its instrument the exercise of revolutionary violence, on both a mass and a vanguard level' (Bobbio 1988: 100).[16]

The shock of Segrate was redoubled on 17 May 1972 when Calabresi was murdered. Never credibly claimed or solved, the murder was widely regarded as a provocation designed to incite the Left to further violence. Neither Potere Operaio nor Lotta Continua lamented the murder, although both stopped short of endorsing terrorism. Potere Operaio welcomed the death of Calabresi but rejected terrorism on tactical grounds: 'this terrorist initiative obliges us all to decide where we stand . . . we need have only one objection: that is, that the mismatch between the number of our deaths and theirs is too great to be made up by these means' (Potere Operaio 1972b).[17] Lotta Continua's position was more nuanced – nuanced, in fact, to the point of ambivalence. 'Political murder is not the decisive weapon for the emancipation of the masses from capitalist dominion, any more than clandestine armed action is the decisive form of class struggle in its current phase. But these considerations cannot induce us to regret the killing of Calabresi, an act in which the exploited

recognise their own will to justice' (*Lotta Continua* 18/5/1972; quoted in
Bobbio 1988: 107).[18] This near-endorsement of the murder provoked strong
dissent; the position was quietly abandoned soon afterwards (Bobbio 1988:
108). Some groups within the organisation took a more favourable view; one
Lotta Continua member who went on to join Prima Linea recalled the murder
as 'a turning point in our choice of the armed route' (Biacchessi 1998).[19]

The organisations which had survived from the first cycle were rapidly
losing membership and influence; the choice of 'the armed route' by small
groups within them accelerated their decline. Potere Operaio, in particular,
lost many members after an April 1973 arson attack killed two children of
an MSI activist (Grandi 2003: 291–7). Although the organisation came to the
defence of the three activists accused of the crime, all three were eventually
convicted (Potere Operaio 1973; Grandi 2003: 342). The organisation was
widely criticised as unable (or unwilling) to exert political control over its
'armed' sub-groups. Internal divisions were also becoming acute. Piperno
and Scalzone, followed by a majority of the organisation, argued that its unity
and ideological clarity enabled Potere Operaio to function as a Leninist vanguard party, organised 'externally but not extraneously' to the working class
(Wright 2002: 137). A minority associated with Negri countered that 'the
problem of the unity of revolutionary forces' could only be addressed after
re-establishing 'working-class direction of the organisation' (Wright 2002:
147). Significantly, both these opposed formulations tacitly acknowledged
Potere Operaio's reduced presence in the workplace.

Lotta Continua, meanwhile, had reversed its 'militarist turn' by the end of
1972, committing itself to participation in factory councils and fraternal relations with other far-left groups. In January 1973 Sofri, the organisation's
informal leader, argued for a combative but constructive engagement with
the PCI. Stating that 'revisionism is not destined to disappear',[20] Sofri proposed a vaguely defined *incontro-scontro* ('meeting/clash') with the PCI
(Bobbio 1988: 126). At the same time as this 'institutional' turn, Lotta Continua had allowed the development of groups using organised violence within
its ranks; as early as 1973, the organisation's paper carried reports of attacks
on factory bosses, not only on the shop floor but outside their homes (Deaglio
1982). The organisation's 'prison commission', formed in 1971, had rapidly
taken on an autonomous existence, organising inside prisons under the name
of I dannati della terra ('The wretched of the earth'); the group rejected
bourgeois legality, arguing that prisoners were entitled to rebel against their
condition. The Lotta Continua leadership's about-turn on the question of
violence, together with the increasing moderation of the organisation's line
on prison reform, led many prison activists to leave the organisation. Two
such were Luca Mantini and Pasquale Abatangelo, a criminal politicised by
his encounter with I dannati della terra. After leaving Lotta Continua in 1973,

Mantini and Abatangelo founded the Collettivo George Jackson: this was both a group agitating publicly for prison reform and a clandestine armed group.

The BR, meanwhile, had carried out a second brief kidnapping in March 1972 and two more during 1973; most victims were factory managers either in Milan or in Turin, where the BR established its second local group at the end of 1972. By now, aspirations to *doppia militanza* had been curtailed. In March 1972 BR member Marco Pisetta was arrested; by June he had turned informer. The BR was forced to implement a cell-based structure, with a rigid division between part-time members and full-time members, living in clandestinity (Jamieson 1989: 77). In December 1973, in the BR's fifth kidnap, Fiat personnel director Ettore Amerio was held for eight days; this was the first occasion on which a kidnap victim was held overnight (Centro di Documentazione 'Fausto e Jaio' 1995).

Sabotage, arson, kidnapping, assault, even selective assassination: by the end of 1973 the possibility of 'pursuing class war, even on the terrain of violence and illegality' lay before the Italian far left. The pressure for this choice derived in part from the successful absorption of the repertoire of the earlier protest cycle. The power of the Communist Party and the unions had not been shaken; if anything, it had been consolidated. Only the most intransigent ideological frames and tactical repertoires, including those deriving from sources outside the first cycle, remained uncompromised.

Autonomia emerges

A similar configuration of constraints and opportunities underlay the coalescence of the 'area of Autonomia', as the origins of two leading autonomist groups suggest. In Rome, the Comitati autonomi operai di via dei Volsci (CAO) formed in 1972. The CAO (widely known as 'i Volsci') brought together autonomous groups from the Policlinico (a major hospital), the state electricity company ENEL, a local Fiat factory and elsewhere (Monicelli 1978: 116). Potere Operaio's group in Porto Marghera, a workerist stronghold, broke away from the increasingly factionalised organisation in 1972; initially it continued to use the name of 'Potere Operaio', before eventually reorganising as the Collettivi politici veneti per il potere operaio (CPV; 'Political collectives of the Veneto for worker's power') (Balestrini and Moroni 1997: 465–6).

The watchword of 'autonomy' evoked the 'left-workerist' stress on building new working-class organisations rather than working within existing groups or parties. More fundamentally, autonomy encapsulated the workerist belief in the primacy of the working class within capitalism development, as well as its commitment to the assertion of proletarian power through the 'refusal of work' (*rifiuto del lavoro*). This was seen not as a way of opposing the employers but as a declaration of independence: 'the working class affirms its "autonomy from capital", inasmuch as it not only refuses wage labour but fights against it, and in fighting reasserts its own otherness, difference and superiority relative to it' (Piazza 1987: 175).[21] Both the surviving groups and those formed by newly disaffected activists aimed to pursue the workerist goals of the late 1960s while avoiding the institutionalisation which had followed the Hot Autumn.

In November 1972 Roman and Neapolitan autonomist groups attended a Convegno sull'Autonomia operaia e sul Mezzogiorno ('Conference on Worker Autonomy and the South') in Naples. After a preparatory conference in Florence in January 1973, March 1973 saw the first national conference of Organismi autonomi in Bologna, with delegates representing autonomous factory assemblies from the industrial centres of Milan and Turin as well as autonomous collectives from Bologna, Rome, Florence and Naples (Piazza 1987: 200–2). A preparatory document proposed three guidelines:

a) the anti-capitalist and anti-productivist nature of the objectives which the movement sets itself – that is, they constitute an attack on the structure of work
b) a terrain not defined by respect for the law but linked to the necessity of struggle which is determined by the objectives we set ourselves and modified solely by our awareness of the relations of force
c) continuous development, in all its aspects, of the capacity for self-management of the confrontation conducted directly by the exploited masses themselves (quoted in Piazza 1987: 201)[22]

The conference's final resolution proposed 'a platform which the organisations of Organised Workers' Autonomy commit themselves to carry forward, not as representatives of Workers' Autonomy as such but so as to create the conditions in which this can be developed further' (quoted in Piazza 1987: 201–2).[23] The development of workers' autonomy could restore to the class an 'awareness of proletarian power which the traditional organisations have destroyed'. This was a programme for action as well as organisation: in conditions of capitalist restructuring and incipient crisis, *'the only path possible is that of attack'* (quoted in Wright 2002: 153; emphasis in original).

What was widely seen as Autonomia's first attack took place at Fiat's Mirafiori factory in Turin, where workers struck during March in defiance of the 1972 contract settlement. An improved offer was produced on 27 March; judging it inadequate, on 29 March the workers occupied the factory. The occupation was justified as legal in terms of the *Statuto dei Lavoratori*, by the expedient of being announced as a 'permanent factory assembly'. However, it was both spontaneous and confrontational, taking place outside the unions and against a union-negotiated settlement. *L'Unità* reported:

> the strike was total from 6 a.m., when a procession of 8–10,000 workers formed, the most imposing of these past five months of contractual struggle. Then the workers split into groups and in a few minutes, in perfect synchronisation, all twelve of the main entrances into the citadel of cars were picketed, with red flags, banners, placards and posters, one of which said 'Emigration, exploitation, repression: this is the violence of FIAT' (Anon. 1973b)[24]

The occupation appeared to be independent of all existing organisations; the presence of Lotta Continua and Potere Operaio amounted to little more than leafleting. As the brief slogan quoted here suggests, the occupation was also remarkable both for its intransigence and for the sophistication of its analysis. The reference to 'the violence of FIAT' is particularly striking, implicitly suggesting that direct violence might be justified in retaliation.

In May and September 1973, the new movement held two further national meetings. The second of these called for united action on a national scale, arguing that '[the] need to relaunch the factory-based struggle [was] one of the main elements which could give impetus to the process of centralisation' (quoted in Piazza 1987: 203–4).[25] The heavily depleted Potere Operaio had disintegrated by the end of the year, after a final conference in June 1973. Piperno in Rome and Scalzone in Milan attempted to sustain an organisation under the name of Potere Operaio, with limited success (Grandi 2003: 305); Many Potere Operaio activists in Rome entered the 'area of Autonomia' in the Comitati Comunisti Romani (CoCoRo; 'Roman Communist Committees'), including the particularly active Comitato Comunista di Centocelle (CoCoCe; 'Centocelle Communist Committee') (Progetto Memoria 1994: 74).

In December 1973 a similar route was followed by the Gruppo Gramsci, a Maoist group based in Milan which produced the influential journal *Rosso*; the group re-emerged within the 'area' as the Collettivi Politici Operai (CPO; 'Workers' Political Collectives'), opening itself to left-libertarian as well as Leninist influences (Wright 2002: 154). In August 1973 Negri organised a week-long meeting in Padua, bringing together sympathising Potere Operaio members and local autonomists; this concluded with the statement: 'We have refused the group and its logic to be within the real movement, to be within Organised Autonomy' (quoted in Piazza 1987: 206).[26] Negri later joined the Collettivi Politici Operai. While Negri had a common workerist background with his geographical neighbours in the CPV, they had shared neither his Leninist turn nor his subsequent conversion to the autonomist model. The dedicated workerists of the CPV held aloof from the 'area' for some time, believing that the programme of Potere Operaio had not been discredited but only abandoned. They eventually entered the 'area' in 1977, but retained their distinctive emphasis on activism, organisation and discipline (Piazza 1987: 250).

The nascent area of Autonomia embodied many of the themes of worker-ism: autonomous working-class power, direct action in workplace and community, transparent organisations functioning through direct democracy. However, there were significant differences between Autonomia and the workerists of the late 1960s, reflecting the filtering of the earlier movement's innovations in the 'engagement' stage of the first cycle. Ideologically, the movement was both more developed and more blunt in its commitment to 'proletarian power'. Developing concepts of 'self-valorisation' and 'the refusal of work', while redefining key terms such as 'sabotage' and 'violence' (Negri 1978), writers such as Negri theorised the decoupling of working-class power from the capitalist system, albeit in increasingly abstract terms. Many autonomists argued that direct action in workplaces and neighbourhoods could develop into the assertion of 'counter-power' and the progressive liberation of territory from capitalism and the State. The Leninist party model, and the associated perspective of moving from economic to political activism under the guidance of an external vanguard, had few adherents. Both this and the mass assembly, the two organisational forms which had dominated the earlier cycle, were displaced by 'committees' and 'collectives': structures which combined the fluidity and openness of the assembly with the permanence and freedom of action of the party form.

The armed milieu in this period was also characterised by ideological and organisational innovation, as well as the key tactical innovation represented by applying clandestine organisation and armed force to sectoral objectives. Organisationally, the milieu was dominated by the antagonistic imperatives of accountability and clandestinity. Successive groups struggled to maintain security while keeping open channels of communication with supporters – or, failing that, to justify their isolation. In 1970 a GAP document argued that 'an action has a mass character, for us, not because the masses carry it out but because the masses come to understand it, because it answers to deep-rooted mass needs and demands' (Progetto Memoria 1996: 23).[27] This 'deep-rooted mass needs' analysis, echoed by Lotta Continua and Potere Operaio's comments on the Macchiarini kidnap, was widely held. To the extent that armed groups managed to maintain informal contacts among 'the masses', it might provide a functional substitute for true *doppia militanza*. In many cases, however, it was no more than a consoling fantasy.

Ideologically, the early armed struggle groups presented a mixed message. Both the BR and the GAP had been formed around a catastrophist analysis: both anticipated an abrupt intensification of class conflict, involving a decisive shift to the right at government level. Each group presented itself as the nucleus of a new type of organisation (whether 'revolutionary army' or 'armed party'), which would be needed in order to conduct the class struggle at the new level of intensity. Both groups believed that a cohesive armed vanguard had a disproportionate capacity to achieve victories over the enemy and mobilise popular support. In order to validate this strategy, the groups needed to strike targets which could plausibly be seen as responding to 'deep-rooted mass needs'. However, while some actions were genuinely popular, their 'sectoral' focus was at odds with the groups' revolutionary project. For the people at whom the armed groups directed their actions, clandestine violence appealed not because it showed the way to revolution, but because it offered the possibility of escalation in force without the risks of an intensified confrontation.

The gap between these two perceptions of the armed groups was bridged by the image of the Resistance. As Potere Operaio's critique suggested, this was double-edged: it could stand for the unfulfilled hopes of the revolutionary wing of the Partisan movement, or it could simply denote 'a form of rebellion which aims to conserve or restore a pre-existing order'. More concretely, the concept of resistance evoked low-intensity asymmetric conflict, maximising the damage inflicted on a more powerful enemy while minimising reprisals: to describe an attack in terms of resistance effectively implied that the enemy was already in control. Reading statements like the BR's call for '*resistance inside the factories*', the armed groups' audience could easily conclude that their goal was to 'conserve or restore' the earlier level of militancy in the factories. While an agenda like this had little in common with the armed groups' revolutionary aspirations, it was more than most of the Left could offer. Ironically, these perceptions may have accounted for much of the armed groups' popularity and promoted the diffusion of their repertoire, which (like the intransigent autonomist repertoire) took root in the wake of the general demobilisation which had followed the earlier cycle of contention.

'Won't pay!' Autonomia leaves the factories

Mirafiori inaugurated a period of renewed militancy, with wildcat industrial action outside and against the unions. The new autonomous committees were supported by a new generation of workers, highly educated and politically unillusioned. As well as using strike forms developed during the earlier cycle, autonomists confronted managers and strikebreakers openly and physically. However, this was increasingly a defensive battle in the face of restructuring. Even Potere Operaio, praising the new movement, acknowledged this context. In November 1973, announcing its own dissolution, the group hailed the formation of 'the party of Mirafiori', which 'shows that it is impossible for the capitalists to use the instruments of repression and restructuring' (quoted in Balestrini and Moroni 1997: 437).[28]

This, moreover, was a huge overstatement of Autonomia's capabilities. Industrial managers were now restructuring entire production processes, farming out tasks to external plants and experimenting with automation. The new movement also suffered from the consolidation of union power following the first cycle of contention. At the Innocenti plant in Lambrate, outside Milan, a campaign against management proposals to increase working hours while sacking a third of the workforce led to a confrontation between the CGIL and the Coordinamento Operaio Innocenti ('Innocenti Workers' Co-ordination'), 'a rank-and-file grouping possessed of a certain following in key shops within the plant' (Wright 2002: 169). After a violent clash between autonomists and CGIL stewards in October 1975, six leading members of the Coordinamento were sacked, throwing resistance to the restructuring proposals into disarray (Wright 2002: 168–9). In retreat, autonomists appear to have adopted covert violence: in April 1976, two successive arson attacks on Fiat plants were attributed to but subsequently disclaimed by the BR (Anon. 1976a, 1976b). Those responsible were almost certainly workplace activists. Autonomia had never had the same roots in the workplace as workerism's first wave; its increasingly defensive factory interventions were now overwhelmed by the CGIL's re-establishment of control. The right-wing *Corriere della Sera* noted in 1976, 'Rigidly marshalled by the unions . . . Fiat workers are ever less receptive to extreme suggestions' (Passanisi 1976).[29]

It was in this period that the repertoire of Autonomia began to diffuse to new groups and areas. Autonomia was characterised by a commitment to organise in the community as well as in the workplace; in the inflationary conditions of the mid-1970s, the autonomist message found a receptive audience in working-class communities. As the movement of 1967 had left the universities, the movement of 1973 now moved outside the factories. Its first great success was *autoriduzione* ('self-reduction'). Beginning with workers at the Rivalta Fiat plant in Turin, who refused to recognise an increase in bus fares, the tactic of 'self-reducing' prices rapidly spread throughout the northern cities and Rome. With 180,000 households in the Piemonte region alone refusing to pay bills in full, *autoriduzione* had mass support. Autonomists advised households to pay the industrial rate, 25 per cent of the domestic rate; a popular slogan was 'We'll pay what Agnelli pays', referring to the head of Fiat.

1974 also saw a wave of occupations of empty properties, beginning in Rome and spreading to Turin. The Turin occupations were remarkable for involving large numbers of factory workers, rather than the unemployed and under-employed groups previously involved in similar actions. Also in 1974, *spese proletarie* ('proletarian shopping') made its first appearance, when a group of demonstrators in Milan forced a supermarket manager to cut prices (Anon. 1974a; Wright 2002: 159). Autonomist activists were also involved in the establishment of *mercatini rossi* ('red markets'), buying staple goods wholesale and selling them at below the retail price. Promoted and sometimes actively organised by autonomist groups, all these tactics had widespread adoption and success over the next two years.

Autonomia also appeared on the streets in this period. Franco's Spain was a focus for autonomist activity, with scattered attacks on Spanish businesses and embassies. In March 1976 autonomists launched a concerted firebomb attack on the Spanish embassy in Rome; in response the police opened fire, wounding one autonomist and killing a passer-by (Anon. 1976c; Irdi 1976). More concerted action had followed a PCI-approved anti-Franco protest. On the morning of 27 September 1975, Franco's Spain executed five convicted terrorists – members of the Basque nationalist Euzkadi Ta Azkatasuna (ETA; 'Basque Homeland and Freedom') and the Maoist Frente Revolucionario Antifascista y Patriótico (FRAP; 'Revolutionary Anti-fascist Patriotic Front'). There were massive protest demonstrations throughout Italy, with the PCI in the forefront; *l'Unità* gave the protests a full page on 28 September (Anon. 1975a). The 'official' demonstrations were followed by rioting in Rome, Naples and Turin. As well as clashing with the police, the autonomists smashed windows and looted shops. The passage from *autoriduzione* to outright *espropriazione* ('expropriation') caused outrage on the Left. Antonello Trombadori, PCI elder statesman and former GAPist (Massari 1979: 188), pronounced anathema: 'People who smash shop windows, like people who encourage attacks on the police . . . must not be allowed a place in the ranks of popular and proletarian mass action' (Monicelli 1978: 56)[30] Lotta Continua's judgment was more measured:

> The so-called area of 'autonomy', which considers the use of violence justified and useful, has existed for years in Italy. While we disagree, we consider them comrades and not provocateurs. Hence, we must take note that the numbers of the 'autonomists' – young people filled with revolutionary impatience, who want to change their own lives without waiting for the seizure of power – are continually growing. And the problem of reabsorbing them is a political problem, not one of public order. (quoted in Monicelli 1978: 56)[31]

This period of diffusion saw the autonomist committee/collective form spreading to new areas of struggle and undermining existing groups from within. The Gruppo Gramsci's statement of dissolution, *'Una proposta per un diverso modo di fare politica'* ('A proposal for a different way of doing politics'), sets out a contrast between the 'group' united around a shared model of society and the 'movement' composed of diverse forces, who might share nothing but their 'extraneousness' from the capitalist productive process but who could come together in a campaign against diverse forms of repression:

> Organising workers' autonomy means identifying and creating space so that the elements of the refusal of capitalist work and the positive contents of extraneousness can emerge and be generalised in a process of ever more mass-based politicisation. It means organising these elements in a proposal for political practice which begins from the factory but is not confined to it . . . Sex and the family, the condition of young people and women, emotional and intellectual repression, the marginalisation of the 'abnormal' are the concrete everyday reality in which the slavery imposed by capital, in the factory and in our lives, manifests itself . . . So, a new way of doing politics? Certainly. We need one. Because it's no longer possible to go on as vanguards talking to vanguards in the parochial language of political 'experts', knowing all the ABC – even the M and the L – of Marxism-Leninism without managing to talk concretely about ourselves and our experiences . . . [and] because we are beginning to create concretely the first beginnings of a different life, of a different way of being ourselves and relating to one another, beyond the roles which capital imposes in order to marginalise, subordinate and divide us. (quoted in Balestrini and Moroni 1997: 507)[32]

In 1974 the CPO threw *Rosso* open to the movement, attracting the participation of diverse tendencies in the northwest, including industrial activists as well as Negri and Scalzone (Monicelli 1978: 120). Towards the end of 1975 *Rosso* also gained the participation of the Roman CAO, briefly becoming something like a national journal of Autonomia. However, the Romans' differences with the influential but abstraction-prone Negri were insurmountable. The CAO abandoned *Rosso* in October 1976 and subsequently launched its own publications, *Rivolta di Classe* and *i Volsci* (Wright 2002: 171).

On a broader level, the CPO's analysis was borne out. Autonomia was not a 'party', aspiring to unite different struggles within a single organisation and political programme, but an 'area': a proliferation of local and sectional organisations, which could nevertheless come together in different configurations to work for shared objectives. Geographical and organisational poles can be identified: the CPV in the northeast; in Rome, the hard-bitten militants of the CAO; in Milan, the different strands of workerism associated with Scalzone and Negri, as well as the veterans of the Lotta Continua *servizio d'ordine*. Bologna, meanwhile, was the centre of the *desiderante* ('desiring') wing of Autonomia, which stressed the transformation of everyday life and was associated with intellectuals such as Berardi, the journal *A/traverso* (launched in May 1975) and the 'free radio' station Radio Alice (launched in February 1976). However, even the most clearly defined of these aspired to represent a plural reality, as suggested by the near-universal use of plural nomenclature (*Collettivi, Comitati*). For most participants Autonomia was a 'galaxy' of groups, built around local issues and affinity relationships, shifting in membership and ultimately innumerable. The vitality of the area is attested to by the range of 'alternative' papers and magazines produced in the period. Echaurren and Salaris list more than 50 titles from the 1972–6 period and another 50 for the year 1977 alone (Echaurren and Salaris 1999: 199, 209).

The movement's intransigence and insistent assertion of 'extraneousness' often degenerated into the celebration of irrationality and disorder, as in the popular slogan '*Disgregazione è bello*' ('Disorganisation is beautiful'). However, the diffusion of autonomist ideology was also accompanied by creative and original thinking about the movement. In May 1975 *A/traverso* analysed the new form:

> The problem of recomposition lies in the passage from diffuse and dispersed extraneousness to the reconstruction of new means of aggregating and collectivising desire. . . . We therefore propose a small group in a process of horizontal multiplication and recomposition. Constituted as a unit of desire, a collective must learn how to interpret the desire for recomposition: the flows which run through the class, which change the everyday life of the masses. Recomposition is not a moral imperative or a political dogma: it is a desire of the movement. (reprinted in Chaosmaleont 2001)[33]

The problematic of 'recomposition' suggested that informal and fluid organisational practices could, perhaps, offer expression to a new kind of political subjectivity.

'Time to rebel': the proletarian youth movement

The challenge of the 'desiring' autonomists was picked up by the 'proletarian youth movement'. In the autumn of 1975 groups of young people began meeting regularly in Milan. Some were students or unemployed; most worked in poorly paid jobs, notably in the small and under-regulated workshops which flourished following the restructuring of Italian industry. Their initial focus was the limited range of leisure activities, particularly given the inhospitality of local bars: 'they threw us out because we had long hair, because we were on drugs, but above all because we drank too little' (quoted in Balestrini and Moroni 1997: 509).[34] The 'proletarian youth circles', supported by *Re Nudo* (which had long defined its readership as 'young proletarians') embarked on a threefold programme of activity: *autoriduzione* of the costs of leisure under the slogan of '*il diritto di lusso*' ('the right to luxury'); self-defence against threats affecting young people; and, least tangibly but ultimately with the most radical implications, *stare insieme* ('being together', 'hanging out').

The movement overlapped and finally merged with the movement for *centri sociali* ('social centres') (Moroni 1994, 1996). The *centri sociali* were empty buildings, occupied by autonomists and Lotta Continua veterans. Their potential as a base for *stare insieme* made them attractive to the 'circles', whose members largely had no living space of their own. Dozens of properties in Milan were taken over by the combined movement and turned into *centri sociali*; *ronde* ('patrols') toured neighbouring streets, scouting out empty properties and assaulting drug pushers, sweatshop employers and neo-fascists. This was the most coherent assertion of autonomy yet made, providing living quarters, companionship, self-expression and the means for the movement to make its presence felt. This combination of 'territorial counter-power' and communal living is vividly evoked in Balestrini's novel:

> an endless coming and going great excitement the noise of cars arriving and leaving music from the radios of cars parked outside and music coming from inside the centre the strumming of guitars the soft sounds of flutes the whistle of pipes the rhythmic beat of bongos every night there were new faces every night there were new things to see and hear and do the security patrol the patrol of the building wall newspapers and new leaflets to read news opinions comments to exchange meetings to arrange general assemblies poster-pasting groups discussions quarrels shy and awkward newcomers self-assured old-timers lunatics and alcoholics to deal with (Balestrini 1987: 200–1)[35]

During 1976 the 'circles' were active throughout Milan; on Sundays, in particular, thousand-strong groups gathered in the city centre, leading to incidents of mass shoplifting and clashes with the police. The circles' programme was set out in the 1976 document *Ribellarsi, è ora? Sì* ('Time to rebel? Yes'):

> Our lives are sucked dry for 8–10 hours of exploitation every day; free time becomes nothing but a miserable ghetto . . . This is why we say, we want everything! This is why we say, it's time to rebel! We hold festivals because we want to have fun, to be together, to affirm our right to life, to happiness, to a new way of being together. We occupy buildings because we want to have places to meet, to debate, to play music, put on plays, make things up, to have somewhere that's a definite alternative to family life. We mount patrols to defend apprentices from hyper-exploitation, to stop heroin pushers and kick out the fascists. (quoted in Balestrini and Moroni 1997: 513)[36]

There followed a series of demands, directed to local and central government: for the requisition of vacant buildings; for the elimination of underpaid work and child labour; for the legalisation and regulation of soft drugs; and for the establishment of state-supported agricultural communes in the south. The document concluded on a 'red/green' note: 'we like nature, greenery, animals, mountains . . . when we succeed in dominating them naturally. Nature must be at the service of people, not profit. It's the law of profit that enables the bosses to poison the air, the water, food, the environment, and workers' minds and bodies' (quoted in Balestrini and Moroni 1997: 519; ellipsis in original).[37]

The new movement also began to develop cultural forms of activity, confronting mainstream society on the level of communication. Radio Alice encapsulated this ambition, combining music and poetry with phone-ins and satirical provocations. The mid-1970s also saw the diffusion of 'Indian' imagery and identities within the movement, culminating in the emergence of the organised 'Metropolitan Indians' in 1976 (Olivier Turquet, personal communication). The 'Indians' represented a lifestyle as much as an organised movement, but one which united the themes of autonomy in a highly developed form. Renowned for spectacular (and often apocryphal) feats of *autoriduzione*, such as visiting expensive restaurants and exercising '*il diritto al caviale*' ('the right to caviar'), the Indians also presented a broader challenge. Their appearance was a standing affront to 'straight' society; their exaltation of a semi-mythical native American culture flew in the face of industrial modernity, amounting in some cases to outright primitivism (Monicelli cites the 'High Plains Indians' who 'find the "Metropolitans" too folkloric and raise the slogan of the "real axe", as distinct from the toy rubber axes brandished by the Indians of the city' (Monicelli 1978: 105)).[38] Above all, their playful use of language was a challenge to the mainstream, including the mainstream of the broader movement. At a press conference in 1977, Massimo d'Alema, the 28-year-old secretary of the FGCI, sat alongside Olivier Turquet, who wore a top hat and theatrical makeup. Turquet began:

> My name is Gandalf the Violet. I shall speak in a strictly personal capacity. As such, I speak in the name of the Elves of Fangorn Forest, the Coloured Nuclei of Red Laughter, the Absent Phantom Political Movement, the Dada-Hedonist Cells, Worker's Joy and Student Rejoicing, the Schizophrenic International, the Disturbed Clandestine Nuclei, the Chicory Tribe, the Cimbles and all the Metropolitan Indians. (quoted in Salaris 1997)[39]

The list of organisations on whose behalf Turquet is (or isn't) speaking satirises the lists of affiliated organisations invoked by left-wing speakers. Beginning in pure fantasy, Turquet's list continues by parodying several movement and armed struggle organisations: the Brigate Rosse, the BR-aligned Movimento Proletario di Resistenza Offensiva ('Proletarian Offensive Resistance Movement'), Potere Operaio, the Movimento Studentesco and the Internazionale Situazionista ('Situationist International'). Most of these had disbanded by 1977; almost none of them were compatible with one another. Turquet concludes (seriously?) by naming two groups of Indians and the movement as a whole. Turquet's pseudonym itself embodied the playful but unyielding 'extraneousness' of the Indians. Its obvious and highly contemporary counter-cultural allusion (Tolkien's *Lord of the Rings* was first published in Italian in 1977 (Vite 2002: 36)) was modified to echo the movement's adoption of the colour violet; this was chosen to distinguish the movement from the red of Communism, the red and black of anarchism and the pink then used by feminists (Moroni 1994: 72).

In June 1976, *Re Nudo* organised the sixth 'Festival of Proletarian Youth' in Milan, in collaboration with the Radical Party, Lotta Continua and a range of other groups including *Rosso*. A five-day pop festival held in Milan's Parco Lambro, the event was a disaster. Over 100,000 young people from all over Italy attended, around 28,000 of whom had tickets. Relations with the Communist-controlled local council were difficult; water and sanitation were not supplied, and at one stage the power supply was cut. The Istituto Molinari, a nearby technical college, was broken into and occupied for shelter. These conditions were aggravated by alternating blazing sunshine and heavy rain, food stalls whose prices rose as the festival went on and the non-appearance of several acts. (Singer Gianfranco Manfredi, writing about the festival for *L'erba voglio*, recalled: 'After the festival a well-known idiot came out with the comment that "people felt the lack of a Weltanschauung". To which a "young proletarian" added, "That's true, and Alan Stivell and Steeleye Span didn't turn up either"'[40] (quoted in Manfredi 2003)). Food stalls were raided, despite appeals from the platform that 'we don't expropriate comrades' (Moroni 1994: 56); there was widespread aggression against the women present, most of whom rapidly abandoned the festival, while a stall belonging to the gay group FUORI was destroyed. An ordinary festival might have survived this turn of events; the idealism of 'proletarian youth' was badly shaken. In the words of a song subsequently written by Manfredi, 'We're all together but everyone's alone. Recomposition's a dream, it isn't here' (quoted in Balestrini and Moroni 1997: 521).[41]

Both the thefts and the profiteering which had prompted them were seen as danger signs for the movement. The issues were extensively discussed during an assembly which dominated the last two days of the festival, beginning on a secondary stage and then taking over the main stage: 'The real problem, comrades, is that the limits we have hit here are the limits of all of us . . . the contradictions which have emerged here are contradictions within the movement' (quoted in Manfredi 2003).[42] As Manfredi later summed up, 'The festival allowed to emerge, with dramatic clarity, the divisions within a movement which up till then had believed itself united, as well as . . . the downright wretched representative capacity of political groups which, however sincere their intentions, could not understand the needs or the very nature of so-called "proletarian youth"' (Manfredi 2003).[43]

The autumn of 1976 saw an attempt by the Maoist MLS to engage with the new movement: MLS local groups were renamed from Comitati antifascisti di quartiere ('Neighbourhood anti-fascist committees') to Circoli giovanili ('Youth circles'). The influx gave new life to the movement, which set up a central 'Coordinamento', complete with sub-committees (medical, legal, housing, anti-heroin, anti-sweatshop) and a journal, *Viola*. On 27 and 28 November a *Happening Nazionale del Proletariato Giovanile* ('National Proletarian Youth Happening') was held at the Statale, an MLS stronghold. A poster announcing the 'happening' featured a tomahawk and the slogan '*Abbiamo dissotterrato l'ascia di guerre*' ('We have unearthed the hatchet'). The Happening led to a parting of the ways with the MLS, whose puritanism had caused friction from the outset: in the words of Manfredi's song, 'they'll beat up the pusher, then beat up the junkie' (quoted in Balestrini and Moroni 1997: 522).[44] More constructively, it made room for reflection on Parco Lambro. The Happening's concluding resolution noted:

> Parco Lambro gave an accurate reflection of a reality of marginalisation, isolation, powerlessness to change things. We suddenly realised that our individual condition is tragically collective; the thoughts which followed led to the need to build a collective force capable of changing . . . We need to have a clash in order to free the contradictions. A clash to affirm the real needs of young people, a clash to define and achieve a real autonomy. A clash to fight a conception of politics and of militancy understood in terms of negation of ourselves and fear of expressing our own needs in life. (quoted in Balestrini and Moroni 1997: 524)[45]

Finally, the Happening agreed on staging a mass protest against the 7 December opening night at La Scala, Milan's world-famous opera house. This protest would bring the new movement into open conflict with a Communist-controlled municipality.

We have no choice: new armed groups

The *disgregazione* and *ricomposizione* characteristic of autonomist groups was echoed in the armed milieu. In 1974, members of I dannati della terra, who had left Lotta Continua following the organisation's 'institutional turn' in 1972, regrouped as the Nuclei Armati Proletari (NAP; 'Armed Proletarian Nuclei') (Balestrini and Moroni 1997: 416); they were joined in the new organisation by members of groups such as the Collettivo George Jackson and the Pantere Rosse ('Red Panthers'), a radical prisoners' network formed in 1972 (Progetto Memoria 1994: 65, 225). The NAP centred on Naples. Early NAP actions included announcements urging prisoners to rebel, broadcast outside prisons from loudspeakers wired to explode after the broadcast

(Progetto Memoria 1994: 65). The NAP's viewpoint has similarities with Bonanno's justification of spontaneous class violence. In 1974 the group wrote: 'We have no choice: either rebel and fight, or die slowly in the prisons, the ghettoes, the asylums where bourgeois society keeps us . . . Revolt and armed struggle as a refusal to accept passively the repression which is being added to the permanent social genocide of our proletarian class' (Progetto Memoria 1996: 233).[46] Both the group's perspectives and its targets (the police, judiciary and prison system) can be related directly to its members' background. As Enrico Deaglio of Lotta Continua commented,

> The NAP represent a group of people who were in prison; the group itself formed because of the impossibility of implementing any reformist solution, of achieving the prisoners' objectives, which in this period were nothing more than prison reform. . . . On the other hand, take Feltrinelli . . . he works out at his desk where he's going to launch the armed struggle, for example at one point he thinks of doing it in Sardinia, he has this *foquista*, Guevarist theory which leads him to make this choice. When you get down to it, even the BR's choice was taken at a desk. The NAP's, no. (Deaglio 1982)[47]

Abatangelo sums up: 'We knew very well what violence was, and we were certain that violence had to be fought with violence' (Pizzo 1997).[48]

After the split with I dannati della terra, the question of organised violence was raised again within Lotta Continua by a group based in Sesto San Giovanni: a working-class area of Milan and historically a PCI stronghold. At Lotta Continua's first national congress in January 1975, the group constituted itself as a tendency known as *la frazione* ('the fraction'). With a second group, composed mainly of members of the Lotta Continua *servizi d'ordine* and known as *la corrente operaia* ('the worker tendency'), the group agitated for the militarisation of the movement. Losing this debate, *la frazione* left Lotta Continua and joined the area of Autonomia under the umbrella name of Comitati Comunisti. Scalzone's rump Potere Operaio later merged with this group to form Comitati Comunisti per il Potere Operaio (CCPO; 'Communist Committees for Workers' Power') (Bobbio 1988: 141; della Porta 1995: 92–3; Balestrini and Moroni 1997: 447; Progetto Memoria 1994: 96; Moroni 1994: 70).

In the 1975 regional elections Sofri recommended a vote for the PCI, arguing that electoral success would exacerbate the party's internal tensions and create opportunities for the radical left. In the national elections of June 1976 Lotta Continua participated in an electoral alliance with Avanguardia Operaia and PdUP; the aim was to form the far-left opposition to a future PCI-led government. Despite their differences, these two strategies both reflected a double overestimation, of the PCI's proximity to power and of the strength of Lotta Continua itself. Meanwhile, the organisation had hosted a violent confrontation within its own ranks. In December 1975 the Lotta Continua section of a national women's march in Rome was invaded by male *servizio d'ordine* members and local autonomists (Wright 1996). The intruders objected to their own exclusion from the event and to the feminists' rejection of their version of radicalism; modifying a familiar workerist slogan, they chanted '*È ora, è ora la fica a chi lavora!*' ('Screw the workers!') (Malaspina 1996). (The slogan was particularly offensive in this context; '*fica*' translates literally as 'cunt'.) Incidents such as this accelerated the *disgregazione* of Lotta Continua, as well as encouraging women-only marches. Lotta Continua's second National Congress in October 1976 broke up as soon as it began, with feminists, autonomists and other groups holding their own meetings; the organisation was dissolved soon afterwards (Malaspina 1996). The activists of *la corrente*, who had attended the congress with the intention of either reorganising Lotta Continua or splitting the organisation, joined the former activists of *la frazione* in CCPO. It has been suggested that the growing weight of *la corrente*, and the leadership's inability to control it, was the real reason for the dissolution of the organisation (Moroni 1994: 70–1).

Between 1973 and 1975, several small armed groups formed and disbanded; as one participant recalled, 'this was a period in which the revolutionary movement was a burning magma, constantly bubbling, with armed groups forming and dissolving' (Maccari 2000).[49] Among the more durable were the Brigata Proletaria Erminio Ferretto (BPEF; 'Erminio Ferretto Proletarian Brigade'), a Veneto-based group named after a local hero of the Resistance and active between 1972 and 1974; Proletari Armati in Lotta (PAIL; 'Armed Proletarians in Struggle'), a group based in San Benedetto del Tronto on the Adriatic coast and active between 1973 and 1975; and Lotta Armata per il Comunismo (LAC; 'Armed Struggle for Communism'), a loose network of Roman activists associated with the CoCoCe and active between 1974 and 1976 (Progetto Memoria 1994: 226–8). BPEF and PAIL both eventually dissolved into the BR; members of PAIL who joined the BR included Patrizio Peci, later a notorious police informer.

In Rome, the Formazioni Comuniste Armate (FCA; 'Armed Communist Formations') formed in 1975 within the CoCoCe/LAC milieu; its targets included the multinational oil companies Chevron and Texaco (Progetto Memoria 1994: 74). In 1976, with the formation of the BR's Roman column, part of the group joined the BR; other members formed a new group, the Unità Comuniste Combattenti (UCC; 'Fighting Communist Units'), which also drew members from the Roman section of CCPO (Progetto Memoria 1994: 74, 81). The UCC's activities consisted mainly of property damage and focused on 'instruments of capitalist command over labour', computing installations in particular (Progetto Memoria 1994: 81). The UCC also related its actions to popular demands: the group denounced sweatshop labour and on one occasion kidnapped a meat wholesaler, demanding the sale of meat at affordable prices (Progetto Memoria 1996: 248–50).

In Milan in 1974, a group of *servizi d'ordine* members close to the CPO and *Rosso* carried out a series of arson attacks and robberies. Early actions were claimed under a variety of signatures, including 'Mai più senza fucile' ('Never again without a rifle') and 'Senza tregua per il comunismo' ('Without quarter for communism'); the group's first action, in 1974, was an arson attack on FACE Standard, a subsidiary of US company ITT. The amateurishness of the action caused some puzzlement: 'It almost seems as if traces have been left on purpose', one commentator remarked in the *Corriere della Sera* (d'Adda 1974).[50] In 1976 the group reorganised as Brigate Comuniste (BC; 'Communist Brigades') (Progetto Memoria 1994: 108).

Also in Milan, the CCPO in 1975 published one issue of a journal called *Linea di Condotta* ('Party Line') followed by the longer-lived *Senza Tregua* ('No Quarter'), named after Pesce's Resistance memoir. Both advocated the concurrent organisation of the 'armed struggle' and the 'political struggle'. Comitati Comunisti Rivoluzionari (CoCoRi; 'Revolutionary Communist Committees'), formed in 1976 out of the Milan CCPO/*Senza Tregua* milieu. Initially, CoCoRi was both a legally organised umbrella group and a body co-ordinating armed struggle initiatives, claimed under multiple different names. In 1976 a 'sergeants' revolt' within CoCoRi pitted the *servizio d'ordine* veterans against Scalzone and other intellectuals. Many members left the organisation and regrouped as Prima Linea ('Front Line'), a national group uniting multiple local collectives, committed to military organisation and industrial *doppia militanza* (Progetto Memoria 1994: 96; della Porta 1995: 94). The name evoked the experiences of the *servizi d'ordine*, who took the lead in marches and bore the brunt of clashes with opponents.

As in the previous period, most actions by the smaller armed groups can be classed as 'sectoral', applying clandestine organisation and armed force to conflicts already being conducted overtly. Armed actions of this type took place in four main areas:

- *industrial* conflict and associated attacks on managers and foremen
- *political* conflict, from street fighting with neo-fascists to ambushes and shootings
- *internationalist* activism, primarily in opposition to US imperialism or Spanish fascism
- clashes with the *police* and criminal justice system.

In industry, overt activism outside the CGIL was becoming more difficult; one result was a rise in covert actions against industrial targets. A former member of Prima Linea recalled:

> In the big factories, as they started to single out the members of the radical groups and to persecute them, the number of sympathisers shrank. Protest action inside the factory became more and more dangerous and difficult to organise. So, the workers told us: 'that one is a bastard, but we can do nothing against him inside the factory, so you have to intervene from outside.' We started therefore this practice of *gambizzazioni* [kneecappings]. (quoted in della Porta 1995: 146)

This was also a transitional period for established armed groups. Following the eight-day kidnapping of Amerio in December 1973, in April 1974 the BR kidnapped the judge Mario Sossi and held him for 35 days; the kidnap was announced as an intensification of the BR's campaign, aiming to 'take the attack to the heart of the state' (Progetto Memoria 1994: 49). In return for Sossi's release the BR demanded the release of eight members of the Gruppo XXII ottobre, whose sentence he had passed. The release was vetoed by the General Public Prosecutor Francesco Coco, on the grounds that 'the powers [of the judiciary] are absolutely unavailable for any use which is radically different from that for which they are ordained' (Anon. 1976d).[51] In June, BR militants who had broken into an MSI office in Padua were confronted by two MSI members, Graziano Giralucci and Giuseppe Mazzola, and shot them dead. While the local BR group claimed responsibility for the killings, the national leadership later issued a statement stressing that the group's target was the state rather than neo-fascism (Progetto Memoria 1994: 375). In 1975 the BR kneecapped the Christian Democrat Massimo de Carolis, attempted to hold the industrialist Vittorio Gancia to ransom and robbed a bank near Padua: respectively, the group's first deliberate wounding, its first kidnapping for 'self-financing' purposes and its first major 'expropriation'. In June 1976, depleted by a police operation which had led to the arrest of almost all of its 'historic nucleus', the BR shot dead Coco and his body-guards: the group's first planned killing.

The NAP, meanwhile, had been shown no quarter. The forces of order appear to have seen the group for what it was at a relatively early stage. On 29 October 1974, a five-person group of NAP activists carried out a bank robbery in Florence. On leaving the bank, the robbers appear to have been ambushed by a group of carabinieri; Luca Mantini and Giuseppe 'Sergio' Romeo, a career criminal, were shot dead. A NAP statement claimed them both as militants of the group (Progetto Memoria 1994: 280). Afterwards a carabinieri official was quoted as saying: 'we are concerned – it's very dangerous when criminals and fanatics start to go hand in hand' (Monti 1974).[52] On 8 July 1975, Mantini's sister Annamaria was shot dead by Antonio Tuzzolino, an officer of the anti-terrorist police, who had been lying in wait in her flat. According to a police statement, on seeing Tuzzolino inside her flat Mantini made to draw a gun and tried to shut the door. When Tuzzolino raised his own gun in self-defence, Mantini slammed the door on his arm; this caused his gun to go off, killing her. The police account was queried by a startling comment piece in the *Corriere della Sera* headed 'The risk of half-truths':

> We know, sadly, that the members of these insane NAP bands are determined to shoot and to kill. . . . The NAP are outside the social fabric of the country; their choice of clandestinity confirms this clearly. But just these certainties force us to ask questions about the death of Annamaria Mantini. Why is the thesis of an accidental death being put about? Why is it being maintained that the girl herself, trapping the officer's arm, caused the shot which hit her in the head? Does the defence of the law perhaps need official versions which soften the truth? Why should a mature public opinion not be told everything, boldly and precisely? (Anon. 1975b)[53]

However 'determined' they might have been, the NAP had not in fact killed anyone at this stage.

The group's active life came to a close in July 1977, when the NAPist Antonio Lo Muscio – who had been on the run since killing a policeman in March – was surprised by carabinieri while eating fruit on the steps of a church in Rome. Lo Muscio attempted to flee, covering his retreat with pistol shots. He was shot with a machine gun, apparently after having emptied and dropped his pistol; he was killed by a bullet in the neck, fired at close range while he lay on the ground (Progetto Memoria 1994: 293). The *Corriere della Sera* hailed the carabiniere who killed Lo Muscio as a 'man of courage', adding that 'he did not shoot until Lo Muscio had opened fire on him and his colleague. Then he pursued the terrorist, loosing multiple bursts from his machine gun and defying the shots from his opponent's Colt Special' (Marrocco 1977).[54] Two years earlier, *l'Unità* had lodged a mild criticism of the shooting of Annamaria Mantini: 'Perhaps the life of Anna Maria Mantini [sic] could have been spared, not only for those legitimate humanitarian motives which weigh on us in all circumstances, but also because the young woman could make a useful contribution to an investigation' (Anon. 1975c).[55] Now the paper dismissed denunciations of a 'shoot-to-kill' policy by *Lotta Continua* and *Il manifesto* in an editorial comment headed 'Cynicism and false piety' (Anon. 1977a).

The effects of the particular 'concern' with the NAP expressed by the carabinieri and underwritten by the *Corriere* (and, latterly, *l'Unità*) are clear. In its three-year existence, the NAP carried out two of the nineteen killings attributed to left-wing armed struggle groups but accounted for seven of the eleven militants who died, including five of the eight killed by police. In the same period the BR killed twelve people and lost two (Progetto Memoria 1994: 65–7, 280–93, 375–90).

From innovation to diffusion

This was an extraordinarily fertile period, in which a ramifying social movement worked out the contradictory implications of two distinct sets of innovations. The organisational forms developed in the area of Autonomia flourished and entered new areas, most notably with the youth movements of 1975–7. Autonomy was embodied in direct and informal democracy within a group accountable only to its members. 'Political macro-groups were increasingly replaced by spontaneous micro-gatherings, which often used forms of intervention more closely related to the "happening", street theatre, or the typical provocations of an artistic avant-garde than to the practical tradition of struggle which had been tried and tested in years and years of demonstrations and other extra-parliamentary rituals' (Echaurren and Salaris 1999: 204).[56] The organisational innovations associated with the new movement diffused by way of a dialogue between old and new types of group, an encounter which changed both. The relationship between the *circoli del proletariato giovanile*, the old hands of the *centri sociali* movement and the MLS is one example of this process.

Writing in 1978, Monicelli distinguished three main elements of Autonomia:

> The first, numerically in the majority, is the 'creative' wing, libertarians with radical leanings . . . These are the 'small-a' autonomists, who at one time or another fight for a 'better quality of life' . . . The second large strand is that of the professors, the intellectuals, the theorists of the new message . . . The third strand, finally, is that of the 'capital-A' autonomists, or Autonomia operaia organizzata ['Organised Workers' Autonomy'] (Monicelli 1978: 208)[57]

The process of organisational diffusion contributed strongly to the formation of the second and third of these – with mixed results. The 'professors' of the workerist groups, who by 1975 had all made the leap into the autonomist milieu, brought with them a Leninist heritage which was easier to repudiate in theory than to shed in practice: as the CAO warned in 1974, 'a new relationship to the movement' would be needed if the group-builders of the first cycle were to do more than build a new set of groups within the area of Autonomia (Wright 2002: 160). Meanwhile, some of the 'capital-A' autonomists stressed organisation and military preparedness to the point where there was little difference between an autonomous committee and an old-style *servizio d'ordine*.

Autonomia's tactical repertoire expanded as it diffused. Increasingly deprived of institutional recognition, autonomist industrial militancy was ever more reliant on physical force. Outside the factories, however, the twin tactics of occupation and *autoriduzione* were massively successful. As with the recurring evocation of 'resistance', both these tactics owed much of their initial success to being framed as defensive or reactive, appealing to ideas of a 'just price'. With the development of the proletarian youth circles and in particular the establishment of *centri sociali*, these tactics merged with other repertoires: the physical force tradition formed in *servizi d'ordine*; the new emphasis on collective creativity and *stare insieme*, sociality as an end in itself; and, not least, the playful tactics previously associated with counter-cultural movements such as the Beats. 'The great organisational machine of the extra-parliamentary Left smashed against the fundamental desire to *change your life*, to stop waiting for a party or a grouplet to show the way to liberation' (Echaurren and Salaris 1999: 203–4; emphasis in original).[58]

Ideological innovation was fostered by initiatives such as Radio Alice, developing the workerist stress on autonomous self-organisation. One was a significant increase in collective self-awareness, with widespread discussion of what the movement itself signified, had achieved and could yet become. The first issue of *A/traverso* set the tone:

> the movement has gone far beyond politics; it's gone far beyond the old problems of struggle and unity; it's situated in a dimension defined by radical extraneousness and refusal . . . the sphere of institutional politics is too wretched, and even antagonistic direct action is a poor thing, compared to the richness that the subject in movement can develop (reprinted in Chaosmaleont 2001)[59]

The ideology of 'maodadaism' offered to encapsulate this outlook. The term was defined in the February 1977 issue of *A/traverso*:

> Dadaism wanted to break the separation between language and revolution, between art and life. It remained an intention because Dada was not inside the proletarian movement, and the proletarian movement was not inside Dada . . . Maoism shows us the process of organisation not as hypostasis of the vanguard-subject, but as the capacity to synthesise the needs and tendencies present in the material reality of work and life. (quoted in Balestrini and Moroni 1997: 604)[60]

Autonomy would be cultural and political, grounded in social needs and expressed in a new language. Perhaps the ultimate extreme of this *disgregazione* of inherited politics was the Metropolitan Indians' rejection of the label of 'maodadaist': 'fighting party or Indian party? Oask! The fighting wowdadaist hypothesis bursts from the metropolitan labyrinth' (quoted in Monicelli 1978: 105).[61]

The armed struggle repertoire also continued to change. GAP's revolutionary dreams were largely forgotten and the BR's developing focus on 'the heart of the state' disregarded; 'sectoral' actions predominated. These, however, were widely seen not as a form of resistance but as a counter-attack in a battle initiated by capital. In particular, the escalation inherent in a violent response to workplace restructuring was justified by playing up the violence inherent in capitalist normality; workplace fatalities, known as *omicidi bianchi* ('white murders'), were a frequent reference point.

Organisationally, the armed groups were increasingly divided over the question of local autonomy. The development of Prima Linea, in particular, suggests that the strategic guidance of a national organisation had a strong appeal: the party model, sidelined by the 'creative' wing of Autonomia and half-disavowed by the 'capital-A' autonomists, resurfaced in the armed milieu. Partly as a result, relations between the armed milieu and the broader movement continued to be problematic. Certainly, the commitment to *doppia militanza* was as widespread as ever. However, while the armed milieu was stronger in 1976 than it had been in 1973, with twice as many groups carrying out five times as many actions, Autonomia in the factories was weaker.

The shifting balance between the two highlights the problematic nature of the concept of *doppia militanza*: if Autonomia had been strong enough for autonomists to sabotage machinery and assault foremen in their own right, it would hardly have needed the support of clandestine groups. The proposed partnership required the autonomist movement to be weak enough to need armed support but strong enough to impose its own priorities on the armed groups: a delicate balance to strike. In practice, the armed groups tended either to assume that the required conditions existed or to adopt a looser model of the relationship, echoing the 'deep-rooted mass needs' model. The 'area' for its part did not see itself as weak enough to require armed support. Thus, for Vincenzo Miliucci of the CAO, the March 1977 looting of an armoury in Rome was a gesture of defiance to the armed groups as well as the state: 'we had no need to use guns, the movement was quite capable of defending itself . . . the looting carried two messages. One for those in power: "When we need weapons, we'll just go and take them from the usual places". The other for the armed groups: "This isn't the time to take up arms and go underground"' (Miliucci 1997: 10).[62]

La Scala, *la cacciata di Lama* and the movement of 1977

By the end of 1976, the size and strength of the new movement had made an engagement with the institutional Left unavoidable. It began with the attack on the first night at La Scala of 7 December 1976. In 1968 a group of around 70 members of the earlier student movement had attacked the same objective, but been repelled by a police blockade (Echaurren and Salaris 1999: 94). On this occasion around 5,000 demonstrators were met by a similar number of police: two concentric rings of police roadblocks around the venue turned away everyone except local residents and ticketholders, while two mobile squads were deployed with the task of breaking up any demonstration which formed. Three groups of around 1,000 did assemble; all three were attacked violently and dispersed by the police, who supplemented beatings with tear-gas grenades. By the end of the night 250 people had been detained by the police, 30 arrested and 21 injured (Balestrini and Moroni 1997: 525). The ultimate responsibility for the operation lay with a PCI-dominated local government and a national government sustained in power by the PCI: rather than attempt to divert or split the movement, the PCI had effectively defined it as criminal and consigned it to the mercies of the police. Following this defeat, the circles and social centres were eroded by pressure from the armed struggle milieu, on one hand, and by general defection to private life and passivity, taken to its extreme in the contemporary growth of heroin addiction. As the movement was criminalised, in other words, the options open to its members narrowed, making the deliberate adoption of illegal violence increasingly attractive.

In October 1976, Berlinguer had called for a *battaglia contro gli sprechi* ('war on waste'), specifically including *lassismo nel lavoro e nello studio* ('laxity in work and study') (Berlinguer 1976); parts of the PCI's own constituency were now among the targets of the party's critique of 'parasitism'. January 1977 saw the promulgation of the doctrine of *austerità*, endorsed emphatically by Lama:

> 'Austerity,' comrade Luciano Lama said later in his contribution, 'is a word that smarts. But we need to say it without fear: it doesn't mean giving up and putting ourselves in the hands of Fate, but making a choice for change.' . . . 'Anyone who says one thing and does another,' Lama added, interrupted by deafening applause, 'doesn't deserve respect or credibility. Therefore we have the fixed intention of avoiding . . . actions which would not be consistent with this choice, such as industrial platforms centred on salary' (Anon. 1977b)[63]

The 'movement of 1977' emerged in February. In December and January, proposals for reform of tertiary education by Minister of Education Franco Maria Malfatti had brought protests and occupations at universities across the country. The Rome federation of the PCI responded with a series of initiatives to combat political violence and those forces which, the federation alleged, were exploiting it in an attempt to 'wreck the democratic state born in the Resistance' (Del Bello 1997: 305).[64] The situation was inflamed by an attack on the University of Rome by a group of armed fascists on 1 February. The following day a protest march attacked and set fire to the nearby MSI headquarters. The march was ambushed by a group of police in plain clothes, who opened fire; an exchange of fire followed, leaving one policeman and two students seriously injured. The wounded students, Paolo Tommasini and Leonardo Fortuna ('Paolo e Daddo'), were arrested for attempted murder (Del Bello 1997: 307).

In reaction, demonstrations and university occupations spread. The University of Rome, occupied and under police siege to prevent any further marches, hosted a spontaneous festival. On 7 February Francesco Cossiga, Minister of the Interior, announced a forthcoming law enabling the government to close the autonomists' *covi* ('dens'); the *Corriere della Sera* noted with some surprise the strong support expressed for Cossiga by Trombadori of the PCI (Padellaro 1977). A 30,000-strong demonstration in Rome on 9 February was followed the next day by a counter-demonstration of school students against extremism in the university, organised by the youth wings of the PCI, PSI, PdUP and Avanguardia Operaia. This was of limited success, as the demonstrators chanted anti-government and anti-PCI slogans (Balestrini and Moroni 1997: 534–5).

On 15 February, PCI members in Rome forced entry to the university and held a meeting, which concluded by proposing a public meeting for two days later. The aim was to break the occupation: on 12 February the local PCI had resolved that 'the resumption of didactic and scientific activity' in the university was 'politically essential and essential for democracy' (Del Bello 1997: 309).[65] The speaker was to be Lama. On the morning of 17 February, a CGIL *servizio d'ordine* arrived early to prepare the ground by painting out the writing on the walls; the Metropolitan Indians' provocatively meaningless slogan '*I Lama stanno nel Tibet*' ('The Lamas are in Tibet') caused particular bafflement and fury. Speaking from the back of a lorry, surrounded by CGIL *servizio d'ordine*, Lama was faced by an absurd and vicious parody: a dummy mounted on a set of library steps, surrounded by Metropolitan Indians and bearing a pink cardboard heart with the message '*Nessuno Lama*' ('Nobody loves him'). Chanting ironic slogans such as '*Più lavoro! Meno salario!*' ('More work, less pay!') and '*È ora, è ora, miseria a chi lavora!*' ('Poverty to the workers!'), the Indians pelted the CGIL *servizio d'ordine* with water and paint. Lama exhorted his audience to save the university from the autonomist provocateurs:

> together we must fight and win the great battle for the renovation for society as a whole; we must fight and defeat fascism, reactionary temptations, subversive provocations, every form of violence and every irrational temptation. Breaking windows and smashing up university buildings doesn't hurt Malfatti, it only damages the students' cause. The workers' movement – and this is in no way rhetoric – also fought against fascism by jealously defending the factories, preventing them from being destroyed (Lama 1977)[66]

After his address the CGIL *servizio d'ordine* counter-attacked, destroying the Indians' dummy. The fighting escalated, with the intervention of CAO activists; by the end of the day the autonomists had driven the Communists out and withdrawn, after which the campus was evacuated and surrounded by police (Rivolta 1977; Villoresi 1997; Balestrini and Moroni 1997: 536–43; Del Bello 1997: *passim*).

What became known as *la cacciata di Lama* ('the rout of Lama') made a deep impression on both sides. For the movement and its sympathisers, the PCI ceased to be seen as even a potential ally; years of increasingly harsh criticism deepened to outright enmity. The events discredited any political repertoire based on dealing with the PCI as an interlocutor, or even pressurising the party to allow it some political space. For the PCI, the movement must now be recognised, and recognised as an enemy.

The 20 February issue of *l'Unità* carried Alberto Asor Rosa's 'New forms of anti-Communism', a long article relating the threat posed by Autonomia to the emergence of a 'second society', unschooled in wage labour and eager for immediate gratification. In the early 1960s Asor Rosa had been a member of Tronti's *Classe Operaia* group, committed (like Tronti) to developing the programme of *operaismo* while working inside the PCI. On 14 February he and Duccio Trombadori (editor of *l'Unità* and son of Antonello) had been threatened by a group of autonomists who broke into a meeting of the Rome University Senate (Del Bello 1997: 309). While the analysis developed in this article was eventually published in book form under the title of *Le due società* ('The two societies') (Asor Rosa 1977a), its original title is significant. The autonomist challenge is effectively defined by its opposition to the PCI, with the implication that it shares common features with other forms of 'anti-Communism'. Indeed, Asor Rosa alleges an 'alliance', 'objective' or even 'subjective' (i.e. conscious), between 'social conservatism and fragmentation'.

On 26 February, an assembly of the occupations movement called a national meeting in Rome on 12 March (Del Bello 1997: 313). The assembly was rapidly dominated by the 'organised' autonomists, who imposed themselves both by superior discipline and by force; groups of Metropolitan Indians and feminists, who left the meeting in protest, were prevented from re-entering the meeting by autonomist *servizi d'ordine* (Monicelli 1978: 142).

On the evening of 28 February, a group of neo-fascists opened fire on a group of young people outside the Mamiani secondary school in Rome, injuring two. Protests were widespread. On 2 March around 2,000 young people staged a protest march in Turin. A group of autonomists broke away from the march and attacked the offices of the right-wing Catholic group Comunione e Liberazione (CeL; 'Communion and Liberation') and the extreme-right Monarchist party (Del Bello 1997: 313). At the rally following the march, FGCI militants were pelted with water bombs and then chased away with iron bars. The next day, the Turin PCI's *servizio d'ordine* retaliated by attacking a group of students outside the university; the paper *Lotta Continua* recorded, '*300 funzionari del PCI attaccano gli studenti a Torino e vengono respinti*' ('300 PCI employees attack Turin students and are repelled') (Novaro 1991: 171). Members of a group of Turin activists who later joined Prima Linea recalled this as a defining moment in their political development (Novaro 1991: 152). The PCI and associated organisations deployed their *servizi d'ordine* against the movement on several occasions during the year, barring movement activists from PCI-endorsed events; one such clash, on 15 February in Rome, predated the confrontation with Lama (Del Bello 1997: 309).

March brought an abortive attempt by the FLM to open a dialogue with the movement. Under the leadership of former *azionista* Bruno Trentin, the FLM was much more open to the movement than was the PCI norm. In February the FLM invited the students to send a delegation to its conference in March. Trentin's comments on the initiative make a striking contrast with *l'Unità*'s contemporary editorial positions: 'We have invited all the student groups, excluding only those who aim to use violence and provocation as a weapon against the unity of students and organised workers. The invitation is open both to those students who are active in definite national political formations and to that part of the movement which aims to develop autonomous forms of expression'('m. m.' 1977).[67] Asked whether he had any suggestions for the student movement, Trentin demurred and offered an apology: 'We are aware of serious delays and errors on our part . . . in understanding the new political demands which the most lively forces in the world of education are expressing, demanding not only to "work" but to count in this society, to count in transforming it, without granting the workers' unions the right to represent them in advance' ('m. m.' 1977).[68]

In practice, Trentin's freedom of manoeuvre was limited; whatever his intentions, the FLM could never offer an inclusive engagement, driven by the absorption of new tactics and ideologies, but at best a distant friendship. Even this was made difficult by the movement's distrust of delegation. The FLM conference took place in Florence on 7 to 9 March; a student delegation attended and held extended discussions with an FLM delegation, without reaching agreement on anything more than a brief statement. As the conference closed, the local movement demonstrated outside the conference hall, denouncing the attempt to hold a 'summit conference' (Del Bello 1997: 315–16).

March also saw two major clashes. On 11 March in Bologna, student activists clashed with members of CeL. CeL activists barricaded inside the university were escorted from the area by police; carabinieri then charged the crowd. Pier Francesco Lorusso, a 25-year-old Lotta Continua militant, was shot dead; carabiniere Massimo Tramontani later admitted to having opened fire, although he claimed to have fired in the air. The movement responded

with rioting, looting and arson. While the PCI denounced 'acts of intimida-
tion, hooliganism and destruction . . . carried out by squaddist groups' (Anon.
1977c),[69] a Radio Alice contributor claimed that: 'today's . . . was a demonstration which everyone chose to make violent, without having a *servizio
d'ordine* . . . all the comrades participated in all the actions which took place
today' (quoted in Balestrini and Moroni 1997: 549).[70]

The following day's march in Rome, with well-organised *servizi d'ordine*
again to the fore, led to widespread clashes with the police, with firearms
used on both sides. A march in Milan on the same day ended in dissension,
with some autonomists advocating an open (and suicidal) assault on the
police headquarters, which was surrounded by heavily armed carabinieri. A
group associated with the CPO proposed an alternative objective, the Assolombarda employers' association; empty and unguarded, the Assolombarda
building was attacked with Molotovs and pistol fire. The same day in Bologna,
the police closed down Radio Alice, arresting five members of staff on
charges of 'complicity in criminal association'; Berardi himself was not
present, but a warrant for his arrest on charges of 'subversive association'
and 'incitement to crime' was issued on 19 March (Del Bello 1997:
317–18).

On 13 March the carabinieri cleared the occupied University of Bologna,
entering the ancient city centre at dawn in armoured cars. The use of armoured
cars against the movement was traumatic; all the more so given that, like the
suppression of the demonstration at La Scala, it was endorsed by a Commu-
nist-dominated local authority. On 16 March the PCI staged a 200,000-strong
demonstration in Bologna 'against violence'; a counter-demonstration
attracted 15,000. The same day, Rome University was cleared of its occupiers
and reopened.

On 21 April four faculties of Rome University were occupied, then evacuated by the police. The police operation sparked off running battles in the
streets around the university. That afternoon, a group of students who had been
charged by a police patrol opened fire; one policeman, Settimio Passamonti,
was shot dead (Del Bello 1997: 323). With the political space available to the
movement vanishing, it was becoming impossible for the movement even to
use violence in collective, and potentially negotiable, terms; for the CPO, the
Assolombarda attack was the last point when violence was subordinated to
the movement's political logic (Balestrini and Moroni 1997: 571). Following
the killing, public meetings were banned in Rome until the end of May; the
ban included Italy's greatest national civic festival, the 25 April commem-
oration of Liberation. Promising to respond to violent disorder by all means
necessary, Cossiga echoed Pasolini's populist attack on middle-class students:
'From now on, we won't have the sons of Southern peasants being killed by
the sons of the Roman bourgeoisie' (Del Bello 1997: 323).[71]

Violence and repression

A national meeting of the movement, held in Bologna at the end of April, was divided between two positions. A large minority held that armed actions by small groups 'apart from abusing the movement's democracy and autonomy, weaken the movement and facilitate the manoeuvres of the Christian Democrats, supported by the Communists, aimed at shattering it through the most violent repression'.[72] By a small majority, the meeting passed a motion that held that violence should be guided by the movement as a whole, but maintained that autonomous groups who carried out violent actions remained part of the movement: 'The movement does not carry out excommunications and does not accept the criminalisation of any of its elements' (both resolutions quoted in Giachetta 1997).[73]

On 12 May, the third anniversary of the referendum legalising divorce, the Radical Party held a 'festival' at Piazza Navona in Rome, in defiance of the ban on public meetings. Clashes with police enforcing the ban were long and bitter. Shots were fired by demonstrators and by police both in uniformed and in plain clothes; a 19-year-old Radical Party supporter, Giorgiana Masi, was shot dead while leaving the area. Two days later, a demonstration in Milan protesting against this shooting ended in violence after a group of autonomists ran into a police unit. Although the main body of the group, led by Scalzone, attempted to avoid a confrontation, a small group began shooting and killed a police sergeant, Antonino Custrà (Del Bello 1997: 327). The shooting of Custrà, which had no defensive justification, polarised public opinion still further. Rossana Rossanda of the Manifesto group had never been a sympathiser with the movement; she now took a position of outright opposition, speaking on 17 May of '*imbarbarimento politico e intellettuale*' ('political and intellectual barbarism') and arguing, 'It's Autonomia Operaia, not just its most recent violent actions, that we need to be rid of. By substituting gestures for politics, indignation for strategy, marches with P.38 [pistol]s for armed struggle, they have put us back twenty years' (Monicelli 1978: 150).[74]

The shooting threw the movement into turmoil. In Milan, CoCoRi split for a second time. Like the majority at Bologna, Scalzone urged the movement to reassert collective control over violent minorities, but not to excommunicate them: 'even the errors of revolutionaries become part of the working class's heritage of struggle' (Monicelli 1978: 209).[75] However, within CoCoRi Scalzone was in the minority. The majority did not reject small-group violence, but urged greater discipline in carrying it out. For the CoCoRi majority the amateurishness of the action simply demonstrated the need for greater militarisation. After splitting with CoCoRi Scalzone briefly revived the CCPO label, upholding the name of Potere Operaio for a third time (Monicelli 1978: 209).

Meanwhile, the movement faced a massive police clampdown in the major cities of Italy. 19 May was one of seven holidays (five religious, two civil) which had been abolished on 5 March (Law 54/1977), a measure which was fiercely opposed as an extension of the working year; on 17 May the movement met in Rome to plan action for the day. A proposal for a peaceful meeting, advanced by Piero Bernocchi, narrowly won out over a CAO proposal for a mass demonstration in defiance of the ban on public meetings; the ban, however, forced a relocation of the proposed meeting to the university. Saturation policing maintained order in Rome (Del Bello 1997: 328–9).

In June, sensing that the movement was blocked, *A/traverso* brought out an issue headed *'La rivoluzione è finita, abbiamo vinto'* ('The revolution is over, we won'). A member of the *A/traverso* group recalled: 'What we wanted to say was: kids, we've got some disastrous years ahead, but there will be a process developing in these years which we can attempt to interpret, in which the processes of autonomy will be able to show themselves in new social strata'[76] (Balestrini and Moroni 1997: 580). The movement's autonomous development had outgrown conventional models of revolution, including the centrality of the worker and the workplace; this had influenced Italian capitalism, which would come to place a premium on creativity rather than manual labour.

In June, the paper *Lotta Continua*, which had outlived its parent organisation, sponsored a conference on the student movement in Rome. The conference called for an international conference against repression in Italy, to be held in September (Del Bello 1997: 335). In July two members of the Radio Onda Rossa ('Red Wave') collective went to Paris; they returned with a statement denouncing attacks on the press, publishers and academics, and signed by Sartre, de Beauvoir, Foucault, Deleuze and Guattari, among others (Del Bello 1997: 337; Balestrini and Moroni 1997: 613–14).

On 16 September, *Lotta Continua* printed a statement by Bernocchi and ten other Roman autonomists; 'the 11' rejected the then-current thesis of 'Germanisation', according to which a capitalist regime was emerging that would incorporate the centre-left (including the PCI) while repressing the radical left. The statement also opposed 'armed spontaneism' and urged the movement to exert control over its violent minorities. The following day, Bernocchi further antagonised parts of the Rome movement (the CAO in particular) by urging that the September conference be devoted to discussion of repression rather than serving as a generic opportunity for mobilisation (Del Bello 1997: 344, 24–5).

The conference against repression opened on 23 September in Bologna, whose Communist mayor had pronounced it 'the freest city in the world'. The week before the conference, Berlinguer had scornfully accepted the implicit challenge to the PCI:

'Essentially, the PCI is the enemy to defeat: this is true both of [MSI leader] Almirante and of the "autonomists" and the "Red Brigades". Even the arguments are often the same: totally grotesque arguments, such as the argument that there exists in Italy an agreement on power-sharing between the DC and the PCI, which paves the way for an out-and-out repressive regime.' [Berlinguer referred] to the conference to be held in the next few days at Bologna, called on the basis of this fiction . . . 'Let them do their worst, even in lying about the PCI,' said Berlinguer: 'it'll certainly take more than these dirty little wretches [*untorelli*] to destroy Bologna! And if, among them, there turn out to be a few people who want to hold a serious discussion, the workers and Communists of Bologna will be ready to debate. But the Communists and all the democrats are right to demand that civilised coexistence and the life of the city should be protected from any possible provocation or attack by the men of violence.' (Berlinguer 1977b)[77]

The resonances of Berlinguer's quip about '*untorelli*' are complex. While '*untorello*' is an abusive term in its own right, translating as 'wretch' or 'punk', Berlinguer's phrasing ('*non saranno certo questi poveri untorelli a spiantare Bologna*') also echoes a line from Alessandro Manzoni's 1827 work *I promessi sposi*. The subject of *I promessi sposi* is a seventeenth-century plague outbreak in Milan, widely believed to have been spread by *untori* (literally 'daubers'): a mythical group who supposedly daubed buildings with infected substances. The phrase '*caccia all'untore*', still current in Italian usage, translates as 'witch-hunt'. At one point Renzo, the protagonist of the book, is saved from lynching after being taken for an *untore*; his rescuer sends him on his way with the words '*Va', va', povero untorello . . . non sarai tu quello che spianti Milano*' ('Go on, you dirty little wretch . . . it'll take more than you to destroy Milan'). The effect here is to present the autonomists as beneath contempt: a rabble of troublemakers who are not even significant enough to be repressed ('this fiction'). The epithet was immediately seized on by the movement; a popular chant ran: '*Siamo tanti! Siamo belli! Siamo tutti untorelli!*' ('We are many, we are beautiful, we are all dirty wretches!')

The practical implications of Berlinguer's call for the protection of 'civilised coexistence' can be gauged from the reception Bologna's Communist council gave to the conference. The day it opened, *l'Unità* described the scene:

large posters carry the appeal from the city council 'to young people, the city and the forces of order'. The appeal is peaceful but firm; it is approved by the Communists, the PSI, the DC, the Social Democrats and the Republicans. Young people are invited to isolate those who want to work to 'subvert the framework of the republic with violence' . . . the forces of order, whose task it is to assure the defence of and respect for democratic legality, are reminded to

carry out the task 'with the solidarity of the citizens and with a quiet mind';
the statement concludes with a phrase which sums up the attitude of the city
towards this conference: 'Bologna accepts discussion and dissent but refuses
violence'. . . . In a quiet but alert city, there is a calm but vigilant PCI. . . . No
intention, either by the PCI or by the other forces working together in the Anti-
Fascist [sic] Committee for Democratic Order, to substitute for the forces of
order . . . there is broad-based democratic mobilisation and alert vigilance,
ready if circumstances require it. (Enriotti 1977a)[78]

The Committee's posters made visible the PCI's administrative grasp on
the city, forcibly reminding conference attenders of the alternatives facing
them: either 'civilised coexistence' under the watchful eye of police force
and PCI, or 'subvert[ing] the framework of the republic'. The point was
emphasised by the heavy ideological freight carried by the name of the committee itself, tending to paint any dissenters as fascists or opponents of
democracy.

The conference, which drew anything up to 100,000 people from all over
the country, was uneventful. Around 10,000 people attended the conference
proper, which, like the April conference, both rejected violence as an end in
itself and refused to dismiss it as a tactic. Monicelli was unimpressed: 'All
the conference can do is give a disorganised thumbs-down to the programme
of the "armed party", patiently hear out floods of letters and statements sent
from prison, boo the message from Bifo [Berardi] in exile . . . and shout
"Free" in unison when somebody calls out "Curcio"' (Monicelli 1978: 173).[79]
Most of those who had come to Bologna ignored the conference, occupying
the city in a confrontational but peaceful spirit.

Ahead where? After the movement of 1977

For Bernocchi, the outcome of the conference was positive, heralding a return
to peaceful protest and a resumed *incontro/scontro* with the PCI: the movement could now 'resume the journey which was interrupted, in a sense, on
11 March',[80] working to 'fragment the PCI's hegemony over the working
class, but without dividing it and exposing it to right-wing threats'[81] (both
quoted in Monicelli 1978: 174). However, this assessment derived mainly
from the discomfiture of currents other than 'the 11': 'Many aspects of Autonomia were swept away: the "creative" and potentially anti-political
area . . . the positions on "Germanisation"; the theories of an armed nucleus
working within the movement. . . . There is no longer a comprehensive
programme' (quoted in Monicelli 1978: 174).[82]

In fact the movement was faltering. The French appeal and the tolerance
of Bologna briefly gave the appearance of health and legitimacy to a
movement which had been systematically marginalised, and had borne the

consequences. The 'organised' autonomists were heading for a break, not only with the old 'new Left' (PdUP, Avanguardia Operaia, the MLS and the remnants of Lotta Continua, all of which were 'expelled' from the movement during 1977) but with parts of the movement itself. As Monicelli saw it, Bologna exhibited 'an unlimited potential for struggle, expressed in half a dozen more or less inspired slogans, but not the shadow of a comprehensible political proposal. Only the sense that the movement was mortally tired of contorted analyses and creative oddities – and thirsty for certainties' (Monicelli 1978: 173–4).[83] A member of the *A/traverso* collective similarly evokes a sense of fatigue:

> The march which closed the conference was imposing and inspiring; it took hours to pass. Despite the verbal combativeness of the slogans, there weren't any clashes with the police. At the end everyone felt a slight sense of bitterness, disappointment, frustration as they went back to their own areas and the places where they lived and fought. Everyone was determined to carry on, to move ahead, but nobody could ignore the crucial question: ahead how? ahead where? (Balestrini and Moroni 1997: 581)[84]

On 2 December, the FLM held a rally in Rome; this was widely seen as an opportunity to mobilise against DC–PCI collaboration and the policy of 'austerity'. The PCI's capacity to manage industrial unrest was fundamental to its alliance with the DC; the demonstration thus threatened not only protest but a positive withdrawal of consent. Discussion within the movement in Rome on 28 November had ended in an outright split: when the majority decided to hold an independent march on the same day, a hundred-strong group associated with 'the 11' withdrew and regrouped in another part of the university. There they agreed to join the FLM march, together with supporters of Lotta Continua, the MLS, the PdUP and other far-left groups (Monicelli 1978: 186–7; Del Bello 1997: 356). The result was ruinous: the police surrounded Rome University and prevented the autonomist majority from leaving, while the FLM's *servizio d'ordine* barred the minority from the rally (Miliucci 1997: 13). The movement was now irremediably divided. The group associated with 'the 11' subsequently held joint initiatives with other far-left groups, moving towards a marginalised legality.

November and December 1977 saw a resurgence of university occupations, 'combative' demonstrations and *spese proletarie*. Armed action was also becoming more prominent. In January 1978 two neo-fascists were ambushed by Roman autonomists and killed; in a movement assembly held a few days later, few disavowed the action. Even the BR, set apart from the movement by its long-term clandestinity and its Maoist politics, was not entirely disowned.

For the armed milieu, the 1976–7 period was marked by three partially contradictory trends. Firstly, the actions of the BR grew more violent and more spectacular, as the group attempted to assert leadership of the milieu. In May 1977 in Turin the trial of the 'historic nucleus' of the BR was suspended, owing to the reluctance of members of the public to expose themselves to reprisals by serving as jurors. Shortly afterwards, the BR launched a campaign aiming to 'disarticulate the counter-revolutionary functioning of the major media'. On 1 June in Genoa, Catholic journalist Vittorio Bruno was shot in the arms and legs. On 2 June in Milan, the veteran conservative commentator Indro Montanelli was shot in the legs. On 3 June in Rome, TV director Emilio Rossi was shot in the legs. Rossi's shooting was demonstratively brutal; his two assailants emptied their pistols into him (22 cartridge cases were found on the scene) and left a leaflet at the scene including the phrase 'We can always raise our aim a little.'[85] This threat was carried out on 16 November, when Carlo Casalegno, former Partisan and deputy director of *La Stampa*, was shot in the head. He died 13 days later.

This was also an active period for the smaller armed groups. Fifteen significant groups were formed in 1976 and 1977, as compared with four in the previous two years. While some of the larger groups attempted to organise and co-ordinate diffuse armed struggle actions, grounding them in activist *doppia militanza*, these attempts fell foul of political divisions and police repression. Prima Linea went underground in mid-1977; in the same period CoCoRi became an armed struggle group in its own right, absorbing former CoCoRo and FCA militants in Rome (Balestrini and Moroni 1997: 447; Progetto Memoria 1994: 88; Moss 1989: 76). CoCoRi went underground in turn in mid-1978 and dissolved at the end of the year (Progetto Memoria 1994: 89). In 1977 a split in the BC, caused in part by the difficulties of *doppia militanza*, led to the formation of the clandestine Formazioni Comuniste Combattenti (FCC; 'Communist Fighting Formations'). The FCC initially worked with Prima Linea, with which it shared the goal of co-ordinating dispersed struggles. The alliance ended following disagreements over the Moro kidnap; the FCC broke up shortly afterwards (Progetto Memoria 1994: 131). While these groups sometimes targeted industrialists and political figures, they increasingly followed the BR in taking as their main enemies 'their own direct antagonists in the police, magistrature and prison staff' (Moss 1989: 59). Isolation and repression fostered the logic of the vendetta.

Thirdly, the repression of Autonomia and the movement of 1977 encouraged the adoption of armed struggle repertoires by new and smaller groups. Monicelli wrote, 'how many of these "territorial" armed nuclei are there? Nobody knows. We only know that they are active in the outer suburbs, they aren't clandestine, they don't target the symbols or the "servants" of the State, like the BR, but personal enemies in flesh and blood, close at hand, in the "territory", adversaries at the level of the area, the district, the neighbourhood' (Monicelli 1978: 190).[86]

Significant groups of this type fell into three main categories. Some represented the militancy of the 'hard' autonomists in clandestine form; a typical group in this category was Proletari Armati per il Comunismo (PAC; 'Armed Proletarians for Communism'), a Milanese group which formed at the end of 1977. PAC's victims included prison officials and shopkeepers who had killed burglars. The rapid recourse to high levels of violence was typical of groups formed at this stage; PAC's first murder was carried out in June 1978, a month after its first action (Progetto Memoria 1994: 138).

A second category represented the youth movement *ronda* in militarised form. The fight against heroin, for example, was carried on by the Squadre Proletarie di Combattimento per l'Esercito di Liberazione Comunista ('Proletarian Combat Squads for the Communist Liberation Army') in Milan and Guerriglia Comunista ('Communist Guerrilla') in Rome: both groups murdered pushers and bombed bars used for selling heroin (Progetto Memoria 1994: 232, 237).

A third category, finally, represented a confluence of the armed struggle milieu with the 'creative', libertarian wing of Autonomia. A significant example was Azione Rivoluzionaria ('Revolutionary Action'), founded in mid-1977 by libertarian workerist Gianfranco Faina and taking its inspiration from anarchist and situationist sources. Most of Azione Rivoluzionaria's attacks were on property; the group carried out several woundings but no murders. The group was unusual in its focus on the press: as well as bombing the mainstream papers *Corriere della Sera* and *la Repubblica*, in 1977 the group shot and wounded Nino Ferrero of *l'Unità*, one of the earliest actions against a Communist target (Progetto Memoria 1994: 123). As well as selecting new types of target, the group maintained the 'creative' aspiration to new forms of 'recomposition', overcoming the separation between the clandestine groups and the broader movement. In the words of a statement distributed at the September conference:

> we, the fighting militants of Azione Rivoluzionaria, are here alongside you to participate in the conference on repression because we do not consider ourselves a 'military party', far removed from real mass struggles . . . Our goal is to build a fighting structure which is as open as possible to the base, allowing the participation on a large scale of the exploited, the marginalised, temporary workers and all those who want to attack the bosses and their servants, without there being a military party sifting the base and assuming control of its struggles. . . . We have attacked the PCI, against which so many verbal revolutionaries have directed stinging critiques, calling it one of the principal sources of reaction . . . we have done no more than put into practice what so many comrades theorise. (Progetto Memoria 1996: 312)[87]

The events of 17 February, from the symbolic erasure of the Indians' graffiti to the physical clash between CGIL stewards and the CAO, had signalled the refusal of any possible dialogue between the PCI and the movement, together with the rejection of any contribution from the movement, whether tactical, ideological or organisational. This rejection was repeatedly restated during 1977, culminating in the double defeat of 2 December. The result was an enforced decline in mobilisation, as the movement was driven from the streets; not only the movement organisers but the mass of participants were left beached. The immediate result was a brief period of prominence for armed groups, from the BR to Azione Rivoluzionaria.

From Segrate to Bologna: a cycle in review

The account given in this chapter occupies a middle ground between long-range determining factors (capitalism, the Cold War, the Catholic Church) and the effects of individual day-to-day decisions (by Feltrinelli, Lama, Scalzone . . .). The cultural, ideological and organisational entities which occupy this middle ground are notoriously hard to define, let alone to incorporate into a causal model. A series of events which appear to form an unbroken causal chain may have had no relationship with one another, each successively resulting from separate combinations of long-range determinants and individual decisions. In the period examined here, we know that Feltrinelli's death preceded Lotta Continua's militarist turn, and that the Mirafiori occupation preceded the first example of *spese proletarie*; what we don't know – and can't know – is whether the second event was in any way related to the first.

That said, we can identify what appear to be a series of trends in this period, which roughly fit the revised model of the cycle of contention developed earlier.

Innovation

The new tactics, ideologies and organisational forms which characterised the cycle can be traced back to the 1972–3 period. 1972 saw the first national conference of autonomists, as well as the formation of what would be two of the key regional centres of Autonomia – the future CPV in the northeast, the CAO in Rome. In 1973 autonomist tactics had their first major success in the Mirafiori strike. The same year, three national conferences were held, the first of which proclaimed the indifference to legality which would characterise Autonomia's actions ('a terrain not defined by respect for the law . . . modified solely by our awareness of the relations of force'). Also during 1973, finally, the dissolution of both Potere Operaio and the Gruppo Gramsci represented the erosion of the 'party' model by the organisational forms of Autonomia – in particular the plural, shifting 'committee'. The Gruppo Gramsci's dissolution statement, in which the former Maoists aspired to 'a different way of being ourselves and relating to one another', is an eloquent illustration of the interdependence of tactical, ideological and organisational forms.

Both Lotta Continua and Potere Operaio gave some consideration to armed struggle tactics in this period, while the BR steadily consolidated and extended its repertoire. However, where the armed milieu is concerned, the key 'innovation' of the period was Feltrinelli's death. This was not because it suggested viable tactics for other groups – Franceschini's perception of the GAP sabotage programme as 'rather eccentric' was widely shared – but because the example of Feltrinelli's personal commitment was impossible to ignore. The events of Segrate, seemingly underscored by the (almost certainly unrelated) murder of Calabresi, created the conditions for widespread experimentation with armed tactics over the next few years – this was the period of Maccari's 'burning magma, constantly bubbling, with armed groups forming and dissolving'.

Diffusion

From 1974 on, the new forms and tactics developed in the earlier period diffused into new areas and developed new characteristics. In 1974, housing occupations, *spese proletarie* and *autoriduzione* of rent and utility bills made their first appearance. The following year saw the escalation of autonomist street protest into rioting and *espropriazione*, as well as the first stirrings of the *centri sociali* and *proletariato giovanile* movements in Milan. It was also in 1975 that the groups of *Autonomia organizzata* first attempted to collaborate on a national scale, and that the *desiderante* wing of Autonomia began to articulate a position of 'radical extraneousness and refusal'. The proletarian youth movement and the metropolitan Indians, both of which took more or less organised form in 1976, represented the 'extraneousness' of Autonomia in its most fully developed and most intransigent forms: the two could be summed up in two slogans, the unapologetically extreme *'Riprendiamoci il lusso'* and the defiantly meaningless *'Oask!'*.

In the case of the armed milieu, the period of diffusion appears to extend from 1974 into 1977. A succession of armed groups and umbrella organisations were formed in the period: some of the more prominent examples were Brigate Comuniste, Formazioni Comuniste Armate, Unità Comuniste Combattenti, CoCoRi, Prima Linea and Formazioni Comuniste Combattenti. These groups and the aspirations of their organisers grew over the period, from the formation of a clandestine 'hit-squad' to the co-ordination of dispersed armed struggle groups throughout Italy, in conjunction with overt and legal activism. This ferment was on a different scale from Maccari's 'burning magma': as many as 85 people were investigated in connection with Brigate Comuniste, for example (Progetto Memoria 1994: 109).

The activities of two other armed groups in this period qualify and extend the model of diffusion. The NAP can be readily understood in terms of the diffusion and emulation of armed struggle tactics within what had been a politically inactive milieu, that of the career criminal. However, in this case the process of diffusion was recognised as a threat at an early stage, and subsequently halted through the brutal suppression of the group. The BR for its part operated with a high degree of independence from the broader milieu. However, the effects of the phase of diffusion can be identified in the group's actions throughout the period, and in particular its attention to its own prestige. The spectacularly ruthless attack on Coco, the proclaimed aim of attacking 'the heart of the state' and the steady extension of the group's own tactical repertoire can all be interpreted in this light; so too can the multiple kneecappings of June 1977, which seemed designed to demonstrate how the non-lethal methods of the smaller armed groups could be combined with the professionalism and national reach of the BR.

Engagement

The la Scala demonstration in December 1976 opened the phase of engagement by the PCI with the mass movements of the cycle. (Engagement with the armed groups would not begin for another year, and will not be considered in detail in this book.) In January 1977 the PCI and CGIL leadership's advocacy of 'austerity' expressed ideological opposition to the movements; in February, with the rout of Lama, this opposition became both physical and mutual. The March riots, the evacuation of Bologna University by carabinieri, the April ban on demonstrations and the shooting of Giorgiana Masi: in each case the PCI identified itself firmly with order and the movements with disorder. In September, finally, a PCI-run council welcomed the Convegno to Bologna under the watchful eye of an Anti-Fascist Committee for Democratic Order; the week before, Berlinguer had made clear that he regarded the movement's politics as politically indistinguishable from fascism, but the movement itself as too weak to take seriously. The outcome of the Convegno can be summed up in the question posed by a contemporary observer – 'Ahead how? Ahead where?'

The PCI, I suggest, played a determining role in the engagement phase, steering it to a conclusion which turned out to be disastrous for the movements and for the party itself. The framing interactions through which this was achieved are the subject of the next chapter.

Notes

1 'Le bombe in un cinema le mettono i terroristi. E questa era un'altra cosa. Le vostre modalità d'azione erano proprie della guerra partigiana.'

2 'i primi punti di aggregazione per la formazione del Partito Armato del Proletariato.'

3 'emanare ed applicare leggi e regolamenti rivoluzionari'.

4 'Le Br non credono ai "cento fiori" della lotta armata. Un solo fiore basta.'

5 'Non possiamo dire: attaccare la merce-capitale è legitimo, non è legitimo attaccare l'uomo che realizza lo sfruttamento; come non possiamo dire attaccare un singolo sfruttatore è legitimo, non è legitimo attaccarne dieci. Che senso avrebbe tutto ciò?'

6 'Se non vogliamo attendere il "gran giorno", e cominciare, ora, subito, a fare qualcosa, a smettere di difenderci e passare ad attaccare il potere? . . . Cosa saremmo, per aver fatto questo, saremmo terroristi?'

7 'La violenza è il *filo razionale* che lega la valorizzazione proletaria alla destrutturazione del sistema e quest'ultima alla destabilizzazione del regime.'

8 'Immediatamente risento il calore della comunità operaia e proletaria, tutte le volte che mi calo il passamontagna. Questa mia solitudine è creativa, questa mia separatezza è l'unica collettività reale che conosco.'

9 'Si tratta di azioni che portano un segno di classe, proletario e comunista, ed esprimono una volontà sovversiva e un bisogno di rivoluzione che è delle masse sfruttate e non di esigue minoranze.'

10 'Noi riteniamo che questa azione si inserisca coerentemente nella volontà generalizzata delle masse di condurre la lotta di classe anche sul terreno della violenza e dell'illegalità'.

11 'non riuscivano a smettere di litigare perché sentivano che la violenza di quella morte creava e imponeva a tutti situazioni irreversibili che erano differenti contraddittorie conflittuali ma irreversibili . . . ci sono duplicità che saltano ci sono ambiguità che saltano una serie di posizioni che non erano ben chiarite ma che potevano coesistere ora non possono più coesistere nell'ambiguità . . . tutti i personaggi si trovano di fronte a questa morte come a una cartina di tornasole uno spartiacque e ne hanno la consapevolezza'.

12 'è qui che avviene il passaggio da una forma di resistenza rispetto alla controrivoluzione rispetto al colpo di stato che è una forma che per i giovani per il movimento non basta più si passa al fatto di volere trasformare radicalmente e violentemente la società cioè la rivoluzione ecco tutto questo dopo la morte dell'editore sotto il traliccio viene drammaticamente allo scoperto'.

13 'Per l'intellighentia rossa, che da anni radicaleggiava sui giornali e nei salotti milanesi, la sua morte fu una cattiva notizia. Ma forse più imbarazzante che cattiva.'

14 'Feltrinelli ha tradito i padroni, ha tradito i riformisti. Per questo tradimento è per noi un compagno. . . . Un rivoluzionario è caduto.'

15 'Un legame che fa dei rivoluzionari lo strumento cosciente dei bisogni delle masse e che a Feltrinelli e ad altri che hanno fatto una scelta simile alla sua, mancava'.

16 'un programma politico che ha come avversario lo stato e che ha come strumento l'esercizio della violenza rivoluzionaria, di massa e di avanguardia'.

17 'questa iniziativa terroristica costringe oggi tutti a prendere posizione . . . dobbiamo avere una sola obbiezione: e cioè che la sproporzione tra i nostri morti e i loro, non è colmabile con questi strumenti'.

18 'L'omicidio politico non è l'arma decisiva per la emancipazione delle masse dal dominio capitalista, così come l'azione armata clandestina non è certo la forma decisiva della lotta di classe nella fase che noi attraversiamo. Ma queste considerazioni non possono indurci a deplorare la uccisione di Calabresi, un atto in cui gli sfruttati riconoscono la propria volontà di giustizia'.

19 'un punto nodale della nostra scelta verso la strada delle armi.'

20 'il revisionismo non è destinato a scomparire'.

21 'la classe operaia afferma la sua *autonomia del capitale*" in quanto non solo rifiuta il lavoro salariato, ma lo combatte, e combattendolo riafferma la propria alterità, diversità e superiorità rispetto ad esso'.

22 'a) la natura anticapitalistica e antiproduttivistica, cioè di attacco della struttura del lavoro degli obiettivi che il movimento si pone b) il terreno non legalitaristico, ma legato alla necessità di lotta che richiedono gli obiettivi che ci poniamo e condizionato solo alla coscienza del nostro rapporto di forza c) sviluppo continuo della capacità di autogestione dello scontro, in tutti i suoi aspetti, condotto direttamente dalle stesse masse sfruttate'.

23 'una piattaforma programmatica che gli organismi dell'Aut. op. org. si assumono il compito di portare avanti, non in rappresentanza dell'Aut. op. in quanto tale, ma per creare i presupposti di una sua ulteriore promozione'.

24 'sciopero è stato totale fin dalle 6 di stamane e si è formato un corteo di 8–10 mila operai, il più imponente di questi cinque mesi di lotta contrattuale. Quindi i lavoratori si sono divisi in gruppi e nel giro di pochi minuti, con perfetto sincronismo, i dodici grandi ingressi della cittadella dell'auto sono stati tutti presidiati con bandiere rosse, striacioni, cartelli, manifesti, uno dei quali diceva: "Emigrazione, sfruttamento, repressione: questa è la violenza Fiat".'

25 '[la] necessità di rilanciare la lotta in fabbrica, uno degli elementi primari per far marciare il processo di centralizzazione'.

26 'Abbiamo rifiutato il gruppo e il suo logica per essere nel movimento reale per essere nell'Autonomia Organizzata'.

27 'un'azione è di massa, secondo noi, non perché è stata fatta dalle masse ma bensì perché essa viene capita dalle masse, perché essa corrisponde a profonde esigenze e rivendicazioni di massa'.

28 'il partito di Mirafiori si forma per mostrare l'impossibilità capitalistica di uso degli strumenti di repressione e di ristrutturazione'.

29 'Inquadrati rigidamente dai sindacati . . . i lavoratori della Fiat cedono sempre meno alle suggestioni estremistiche.'

30 'Chi spacca le vetrine del negozi come chi incita allo scontro con la polizia . . . non deve trovare spazio nelle file dell'azione di massa proletaria e popolare.'

31 'In Italia esiste da anni un'area cosiddetta dell'"autonomia" che considera giusto e utile ricorrere alla violenza. Noi pur dissentendo li consideriamo dei compagni e non li giudichiamo provocatoria. Dobbiamo anzi prendere atto che gli "autonomi", i giovani affetti da impazienza rivoluzionaria, che non vogliono

aspettare la presa del potere per modificatre la propria esistenza, sono sempre di più. E il problema del loro ricupero è politico e non di ordine pubblico.'

32 'Organizzazione dell'autonomia operaia significa identificare e creare lo spazio perché emergano e si generalizzino a politicizzazione sempre più di massa gli elementi del rifiuto di lavoro capitalistico e i contenuti dell'estraneità. Significa organizzarli in una proposta di pratica politica a partire dalla fabbrica, ma non confinata ad essa . . . Famiglia e sesso, condizione giovanile e femminile, repressione affettiva e intellettuale, emarginazione di chi non è "normale" sono la concretezza quotidiana in cui si manifesta la schiavitù di fabbrica e di vita imposta dal capitale. . . . Dunque un nuovo modo di fare politica? Certo. È necessario. Perché non è più possibile rivolgersi da avanguardie a avanguardie con un linguaggio parrocchiale da "esperti" della politica, saper tutto l'abc – e anche la m e la l – del marxismo leninismo e non riuscire a parlare concretamente di noi e delle nostre esperienze . . . [e] perché si giunga a porre concretamente i primi embrioni di vita diversa, di un modo diverso di essere noi stessi e di avere rapporti personali, al di là dei ruoli che ci impone il capitale per emarginarci, subordinarci, dividerci'.

33 'Il problema della ricomposizione è nel passaggio dall'estraneità diffusa e dissoluta alla ricostruzione di nuovi strumenti di aggregazione e di collettivizzazione del desiderio. . . . Progettiamo dunque un piccolo gruppo in moltiplicazione e in ricomposizione trasversale. Costituendosi come unità desiderante un collettivo deve cominciare a saper interpretare il desiderio di ricomposizione: i flussi che percorrono la classe, che muovono il vissuto quotidiano delle masse. La ricomposizione non è un imperativo morale, un dogma politico; è un desiderio del movimento'.

34 'dai bar ci cacciavano perché capelloni, perché drogati, ma soprattutto perché si consumava poco'.

35 'un via vai continuo una grande animazione rumori di macchine che partono e che arrivano la musica delle autoradio ferme lì davanti e la musica che esce da dentro la sede la musica strimpellata delle chitarre i suoni dolci dei flauti i fischi del pifferi il tamburellare ritmico del bonghi ogni sera ci sono facce nuove ogni sera cose nuove da vedere da sentire da fare il giro del saluti il giro delle stanze i tazebao e i volantini freschi da leggere le notizie le informazioni i commenti da scambiare le riunioni da fare l'assemblea generale gli attacchinaggi di manifesti in carovana le discussioni gli scazzi l'impaccio e la timidezza del nuovi venuti la sicurezza del vecchi compagni l'arrivo del pazzo o dell'alcolizzato'.

36 'La nostra vita viene risucchiata da 8–10 ore giornaliere di sfruttamento; il tempo libero diventa solo uno squalido ghetto . . . Per questo diciamo che vogliamo tutto! Per questo diciamo che ribellarsi è ora! Facciamo le feste perché vogliamo divertirci, stare insieme, affermare il diritto alla vita, alla felicità, a un nuovo stare insieme. Occupiamo gli stabili perché vogliamo avere dei luoghi di incontro, di discussione, per suonare, fare teatro, inventare, per avere un luogo preciso alternativo alla vita in famiglia. Facciamo le ronde per difendere gli apprendisti dal supersfruttamento, per impedire lo spaccio di eroina e per spazzare via i fascisti.'

37 'ci piace la natura, il verde, gli animali, le montagne . . . quando naturalmente
   riuscimmo a dominarle. La natura deve essere al servizio dell'uomo e non del
   profitto. È per la legge del profitto che i padroni inquinano l'aria, l'acqua, i cibi,
   l'ambiente, il corpo e la mente dei lavoratori.'

38 'indiani dei "pascoli alti", i quali trovano i "metropolitani" troppo folcloristici e
   adottano slogan del tipo "ascia vera", in contrapposizione alle asce-gioccatolo di
   gomma, brandite dagli indiani di città'.

39 'Mi chiamo Gandalf il Viola. Parlerò a titolo strettamente personale. Perciò parlo
   a nome degli Elfi del bosco di Fangorn, dei Nuclei Colorati Risate Rosse, del
   MPFA (Movimento Politico Fantomatico Assente) delle Cellule Dadaedoniste, di
   Godere Operaio e Godimento Studentesco, dell'Internazionale Schizofrenica, dei
   NSC (Nuclei Sconvolti Clandestini), della Tribù di Cicorio, dei Cimbles e di tutti
   gli indiani metropolitani.'

40 'un noto idiota se ne uscì dopo il festival con questo commento: "La gente sentiva
   l'assenza di una Weltanschauung", al che un "proletario giovanile" ha aggiunto:
   "Sì è vero, anche Alan Stivell e gli Steeleye Span li avevano promessi e invece
   non c'erano".'

41 'E siamo tutti insieme ma ognuno sta per sé/La ricomposizione si sogna ma non
   c'è'.

42 'Il problema vero, compagni, è che i limiti qui verificati, sono dì tutti noi . . . le
   contraddizioni che sono emerse qui sono le contraddizioni che ci sono all'interno
   del movimento.'

43 'emersero con drammatica chiarezza al festival le divergenze di un movimento
   che fino ad allora si credeva unito . . . e la ben misera rappresentanza dei gruppi
   politici incapaci, pur nella sincerità dei loro intenti, di comprendere le esigenze
   e la natura stessa del cosiddetto "proletariato giovanile".'

44 'E con lo spacciatore ti spranga lo spaccato'.

45 'Il parco Lambro è stato specchio fedele di una realtà di emarginazione, di solitudine, assenza di forza per cambiare le cose. Ci si è resi improvvisamente conto
   che la nostra condizione individuale è tragicamente collettiva: le conseguenti riflessioni hanno portato al bisogno di costruire la forza collettiva capace di cambiare . . . È necessario aprire uno scontro, liberare le contraddizioni. Uno scontro
   per affermare i bisogni reali dei giovani, uno scontro per definire e conquistare
   una vera autonomia. Uno scontro per battere una concezione della politica e della
   militanza intesa come negazione di se stessi e come paura di esprimere i propri
   bisogni di vita.'

46 'Noi non abbiamo scelta: o ribellarsi e lottare o morire lentamente nei carceri, nei
   ghetti, nei manicomi dove ci costringe la società borghese . . . Rivolta e lotta
   armata come rifiuto di accettare passivamente la repressione che si aggiunge al
   genocidio sociale permanente del nostro strato proletariato.'

47 'I NAP rappresentano un gruppo di persone che sono stati in galera . . . e rinascono
   dalla impossibilità di praticare qualsiasi soluzione riformista, di raggiungere obiettivi che avevano i carcerati, che non erano niente altro in quel periodo che la
   riforma carceraria. . . . Da una parte, prende Feltrinelli . . . studia al tavolina il
   posto dove fa nascere la lotta armata, per esempio in un certo punto pensa di farla

in Sardegna, ha questa teoria focista, gueverraista che lo porta poi a fare questa scelta. Le BR, tutto sommato, anche la loro era una decisione presa alla tavolina. Quella dei NAP no.'

48 'Noi sapevamo bene cosa era la violenza ed eravamo certi di doverla combattere con la violenza.'

49 'è un periodo storico in cui il movimento rivoluzionario è un magma incandescente in continua ebollizione, ci sono bande armate che si formano e che si sciolgono'.

50 'Pare quasi che si siano volutamente lasciate delle tracce.'

51 'i poteri sono assolutamente indisponibili per ogni uso radicalmente diverso da quello cui sono ordinati'.

52 'siamo preoccupati, quando malviventi ed esaltati si metttono ad andare a braccetto è molto pericoloso'.

53 'Sappiamo purtroppo che gli appartenenti a queste folli pattuglie dei NAP sono decisi a sparare e a uccidere. . . . I NAP sono fuori del tessuto sociale del paese e la scelta della clandestinità ne è la più chiara conferma. Ma proprio queste certezze inducono ad avanzare domande sulla fine di Annamaria Mantini. Perché rispunta la tesi di una morte per fatalità? Perché si sostiene che è stata la ragazza stessa, imprigionando il braccio dell'agente, a provocare il colpo che l'ha raggiunta alla testa? La difesa della legge ha forse bisogno di versione ufficiali che mitigano la verità? Perché a un'opinione pubblica matura non si racconta tutto con precisione e con coraggio?'

54 'Per sparare, ha aspettato che Lo Muscio facesse fuoco contro di lui e contro il collega. Poi ha inseguito il terrorista lasciando tante raffiche dal suo mitra e sfidando i colpi della *Colt special* dell'avversario.'

55 'Forse la vita di Anna Maria Mantini poteva essere risparmiata e non soltanto per legittimi motivi di umanità che si impongono in qualsiasi circonstanza, ma anche perché la giovane poteva fornire elementi utili ad un'inchiesta'.

56 'Ai macrogruppi politici si vanno sostituendo microaggregazioni spontanee che si servono spesso di metodi d'intervento più legati all'happening, al teatro di strada, alla provocazione tipica delle avanguardie artistiche che non alla tradizionale pratica di lotta ormai collaudata in anni e anni di manifestazioni e altri rituali extraparlamentari.'

57 'Il primo, numericamente maggioritario, è quello "creativo", libertario e radicale ggiante. . . . Si tratta degli autonomi "minuscoli", che di volta in volta si battono per una "migliore qualità della vita" . . . Il secondo grande filone è quello dei professori, degli intellettuali, dei teorizzatori del nuovo messaggio . . . Il terzo filone è, infine, quello degli autonomi "maiuscoli", o Autonomia operaia organizzata'.

58 'La grande macchina organizzativa extraparlamentare si infrange così contro il desiderio primario di *cambiare la vita*, di non aspettare più che siano il partito, il gruppuscolo a indicare la via della liberazione'.

59 'il movimento è andato molto più avanti della politica; è andato molto più avanti dei vecchi problemi della lotta e dell'unità; si colloca in una dimensione che è quella dell'estraneità radicale e del rifiuto. . . . è troppo misera la sfera della

politica istituzionale, e anche l'azione antagonista è povera cosa, a fronte della ricchezza che il soggetto in movimento può sviluppare.'

60 'Il dadaismo voleva rompere la separazione fra linguaggio e rivoluzione, fra arte e vita. Rimase un'intenzione perché Dada non era dentro il movimento proletario, e il movimento proletario non era dentro dada . . . Il maoismo ci indica il percorso dell'organizzazione non come ipostatizzazione del soggetto-avanguardia, ma come capacità di sintetizzare i bisogni e le tendenze presenti nella realtà materiale del lavoro e delle vita.'

61 'partito combattente o partito indiano? Oask! Fuori dal labirinto metropolitense esplode l'ipotesi combattente wowdadaista'.

62 'non si ebbe bisogno di sparare, anche perché il movimento si seppe difendere . . . il gesto dell'armeria aveva un duplice significamento. Uno rivolto al potere: "Quando si avrà bisogno di armi, le si prenderà tranquillamente nei luoghi usuali". L'altro, rivolto alle formazioni armate: "Non è il tempo della clandestinità, del passaggio all'armamento".'

63 'Austerità – ha detto più tardi nel suo intervento il compagno Luciano Lama – è una parola che scotta. Ma dobbiamo pronunciarla senza paura: non vuol dire cedimento, accasciarsi al destino, ma scelta per cambiare. E poi si tratta di qualcosa che occorre fare, e non dire soltanto. . . . Chiunque dica certe cose e ne faccia altre – ha detto a questo punto Lama, interrotto da un fragoroso applauso – non merita rispetto, credibilità. Per questo siamo fermamente intenzionati ad evitare . . . azioni non coerenti con questa scelta, come sarebbero piattaforme aziendali incentrate sul salario'.

64 'scardinare lo Stato democratico nato con la Resistenza'.

65 'ritiene "una necessità politica e democratica al ripresa delle attività didattiche e scientifiche" nell'Università occupata'.

66 'dobbiamo lottare e vincere assieme la grande battaglia per il rinnovamento dell'intera società, battere e vincere il fascismo, le tentazioni reazionare, le provocazioni eversive, ogni violenza o tentazione irrazionale. Chi rompe i vetri, chi sfascia le facoltà non colpisce Malfatti ma danneggia la causa degli studenti. Il movimento operaio, e non c'è retorica in tutto ciò, ha combattuto il fascismo anche difendendo gelosamente le fabbriche, impedendone la distruzione.'

67 'Abbiamo invitato tutte le forze della scuola, escludendo soltanto quanti intendono fare della violenza e della provocazione un'arma rivolta contro l'unità degli studenti e dei lavoratori organizzati. È un invito che coinvolge tanto gli studenti che si riconoscono in determinate formazioni politiche nazionali quanto quella parte del movimento che intende darsi delle forme autonome di espressione'.

68 'Abbiamo coscienza infatti dei gravi ritardi e degli errori che sono stati compiuti anche da parte nostra . . . nel comprendere le domande politiche nuove che le forze più vive del mondo della scuola esprimono quando chiedono non solo di "lavorare" ma di contare in questa società; di contare per trasformarla, senza concedere a priori una delega al sindacato operaio.'

69 'atti di intimidazione, di teppismo e di devastazione . . . compiuti da gruppi squadristici'.

70 'quella di oggi . . . era una manifestazione che tutti avevamo scelto di fare violenta, senza avere un servizio d'ordine . . . perché tutti i compagni hanno partecipato a tutte le azioni che si sono svolte oggi'.

71 'Non sarà più consentito che i figli di contadini meridionali siano uccisi dai figli della borghesia romana'.

72 'azioni armate minoritarie, che, oltre a prevaricare la democrazia e l'autonomia del movimento, lo indeboliscono, facilitando le manovre della DC, avvallate dal PCI, tese a stroncarlo nella repressione più violenta'.

73 'Il movimento non fa scomuniche e non accetta la criminalizzazione di nessuna sua componente'.

74 'Di Autonomia operaia e non solo delle sue violenze ultime occorre liberarsi. A forza di scambiare la politica con il gesto, la strategia con l'indignazione, la lotta armata con le processioni a P. 38, ci si ritrova indietro di vent'anni.'

75 'anche gli errori dei rivoluzionari diventano patrimonio di lotta della classe operaia'.

76 'Quello che avevamo da dire era: ragazzi, ci aspettano degli anni disastrosi, però in questi anni si dispiegherà un processo futuro che noi possiamo tentare di interpretare, in cui i processi d'autonomia potranno manifestarsi nei nuovi strati.'

77 'Il PCI è insomma il nemico da battere: sia per Almirante, come per gli "autonomi" e le "Brigate rosse". E anche gli argomenti sono spesso gli stessi: argomenti del tutto grotteschi, come ad esempio quello secondo cui esisterebbe in Italia un accordo di potere tra DC e PCI che darebbe luogo a un vero e proprio regime repressivo. Riferendosi alla convocazione, su questa invenzione, del convegno che si terrà nei prossimi giorni a Bologna . . . Che si esercitino pure, costoro, anche nelle calunnie contro il PCI, ha detto Berlinguer: non saranno certo questi poveri untorelli a spiantare Bologna! E se fra di essi ci sarà davvero qualcuno che vorrà discutere seriamente, i lavoratori bolognesi, i comunisti, non si sottrarranno al dibattito. Ma bene hanno fatto i comunisti e tutti i democratici a esigere che la convivenza civile e la vita della città siano protette da ogni eventuale provocazione e attacco dei violenti.'

78 'i grandi manifesti con l'appello del Consiglio comunale "ai giovani, alla città, alle forze dell'ordine". È un appello pacato, ma fermo approvato dai comunisti, dal PSI, dalla DC, dai socialdemocratici e dai repubblicani. Si invitano i giovani ad isolare chi volesse operare per "sovvertire con la violenza l'ordinamento repubblicano" . . . si ricorda alle forze dell'ordine cui spetta il compito di assicurare la difesa e il rispetto della legalità democratica di esercitarlo 'con la solidarietà dei cittadini, in serena coscienza' e si conclude con una frase che riassume l'atteggiamento della città verso questo convegno: "Bologna accetta la discussione e il dissenso, rifiuta la violenza". . . . In questa città tranquilla, ma attenta, c'è quindi anche un PCI sereno, ma vigile. . . . Nessuna intenzione, nè da parte del PCI nè da parte delle altre forze che si riconoscono nel comitato per l'ordine democratico e antifascista, di sostituirsi alle forze dell'ordine. . . . la mobilitazione democratica è ampia, la vigilanza attenta, pronta se la situazione lo richiedesse.'

79 'L'assemblea . . . si limita a opporre un no caotico alla linea del "partito armato",
ad ascoltare paziente alluvioni di lettere-testimonianze spedite dalle carceri, a
fischiare il messaggio di "Bifo" dall'esilio . . . a rispondere in coro "libero!"
quando uno grida "Curcio".'

80 'riprendere quella strada che, in qualche modo, si era interrotta l'11 marzo'.

81 'disgregare l'egemonia del Pci sulla classe operaia, senza però dividerla e senza
esporla a pericoli di destra'.

82 'Molte cose dell'Autonomia sono state spazzate via; l'area "creativa", potenzial-
mente anti-politica . . . le posizioni sulla "germanizzazione"; le teorie sul nucleo
armato che lavora all'interno del movimento. . . . Oggi non c'è un programma
complessivo'.

83 'Un potenziale di lotta smisurato, che si scarica in una mezza dozzina di slogan
più o meno ispirati; ma neanche l'ombra di una proposta politica decifrabile. Solo
la sensazione che il movimento sia mortalmente stanco di analisi contorte e di
bizzarrerie creative; e assetato invece di certezze'.

84 'Il corteo che chiude il convegno, imponente e suggestivo, sfila per ore e ore.
Nonostante l'aggressività verbale degli slogan non c'è scontro con la polizia. Alla
fine un sottile senso di amarezza, di delusione, di frustrazione riaccompagna la
gente nei propri territori e luoghi di vita e di lotta. Tutti si ripromettono di con-
tinuare, di andare avanti, ma nessuno sa nascondere da se stesso la drammatica
domanda: avanti come? avanti dove?'

85 'Possiamo sempre alzare il tiro di una spanna'.

86 'Quanti sono . . . questi nuclei armati "territoriali"? Nessuno lo sa. Si sa soltanto
che agiscono in periferia, non sono clandestini, attaccano non i simboli o i "servi"
dello Stato, come le Br, ma i nemici personali, in carne e ossa, vicini, nel
"territorio", gli avversari di rione, di quartiere, di borgata.'

87 'noi militanti combattenti di Azione Rivoluzionaria siamo qui, accanto a voi, per
partecipare al convegno sulla repressione perché non ci consideriamo un "partito
militare" avulso dalle lotte reali di massa . . . Il nostro scopo è quello di realizzare
una struttura combattente il più possibile aperta verso la base, che consenta la
massiccia partecipazione degli sfruttati, degli emarginati, dei non garantiti e di
tutti che coloro che vogliono attaccare il padronato e i suoi servitori, senza che a
filtrare questa base ci sia un partito militare che assume la direzione delle
lotte. . . . Abbiamo attaccato il Pci, contro cui tanti rivoluzionari a parole rivol-
gono delle critiche brucianti, chiamandolo fonte tra le principali della reazione . . . non abbiamo fatto altro che realizzare quello che tanti compagni
teorizzano.'

5

'Repudiate all forms of intolerance': how the movements were framed

Framing the news, framing disorder

This chapter analyses the key framing strategies employed by the PCI's daily paper *l'Unità* in relation to the key movements of the second cycle. The period has been divided into three phases: innovation, running roughly from March 1972 to the end of 1973; diffusion, from 1974 to the end of 1976; and engagement, from December 1976 to December 1977.

L'Unità makes a good source on the PCI's framing strategies for three main reasons. The paper at this time was a vehicle of 'orientation' as much as a news organ: both in its explicit editorial comments and in the rhetoric used in news stories, *l'Unità* offered PCI members continual guidance based on party policy. Moreover, *l'Unità*'s attempts at orientation were character-ised by their immediacy: the paper recorded the party's instant responses to events, making it possible to trace the frames used and how these changed under the pressure of circumstances. The choice of *l'Unità*, finally, makes it possible to make comparisons with a second daily newspaper; while this cannot realistically provide a neutral 'control', it does give some idea of when particular themes were unique to the PCI and when they were widely shared within Italian society. *L'Unità*'s presentation of events has been contrasted with that of the *Corriere della Sera*: a long-established mainstream daily paper known historically for a position of enlightened conservatism, firmly anti-fascist and occasionally critical of the DC.

To understand the significance of frame analysis in the news media, it is worth looking at an earlier example of news media analysis in this area. Howard Davis and Paul Walton of the Glasgow University Media Group analysed coverage of the assassination of Aldo Moro in British, US and West German newspapers (Davis and Walton 1983). Davis and Walton showed that the BR were repeatedly referred to using a limited range of characterisa-tions: they were characterised as criminal ('killers', 'gunmen', 'murderers'); as a military organisation ('guerrillas', 'urban guerrillas'); as political extre-mists ('Marxist revolutionaries'); and, to a lesser extent, as insane ('crazies')

(Davis and Walton 1983: 40–1). Davis and Walton argue that these characterisations exemplify 'the "ideological work" which is routinely performed
at the boundaries of *inclusion* and *exclusion*' (Davis and Walton 1983: 43;
emphasis in original), ensuring 'the isolation of the Red Brigades from
"everyday" explanations, the normal run of events and social processes'
(Davis and Walton 1983: 14).

This is a powerful analysis, but fails to take account of the broader social
and cultural context of these framing operations. On one hand, the BR themselves had contributed to setting the limits of representation of the group
within news discourse. While Davis and Walton's comment that 'the activities of the armed groups are one expression of quite general opposition to
unresolved social issues' (Davis and Walton 1983: 13) is valid, it should also
be acknowledged that the BR were self-proclaimed 'urban guerrillas' and
'Marxist revolutionaries': the BR itself had worked hard to dissociate the
organisation from '"everyday" explanations'. Moreover, at this time the BR
had just carried out a killing in cold blood. The event was both shocking and
alien to what news professionals might reasonably suppose their audience's
values to be: exclusionary framings were very much to be expected. The
interest of the framings under discussion lies in the traces or side effects of
this operation, in which the BR are not merely labelled as urban guerrillas,
revolutionaries or killers but assimilated to pre-existing frames. Thus the
criminality of the BR allowed them to be described as 'a handful of violent
criminals and psychopaths', while their revolutionary politics was rendered
by the phrase 'violent anarchists' (Davis and Walton 1983: 40). The function
of framings such as these was to isolate the BR from any possible identification, even in their role as violent Marxist revolutionaries.

It should also be taken into account that the isolation and exclusion of the
BR was not merely the work of the news media, but a political fact resulting
from the strategies of major political parties. The media dimension of this
operation was a reflection (if not a direct expression) of stances taken by
political parties, and of projects pursued by those parties at a given time. Here
again, what is of interest is not so much the fact that media outlets chose to
maintain the exclusion of the BR from political debate as the specific terms
in which particular media operations did so at given times. For instance, we
would not expect a PCI-aligned paper to condemn the BR as 'Marxist revolutionaries'; during 1977, on the other hand, we might expect the demands
of the PCI's alliance with the DC to lead to a stress on 'law and order' issues,
and hence to see the BR branded as criminals rather than as neo-fascists.

My argument is that the PCI's ideological requirements led *l'Unità* to
develop a hostile and internally coherent set of framings for the movements
of the second cycle. This framing strategy can be seen to develop as
the second cycle progresses, with the party's hostility intensifying as the

movements approach engagement with the institutional Left. This sequence of framing transactions correlates with the exclusion of the movements from political legitimacy, suggesting that the PCI's framing operations, carried out in its role as gatekeeper, had direct political efficacy.

A vivid illustration of the effects of different framing strategies, and the context in which they were adopted, is provided by reports of an event at the height of the first cycle of contention. On 27 February 1969, the then US President Richard Nixon made a state visit to Italy. A large protest demonstration in Rome ended in running battles with the police. Students occupying the University of Rome repeatedly attempted to join the demonstration but were blocked by police. The following day, *l'Unità*'s front page lead was headed 'ROME TAKES TO THE STREETS TO DEMONSTRATE/Police violence unleashed in the streets to suppress a powerful anti-imperialist protest' (Anon. 1969a).[1] A front-page comment piece headed 'The politics of the truncheon' announced: 'Violence instead of solving problems . . . the break-up of democracy opening the way for authoritarian initiatives and arousing repression, the arrogance of the truncheon substituting for politics: we won't allow it. Workers, students, democrats cannot allow it' (Anon. 1969b).[2] According to a first-person report:

> The demonstration [was] passionate and vibrant, but composed, controlled by the young people themselves . . . the demonstrators demonstrated their determination to avoid a confrontation . . . As the police charges continued, the young people blocked via della Panetteria and via dei Crociferi with cars. Some cars were burned out . . . Again and again, the students made sorties from the besieged university; every time, they had to face police violence. In the evening, to protect themselves from the charges of police jeeps, the students blocked all the streets around the university with makeshift barriers; police charges took place throughout the area. (Marzullo 1969)[3]

A key point about the stance of the paper's reports of the protest is that it consistently condemned disorder: both the PCI's commitment to the 'republic born in the Resistance' and its role of institutional 'gatekeeper' made it impossible for the party to take a role of systemic opposition, or to give outright endorsement to political disorder. However, order is represented here by the 'composed, controlled' demonstration and disorder by police tactics: the 'arrogance of the truncheon' which 'democrats can't allow'. Thus demonstrators who are set on avoiding confrontation are subjected to gratuitous 'police violence', blockading streets with cars only in self-defence. On the same day, the *Corriere della Sera* condemned the disorder created by 'Communist activists' (Madeo 1969).

A different framing strategy is in evidence as early as March 1972, when *l'Unità* harked back to the February 1969 demonstration. The context was a

report on three neo-fascists, alleged to have masqueraded as leftists and operated as provocateurs: 'the tactic is always the same. Once infiltrated, the fascists play the double role of informer for their "comrades" and provocateur,
carrying out attacks for which the "grouplets" can be blamed or attempting,
at every opportunity, to create incidents with the police. . . . [the three neo-
fascists] turned up at the demonstration against Nixon's visit complete with
red kerchiefs; during the police charges they missed no opportunity to create
still more confusion and carry out acts of vandalism' ('R. Ga' 1972).[4] Ret-
rospectively, the demonstration of February 1969 had been characterised by
gratuitous clashes with the police, acts of vandalism and general 'confusion'.
The blame, moreover, fell on an element among the demonstrators (albeit a
neo-fascist element); the police charges, central to the paper's contemporary
coverage, were now a background detail.

The shift marks a passage from the PCI's engagement with the first cycle
of contention to the 'aftermath' phase, with the reimposition of a division
between acceptable and unacceptable tactics, ideologies and groups. It also
sets the scene for the second cycle. Denunciation of disorder and condemnation of the group responsible, identified as an irremediably hostile and destructive element within a social movement: this is the starting point for the PCI's
framing of the second cycle of contention.

Framing the news, reading the frames

I have carried out an extensive qualitative analysis of the coverage by *l'Unità*
of key events in the second cycle of contention. In total, 142 news stories
and 45 comment pieces have been analysed, over a period ranging from
2 March 1972 to 14 December 1977. A smaller number of pieces in the
Corriere della Sera, addressing the same key events, were also analysed.
Table 5.1 gives a breakdown of the news articles analysed in each phase.

The news stories analysed were chosen for relevance to a series of pre-
selected key events; these are listed in table 5.2. Using the national press as

Table 5.1 Number and type of news articles analysed in *l'Unità*, March 1972–
December 1977

	3/72–12/73	4/74–11/76	12/76–12/77	
	Innovation	Diffusion	Engagement	Total
News				
front page	12	14	48	74
inside	17	17	34	68
Comment	10	6	29	45
Total for period	39	37	111	187

Table 5.2 Subject matter of news articles analysed in *l'Unità*, March 1972–December 1977

Period	Year	Type	Event
Innovation	1972	Armed	Brigate Rosse kidnap Idalgo Macchiarini
	1972	Armed	Death of Giangiacomo Feltrinelli
	1972	Armed	Murder of Luigi Calabresi
	1973	Mass	Occupation of FIAT Mirafiori
	1973	Armed	Brigate Rosse kidnap Ettore Amerio
Diffusion	1974	Armed	Brigate Rosse kidnap Mario Sossi
	1974	Armed	Brigate Rosse kill Giralucci and Mazzola
	1974	Armed	Police kill Luca Mantini
	1974	Armed	Attack on FACE Standard
	1975	Armed	Police kill Annamaria Mantini
	1975	Mass	Anti-Franco rioting
	1975	Mass	Demonstration at Innocenti
	1976	Mass	Spanish Embassy firebombed
	1976	Mass	Arson at FIAT
	1976	Armed	Brigate Rosse kill Francesco Coco
	1976	Mass	Parco Lambro
	1976	Mass	Proletarian Youth Happening
Engagement	1976	Mass	La Scala
	1977	Mass	The rout of Lama; rioting in Rome
	1977	Mass	Rioting in Turin
	1977	Mass	Police kill Francesco Lorusso; rioting in Bologna
	1977	Mass	Rioting in Rome
	1977	Mass	Autonomists kill Settimio Passamonti
	1977	Mass	Police kill Giorgiana Masi
	1977	Mass	Autonomists kill Antonino Custrà
	1977	Armed	Brigate Rosse attack journalists
	1977	Armed	Police kill Antonio Lo Muscio
	1977	Armed	Azione Rivoluzionaria attack Nino Ferrero
	1977	Mass	Bologna conference
	1977	Mass	Metalworkers' march

a source inevitably imposes a bias towards the exceptional or spectacular. In the earlier years of the cycle, in particular, this has meant a focus on reports of actions by the armed groups, rather than *l'Unità*'s scattered references to the activities of the early autonomist committees. This is less of a problem for the analysis of framing strategies than might appear; as we shall see, many of the same framings are applied to both armed groups and mass movements.

My goal in analysing these news stories was not to establish whether *l'Unità* (and by extension the PCI) had a positive or negative attitude to these

events, or even who the paper blamed for the disorder caused. I began from
three assumptions (which were seldom challenged): that the paper would be
hostile towards the mass movements and the armed groups; that it would
make little distinction between the two; and that it would not blame the police
for any harm done while policing the movements and the armed groups.
Beyond this, I wanted to identify the terms in which *l'Unità* set the movements and the armed groups beyond the pale, and how these terms changed
over time.

In short, I wanted to identify the ways in which the cycle of contention
was framed by the PCI. The significance of this analysis is twofold. Firstly,
following Schutz's phenomenological analysis of types and typification, I
argue that framing social reality is a constituent part of the practical, self-
interested activity of individuals and groups. We structure our perceptions,
and communicate how they are structured, as a continuing element of normal
activity. It follows that the ways in which PCI loyalists perceived and portrayed the second cycle of contention will have been responsive to the contemporary priorities of the party. This does not imply, however, that *l'Unità*'s
correspondents are likely to reproduce party policy in a logically coherent
way; rather, we should expect the party's concerns to be echoed in images
and turns of phrase as well as in sustained arguments.

Secondly, following the lead of critical realists such as Sayer, I argue that
the production of knowledge is both determined by and tends to reproduce
structures of social relations. The social position of an institution such as a
political party is sustained in part from its ability to tell a coherent and usable
story. It follows from this that, for a political party playing the role of 'gatekeeper' to a political system, the framing of disorderly social movements and
their repertoires is a priority in itself. This in turn will lead us to expect the
use of persuasive rhetoric in describing the movements, again in ways which
respond to the party's contemporary concerns.

Framing can thus be analysed on two levels, focusing firstly on the vocabulary associated with particular topics and secondly on the ways in which this
vocabulary is articulated. As an example of this double approach, we can
look at *l'Unità*'s coverage of the BR's 1972 kidnapping of Idalgo Macchiarini. On 4 March the paper announced: 'A banditesque provocation took place
late yesterday afternoon in Milan';[5] the piece concluded by identifying the
BR as 'a mysterious organisation which makes itself known in moments of
heightened union-related tension with serious acts of provocation in an
attempt to make the workers and the unions take the blame for acts and initiatives which have nothing to do with the workers' movement and its struggles'
(Anon. 1972a).[6] Three days later, the paper stated: 'Idalgo Macchiarini was
kidnapped by an unknown group which defined itself as "red brigades", but
which was clearly fascist and in the service of the bosses' provocations'

(Anon. 1972b).[7] Further, the paper reported Lotta Continua's approval of the action ('an incredible and insane statement in which this episode of hooliganism is justified and exalted' (Anon. 1972b)).[8] Phrases and images associated with the struggle against Fascism ('clearly fascist', 'the bosses' provocations') appeared together with images of criminality ('banditesque provocation', 'this episode of hooliganism') and allegations of insanity ('this incredible and insane statement'). The central proposition is that the BR should be shunned: whoever they are, they 'have nothing to do with' *l'Unità*'s readership.

L'Unità is not advancing the proposition that the BR should be shunned on the grounds that they are, as a statement of fact, neo-fascist provocateurs who are also insane bandit hooligans. Rather, what we see here is the full range of the paper's vocabulary of condemnation for its disorderly rivals; we can also see the outline of a persuasive rhetorical framing which would pull these terms together so as to encourage the paper's readers to reject the BR. The frame being developed here can be summed up roughly as 'criminal provocateur': the persuasive message is that the BR are both breaking the law and acting as agents provocateurs within the Left. Having positioned its readers as members of 'the workers' movement', *l'Unità* warns that the BR are an enemy of the workers' movement; that their activities are a threat to the movement (which would suffer from any retaliatory clampdown by the state); and that this threat is associated with disregard for the law. This last point, in turn, exemplifies the danger for the movement of departing from the PCI's strategy of law-abiding constitutional politics.

My procedure in analysing *l'Unità*'s coverage follows this two-step approach. I identify thematic clusters of adjectives, epithets and characterisations which occurred regularly throughout the period. A count of the number of occurrences of keywords in each cluster gives a sense of the main themes of the paper's coverage of the second cycle. It is then possible to identify the framings which are used at different times to marshal these keywords into a coherent image, and hence to trace the connections between particular framings and the political context in which they are used.

The principal thematic clusters identified in *l'Unità*'s coverage of the cycle are as follows.

Terrorism is, unsurprisingly, a frequent point of reference in coverage of the armed groups. As well as 'terrorism' and 'terrorist', key words here include 'attack' (*attentato*) and 'guerrilla'. Later in the cycle, framings associated with terrorism also appear in coverage of the mass movements.

Provocation, defined as covertly attempting to induce the Left to use illegal and violent tactics, is a constant concern for *l'Unità* in this period. The possibility that the extreme right was exploiting the left-wing armed groups was widely entertained in the period; *l'Unità* elevated this possibility to the level of near certainty, and applied it to the mass movements as well as the armed milieu. Key words include 'mysterious', 'self-styled', 'murky' (*torbido*), 'tension' and 'plot'.

Extreme left origins are sometimes assigned to the movements of the cycle, particularly earlier in the cycle. Key words here include 'ultra-left' (*ultra-sinistra*), 'extremist' and 'adventurist'. Groups such as Lotta Continua are taken to exemplify 'adventurism', an irresponsible revolutionary maximalism which leads impressionable workers astray.

Extreme right forces, real or imagined, are frequently invoked by *l'Unità*. As well as 'fascism' and 'fascist', key words include 'reactionary', 'subversion' (*eversione*) and 'squaddism' (*squadrismo*).

Crime is an apolitical frame of reference which can be evoked in the context of many of the events of the cycle. Key words include 'bandit' and 'hooliganism'.

Irrationality, finally, is a theme repeatedly used to mark out a group as incorrigibly deviant, or simply to register the writer's incomprehension. Key words include 'folly', 'delirium' and 'raving'.

Table 5.3 and figure 5.1 give a summary of the number of occurrences of key terms in these clusters in the news stories selected for analysis, in both *l'Unità* and the *Corriere della Sera*.

For the *Corriere* the leading category, amounting to nearly one in three of all characterisations, is terrorism; the next is 'provocation' (reflecting the widespread concern caused by the emergence of the armed groups in particular), followed by 'extreme left'. These three account for over 75 per cent of all characterisations. The remainder is mostly accounted for by the apolitical categories of 'crime' and 'irrationality'; terms in the 'extreme right' category appear only nine times in the five-year period.

The weighting of *l'Unità*'s conceptual vocabulary for dealing with the period is very different. The single category of 'provocation' accounts for

Table 5.3 Key words used to characterise events and actors in news stories studied in *l'Unità* and *Corriere della Sera*, 1972–7

	l'Unità		*Corriere*	
	Count	%	Count	%
Terrorism	49	10.0	53	32.1
Provocation	221	44.9	43	26.1
Left	34	6.9	28	17.0
Right	91	18.5	9	5.5
Crime	78	15.9	17	10.3
Irrationality	19	3.9	15	9.1

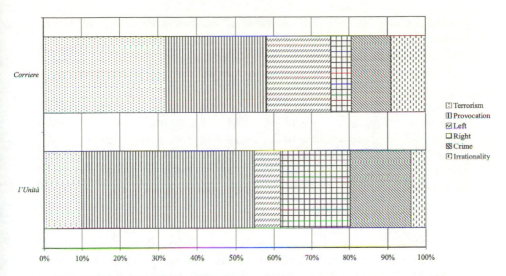

Figure 5.1 Key words used to characterise events and actors in news stories studied in *l'Unità* and *Corriere della Sera*, 1972–7

nearly half of a much larger number of characterisations. (As well as a larger number of stories being taken into account, *l'Unità* showed a much heavier use of evaluative characterisations than the *Corriere*, owing to its role as a vehicle of orientation.) The next largest category is 'extreme right', a closely related concept for the PCI. The only other characterisation to account for more than 10 per cent of the total is 'crime', evincing the importance of constitutional and legal politics for the PCI. 'Terrorism' is a relatively insignificant category for *l'Unità* and 'extreme left' even more so; 'irrationality' occupies last place.

As table 5.4 shows, there are some interesting differences of emphasis if we divide the material studied in *l'Unità* according to the three phases of the cycle of contention.

In all three phases, 'provocation' is the leading category; in the first and second phase it accounts for more than 50 per cent of all characterisations. The second and third categories overall, 'extreme right' and 'crime', account for less than a quarter of all characterisations in the first phase, but over 30 per cent in the second and over 40 per cent (a higher proportion than 'provocation') in the third. The category of 'crime' accounts for only 7.6 per cent of all characterisations in the first phase, but nearly 20 per cent in the third. This suggests that the PCI's attempts to frame the movements of the cycle in terms of either neo-fascism or apolitical criminality grew in intensity over the period, leading to some diversification away from the straightforward

Table 5.4 Characterisation of events and actors in news stories studied in *l'Unità*, 1972–7 (by period)

	Innovation		Diffusion		Engagement	
	Count	%	Count	%	Count	%
Terrorism	14	11.8	11	10.1	24	9.1
Provocation	62	52.1	57	52.3	102	38.6
Left	10	8.4	2	1.8	22	8.3
Right	19	16.0	15	13.8	57	21.6
Crime	9	7.6	18	16.5	51	19.3
Irrationality	5	4.2	6	5.5	8	3.0

'provocateur' framing. The 'extreme left' category, interestingly, almost entrely disappears in the second phase before returning, in the third phase, to a residual level similar to the first. Characterisations of 'terrorism' and 'irrationality' are an unchanging and marginal presence throughout.

'Disconnected, irresponsible and provocative': framing the phase of innovation, 1972–3

L'Unità uses two main framing strategies during the phase of innovation. As we have seen, in the paper's coverage of the Macchiarini kidnapping, the BR were characterised as provocateurs: neo-fascists working covertly to engineer clashes from which the Left could only lose. Provocateurism was further associated with disorderly and criminal behaviour. Thus, two days after Feltrinelli's death, an unsigned commentator in *l'Unità* wrote:

> Everything about the tragic events at Segrate involving Giangiacomo Feltrinelli is profoundly obscure. . . . One thing, however, seems as clear as day: that is, that the episode arrives at the best and most opportune moment for reactionary and conservative forces, for the ruling classes, for all those who want to distract public opinion yet again from the real problems of the country and create a troubled climate of fear, of violence, of tension (Anon. 1972c)[9]

Two days later *l'Unità* identified the PCI not only as the guardian of Italian society against 'provocation' but as its target:

> We should never forget that Italy is, today, the 'western' country with the most advanced democratic system, the strongest and most united workers' and people's movement, the strongest Communist Party. The machine of provocation has been set in motion against all this. And this is why we have been so firm in denouncing the extreme positions which can provide this machine of provocation with alibis and victims. (Anon. 1972d)[10]

Similarly, in December 1973, *L'Unità* was in no doubt regarding the BR's kidnap of Amerio:

> Here we are again. Once again, in the midst of union negotiations at FIAT, as punctual as a Swiss watch, we are faced with a serious provocation. . . . The political and trade union history of the last few years in our country is full of episodes which had the self-styled 'red brigades' [*brigate rosse*] for protagonists. . . . Whatever the political coloration this organisation assumes, its activities are now interwoven perfectly with the subversive schemes of neo-fascist groups. (Anon. 1973c)[11]

Following Italian capitalisation conventions, the BR referred to itself as 'Brigate rosse'; coverage in the *Corriere* invariably followed suit. *L'Unità*'s dismissive use of the lower-case B reflects the paper's 'provocateur' framing. Variants on this frame will be central to the PCI's framing strategies, regarding the mass movements as well as the armed groups, throughout the second cycle of contention.

A second framing, centring on disorder but associating this with undesirable forms of left-wing politics, also appears in this period; the reference quoted above to 'the extreme positions which can provide this machine of provocation with alibis and victims' is an early example. *L'Unità* developed this 'adventurist' framing further in its response to Potere Operaio's tribute to Feltrinelli:

> they have given the label of 'armed struggle' to a series of actions which are disconnected, irresponsible and provocative, which fit perfectly into the strategy of the most reactionary forces and are carried out by groups which form an out-and-out breeding-ground for every kind of adventurist, spy and agent pro-vocateur (Anon. 1972e)[12]

The theme was stated more fully in May 1972, in response to the near-endorsement of the murder of Calabresi by Lotta Continua, another survivor of the first cycle of contention. A front-page comment article signed by the PCI's Aldo Tortorella argued:

> It's obvious that this phrase will be taken as an excuse by the worst forces of the right, validating their own positions. But even that isn't the worst thing about it. The worst thing is the absolute void – cultural, intellectual and political – which these positions represent: a void which makes them dangerous tools, anti-worker, anti-popular and counter-revolutionary by their nature. Those who uphold these positions and represent themselves as ultra-left are not only, in reality, the bitterest enemies of our party; they are, before anything else, adversaries of all the progress achieved by the workers' and Communist movement (Tortorella 1972)[13]

Here the charge of provocateurism is secondary; Lotta Continua's adventurism is condemned in its own right. For Tortorella, the apparent extremism represented by the group's endorsement of violence was actually a denial of the leading role of the organised working class, and hence disqualified the group from membership of the Left. However, this 'adventurist' framing is unstable from the outset; it is associated first with allegations of irrationality and provocateurism, then with suggestions that left-wing adventurism is itself objectively right-wing.

Towards the end of the period a composite framing was attempted, combining left-wing adventurism with irrationality, criminality and provocateurism. Thus an unsigned comment piece in response to the Amerio kidnapping quoted dismissively from a BR statement:

> The 'political' motivation of this action is supposedly that the choice, today, must be between 'historic compromise and armed proletarian power' since 'the middle ways have been destroyed' and that 'there is a division in the heart of the workers' movement' as 'the unity of a revolutionary front grows from this division'. . . . The attempt to split the front of the workers' struggle . . . attests to provocative intentions. It hardly matters, at this point, if we are dealing with phrases produced by frenzied delirium or by calculating professionals: the result is the same. It is the work of people who, in effect, have become the accomplices and the protagonists of the murky subversive schemes which attempt to block the path of the working class and the workers, and to undermine the democratic achievements of the nation. (Anon. 1973d)[14]

The BR's evocation of 'a division in the heart of the workers' movement' is rejected simply because it is divisive: wooing the PCI's working-class base is by definition a provocation. The anonymous writer allows that the BR might not be knowingly operating as provocateurs; they might instead be insane. However, even in this case the BR would be working 'in effect' as a tool of the extreme right. The paper also carried a brief statement by Lama: 'This is an action which has nothing to do with the union movement. Ours is a democratic struggle. Those who set themselves outside the law, whichever political position they claim to occupy, must be rapidly struck and punished' (Lama 1973).[15]

As we have seen, this contrast between orderly and disorderly forms of radicalism enabled the PCI to adopt and absorb the repertoires and activists of the first cycle, even while it dismissed groups such as Potere Operaio as irredeemably disorderly. As the party faced new and more intransigent forms of activism, however, it was beginning to define itself in terms of patriotism, legality and political moderation as well as orderly reform. As the PCI distanced itself decisively from the disorderly Left and the unrest associated with it, the 'provocateur' and 'adventurist' frames began to merge. The anathema pronounced by Lama against any form of law-breaking is particularly significant in this respect, explicitly adding criminality to the 'adventurist' frame and suggesting that this in itself is a sign of opposition to the PCI.

This shift suggests a significant modification of the PCI's implicit self-presentation; after all the activists of the first cycle had precisely 'set themselves outside the law'.

'Typical fascist violence': framing the phase of diffusion, 1974–6

The 'diffusion' phase of the second cycle is marked by the spread of autonomist repertoires to different areas: in this phase we see the first armed struggle groups associated with the area of Autonomia and the adoption of autonomist repertoires by new groups, notably the 'proletarian youth movement' of Milan. There are four main developments in the period. Firstly, Autonomia makes its presence felt on the streets, just as the PCI and CGIL are re-establishing control in the factories; the latter development is marked by a decline in openly organised 'autonomous' activity and a rise in covert actions such as sabotage. Secondly, the Milan-based 'proletarian youth movement' forms and grows to the point of gaining national attention. Thirdly, from 1974 smaller 'armed struggle' groups begin to gain prominence. The BR, lastly, reassert their claim to leadership of the armed milieu by attacking more ambitious targets and making greater use of personal violence.

There are three main framing strategies in use during this period. The 'provocateur' frame dominates: it is applied, with some differences of emphasis, to the BR, the smaller armed groups and Autonomia on the streets. Following the April 1974 kidnapping of Sossi, *l'Unità* wrote:

> Whoever may be putting it into practice, it is perfectly clear that this strategy is willed by people who wish to attack Italian democracy . . . and to terrorise the country in a bid to impose a reactionary turn (Anon. 1974b)[16]

The FACE Standard arson attack in October 1974 was interpreted along similar lines:

> With absolute and lamentably predictable punctuality, just as the right is making its moves to attack Parliament and increase confusion in the country, provocation masked as 'left-wing' has been set off. . . . What is harder to understand is whether we are dealing with outright fascists who act in their own right and then hide behind 'revolutionary' trappings and phrases, or with crazed fanatics who have lost all contact with reality and are now deep in the swamp of anti-worker and anti-democratic irresponsibility. The very fact that this question can be asked brands the authors of the action, whoever they may be (Anon. 1974b)[17]

The writer conceded that the attackers might not be fascists, only to argue that in that case they must be insane ('crazed fanatics') – and, if they were insane, they must be a tool of unknown fascists.

Autonomists were also provocateurs, in the workplace and out of it. The April 1976 arson attacks at Fiat were part of 'a vast criminal plan of provocation' (Anon. 1976b).[18] The March 1976 firebombing of the Spanish Embassy in Rome could also be assumed to be the work of provocateurs, if only because it was an unclaimed attack using Molotov cocktails: 'It is certainly not for us to show even the slightest tolerance towards commando-style initiatives and provocative techniques such as firebombing. And then, who were the protagonists of this escapade, unannounced and unclaimed by anyone, not even the wildest extremist groups?' (Anon. 1976e).[19] Even *autoriduzione* was carried out by provocateurs. In October 1974, *l'Unità*'s Milan edition covered the first known episode of *spese proletarie*: 'Under the pretext of protesting against price rises, a group of provocateurs yesterday evening made a disgraceful scene in front of the Cantalupo neighbourhood co-operatives store in Monza, preventing normal access for shoppers. Several local PCI members arrived on the scene and vigorously rejected the hooligans' repeated attempts to provoke a fight' (Anon. 1974a).[20] On this occasion the PCI offered ideological as well as physical resistance, joining the local DC and PSI in drafting a notice denouncing the 'provocation'. Two years later, in a lengthy account of the Parco Lambro festival published in the local edition of *l'Unità*, the autonomists responsible for 'expropriating' stalls and occupying the Istituto Molinari could be confidently identified as provocateurs:

> On Sunday afternoon, groups of so-called 'autonomists' did no more than 'collect' frozen chickens without paying the bill . . . and mount a 'vigorous' protest against the prices charged by 'Uncle Tom's Cabin', the bar which had the bad luck to find itself in the middle of the festival. . . . The true intentions of certain groups of young people, who had arrived at Parco Lambro with their ski-masks in their rucksacks alongside their spanners and bottles of petrol, became clear yesterday afternoon. . . . Episodes of provocation with regard to the technical and industrial institute were recorded as early as Saturday night when, using the weather as a pretext, some of those who had taken shelter under the awning of the building took the opportunity to force several doors and windows, break in and commit acts of vandalism. Yesterday afternoon, though, there was the sense of an organised manoeuvre, in the true sense of the word, and police intervention became inevitable: stones were thrown from one side, tear-gas grenades from the other. . . . The police avoided a confrontation for as long as possible, enabling the stewards to prevent yet another excursion by these 'autonomists', whose presence at public demonstrations is regularly accompanied by the worst of provocations. Police officers and organisers were jointly discussing what to do when a 'commando' group broke away from the group of 'autonomists' . . . Once again, police intervention was inevitable. This time the tear-gas grenades were met with two petrol bombs and . . . apparently with pistol shots. (Anon. 1976f)[21]

This story in particular demonstrates that the label of 'provocateur' is not simply a term of abuse. To be a provocateur is to have a hidden agenda ('true intentions') and to be determined to cause trouble, and above all to induce the police to respond violently ('police intervention was inevitable'). Moreover, provocateurs plan their actions in advance ('the sense of an organised manoeuvre'). This complex and highly specified frame is imposed on autonomists and armed struggle militants alike.

Provocateurism is also associated with the charge of fascist sympathies. For obvious reasons, this identification is generally either left implicit or asserted without supporting argument, but it is occasionally spelt out. Thus, after the BR's killings of the fascists Giralucci and Mazzola, *l'Unità* denounces both the murder and the claim of responsibility:

> the mysterious double murder in Padua was and is an episode set, without the shadow of a doubt, in the context of the climate of tension and shady manoeuvring which represents a continual menace and a danger to the democratic life of Padua and of the entire nation. . . . These messages from the self-styled 'Red Brigades' have the same Nazi-fascist logic: not only in the attempt to confuse the tracks (a quite impossible goal), but in the very idea of revenge [*vendetta*], feud, assassination which is an idea, precisely, whose origins lie in the infamous baggage of Nazi doctrines. (Anon. 1974c)[22]

The BR are accused of fascism (more precisely, of the un-Italian allegiance of Nazism, associated oddly with the idea of revenge) both for carrying out an assassination and for claiming to be left-wing. (Denying being a Nazi is just the kind of thing a Nazi would do.)

Provocateurism is also associated with opposition to the PCI, in a complex framing which associates the PCI both with the working class and with democratic progress. During the period of diffusion, the emphasis shifts from one element of this framing to the other. Commenting on the BR's statement claiming the Sossi kidnap, the paper accuses the BR of 'attempting to speak in the name of the class which, more than any other and earlier than any other, has branded these fascist methods and acts' (Anon. 1974d).[23] By contrast, two years later, the BR's murder of Coco (the judge who had refused the BR's demands during the Sossi kidnap) was seen as an attempt to 'upset the ordered and civilised conduct of the electoral campaign . . . so as to strike at the democratic regime and prevent the Italian people from freely making new choices which can bring the nation out of crisis and disorder' (Anon. 1976g).[24] Here the BR are framed as enemies of democracy, striking with ruthless efficiency against the imminent general election and the PCI which upholds democracy ('new choices' here refers to the PCI's prospects in the election).

By now opposition to the 'provocateurs' was becoming synonymous with defence of the Italian Constitution. Thus *l'Unità* eulogised the dead Coco (in life a committed right-winger): 'Coco replied to the kidnappers negatively and with the "voice of the State": "I consider that . . . the powers [of the judiciary] are absolutely unavailable for any use which is radically different from that for which they are ordained, not to say incompatible and opposed . . .". This strong "sense of the State", which must not and cannot give in, was always present in the work of Francesco Coco' (Anon. 1976d).[25] As the PCI aspired to a role in a DC-led government, the party's self-presentation was dominated by an insistent commitment to legality; this was now extended to include the defence of the existing Italian state, presented as a repository of republican principle. After the April 1976 Fiat arson attacks, *l'Unità* even evoked that touchstone of Italian Communist history, the Resistance: '"We are struggling to defend jobs," said one worker, "and whoever is doing these things wants to destroy them." "In 1945," another recalled, "it was the workers who saved the factories which the Germans wanted to destroy. Today, the workers have the same task"' (Anon. 1976h).[26] The sheer range of groups and actions associated with provocateurism in this period, together with the shift in the connotations of this framing, demonstrate that the use of a given frame by the PCI in this period was a deeply political choice, corresponding to the changing ways in which the party interprets the contemporary situation and attempts to mobilise its followers.

The 'ultra-left adventurist' frame is also present in this period: it is applied, in particular, to Autonomia in the workplace and on the streets. The September 1975 rioting which followed Spain's execution of ETA militants is condemned in a column headed 'Hooliganism and provocation', but condemned in a tone unlike that of the stories cited above:

> These displays of gratuitous violence . . . have nothing to do with the united democratic political struggle manifested in the past few days to condemn the infamous assassination of the five young Spanish patriots [sic]. Whatever their inspiration, objectively these actions can only lead to a slackening of the isolation of the fascist executioner and to serious rifts in the vast front of anti-fascist solidarity (Anon. 1975d)[27]

The PCI's role in the patriotic anti-fascist coalition of the Resistance, and hence its status as a bulwark of orderly left-wing politics, is an implicit point of reference. However, the rioters are not denounced as provocateurs or covert neo-fascists; the left-wing origins of their actions is even, grudgingly, conceded. That said, it is worth noting that these events preceded the Spanish embassy firebombing, suggesting a subsequent change of emphasis. The hooligans responsible for that attack were branded as provocateurs, if only by their violent and 'commando-style' tactics; *l'Unità* even insinuated that they were fascists in their own right. *L'Unità* was moving towards a simplified framing, presenting a disorderly extreme left purely in terms of criminality, provocateurism and neo-fascism.

The paper's response to the disturbances at Innocenti in 1975 evokes both provocateurism and adventurism, stressing the PCI's own commitment to order:

> Yesterday at the appointed time, the various extra-parliamentary groups were also present outside the station at Lambrate.... [later] they headed for Innocenti-Leyland and made it through the gates.... Many of them had kerchiefs covering their faces, many were armed with knotty staves. The workers' response was firm: the strangers were thrown out at the gates. A little later all the workers of Innocenti Leyland met in a general assembly, restating their will to confirm their own priorities in struggle, rejecting all adventurism and all traps of provocateurs, calling for the withdrawal of union membership from the three workers who led the 'attack' on the factory (Anon. 1975e)[28]

In the event, six autonomists working at Innocenti were sacked (Wright 2002: 169). Ironically, the *Corriere*'s much briefer account gives more details:

> The Lambrate workers' return to the factory . . . was marked by a few incidents. A group of young people got past the gates of the factories and made a circuit of the work areas. The 'intruders' were expelled by the same Innocenti workers who had blockaded the factory's gatehouses. Scuffles broke out during this operation, leaving some workers with bruises. (d'Adda 1975)[29]

L'Unità mentions neither the intruders' attempt at a *corteo interno* (a classic technique of the first cycle) nor the violence of the Innocenti workers, which is tacitly celebrated as 'firmness'. The apparent urgency of rejecting the outsiders is striking: the mass meeting described appears to have been devoted, not to the continuing conflict with the plant's owners, but to restating the workers' rejection of 'all adventurism and all traps of provocateurs'. The PCI's self-framing has taken a 'legalist' turn; the movement which the party aspires to lead is implicitly defined as law-abiding. Further, the combined reference to adventurism and provocateurism carries the implication that these are two aspects of the same threat. This is particularly apparent in *l'Unità*'s coverage of the Fiat arson attacks:

> the episodes of provocation with which the last few months of struggle at FIAT have been studded (the burning of foremen's cars, attacks on team leaders, sabotage, distribution of insane-sounding material, arson and attempted arson) have always found the workers and their united union movement in the front line
>
> . . .
>
> we need to go beyond simple denunciation . . . to build within the workshops and offices a tangible and permanent network of democratic vigilance, giving the workers an active part in the battle to defend democracy. (Anon. 1976i)[30]

All violence and 'adventurism', from arson to the distribution of radical literature, can be traced back to provocateurism. The effect is to evacuate unruly workplace activism of all political content, presenting it solely as a threat to order. By this stage, the 'adventurist' framing appears only as a weakness which makes a group liable to foster provocation. Thus the Parco Lambro story quoted above refers to clashes between autonomists and 'groups which, until the day before yesterday, had either theorised or at least tacitly approved of expropriation';[31] the phrasing evokes the PCI's rivals from the first cycle of contention only to dismiss them with derision. The writer quotes a statement by the FGCI cell at the Istituto Molinari: 'without lingering over the political background which these groups like to give themselves, we say again that these actions are typical fascist violence. Moreover, we condemn all those political forces which, while dissociating themselves from these groups, too often give space to elements whose actions put them in decisive opposition to the workers' movement' (Anon. 1976f).[32] This argument takes anti-fascist vigilance to the rather alarming length of casting doubt on explicit dissociation: whatever the stance of a given group, far-left policies in themselves 'give space' to the autonomists.

The instability and decline of the 'adventurist' framing may be related to the fact that by the time of Parco Lambro all the significant *gruppuscoli* of the first cycle of contention had either dissolved or entered Parliament ('Perhaps the fact of having representatives in parliament demotivates the kids who came to camp out in this dusty park in Milan', a reporter in the *Corriere* commented (Borgese 1976)[33]). The PCI, meanwhile, had made gains unparallelled before or after in the June 1976 general elections; with the 'historic compromise' strategy apparently on the point of success, the party now accentuated its opposition to the disorderly Left.

Towards the end of the period, a new 'disorganised lumpenproletariat' frame was applied to the nascent 'proletarian youth movement', particularly in the context of the November 1976 'Happening'. It is worth comparing *l'Unità*'s coverage of the event with that of the *Corriere*, which presented the 'proletarian youth' as disorganised fantasists united by an ineffectual opposition to the status quo:

> 'They annihilate us, they want to exterminate us, they put us in reservations,' says a young man with long hair and a floral shirt. The reservations are dormitory suburbs, shanty towns on the foggy and hostile outskirts. . . . There's an anger lurking beneath a mass of profoundly different individuals, who are trying to present themselves as united by defining themselves as 'young'. . . . They will continue to dance in illegality around the totem pole of revolution, shooting the arrows of expropriation against their own apathy. (Nava 1976)[34]

L'Unità was more severe:

> Around two thousand kids, many of them extremely young . . . created a sort of small-scale Parco Lambro which few found satisfactory. The problems of youth were discussed very little and in extremely confused terms; any talk of organisation was rejected; nobody really knew what to say . . . The interventions of members of the 'youth circles', followed with little enthusiasm by an audience which changed rapidly, remained superficial, attesting to a dramatic confusion of ideas. . . . Amid this confusion, in which even some justifiable aspirations failed to go beyond the limits of protest, it's no accident that the themes of *autoriduzione* and appropriation had a lot of exposure, and not only in theory. (Anon. 1976j)[35]

Behind this apparent confusion and disorganisation lay the diffusion of new tactics and cultural forms, as the *Corriere* recognised rather more clearly than *l'Unità*. To lecture the movement about the need to discuss 'problems of youth' and attend to 'talk of organisation' was, at best, to express incomprehension of what the movement actually was and had already achieved. Where *l'Unità* does acknowledge the movement's innovations, they are treated as a lapse into simple criminality, encouraged by the anomic confusion of the movement. The minatory tone of the last sentence of the paragraph quoted clearly suggests that the devil would find work for idle young proletarians to do.

This reading is borne out by *l'Unità*'s representation of *autoriduzione* in practice. Once again, it is instructive to compare the paper directly with the *Corriere*. On 28 November, the Milan editions of both papers carried accounts of *autoriduzione* in practice; the *Corriere* focused on a series of raids on restaurants, *l'Unità* on the robbery of a pork butcher.

> There was no violence, although in some cases the reaction of the owners of the restaurants minimised the damage, obtaining rather more from the extremists than they had intended to pay. . . . [At one pizzeria] seventeen young people went in . . . took up all the available seats, ate seventeen pizzas and drank nineteen beers, then got up and were about to leave when the owner presented them with the bill: 48,000 lire. 'We're students,' they replied, 'we can only afford 8,000 lire'. After putting the money on the table, they all fled before the owner could recover from the shock. (Anon. 1976k)[36]

> a group of around 30 young people burst into Giuseppe Vecchi's pork butcher's shop . . . Shouting, 'This is a proletarian expropriation, nobody move,' the young people took possession of various foodstuffs. The proprietor of the shop called the police from the back room, and several patrols from the flying squad and the police's political section arrived on the scene. Nine young people who were still in the area were arrested and taken to the police station. They were later released, after paying the owner of the shop a part of the cost of the goods taken. (Anon. 1976l)[37]

The *Corriere*'s account opens by stressing that there was no violence and that the participants did not get away scot-free; thus reassured, the reader can follow the episode at the pizzeria as comedy, from the detail of the 17 young people getting through 17 pizzas and 19 beers to the slapstick conclusion. For *l'Unità*, the raid on the pork butcher's took the form of a hold-up, from the shout of 'nobody move' to the arrival of the police and the arrest of the wrongdoers. The *Corriere* presents *autoriduzione* as a new and amusingly bizarre form of behaviour; *l'Unità* presents it as a reversion to lumpenprole-tarian petty criminality. The movement itself is presented as an formless mass of young people, wilfully maintaining the confusion in which their margin-alisation has left them, and with no outlet but the pursuit of immediate gratification through crime. That said, the disorganisation and apathy of 'proletarian youth' seemingly makes them no great threat: *l'Unità*'s report notes that nine people were still on the scene when the police arrived, as distinct from the *Corriere*'s 'gastronomic raid' from which the participants got clean away.

Within the period 1972–80, these were the years when the PCI made its greatest electoral advances. This was also the period when the PCI leadership fixed on a cautious and conciliatory approach to the DC, stressing the party's patriotism and economic responsibility while offering co-operation in local government and discipline in the workplace. After the election results of 1975 and 1976, the leadership (and many party loyalists) must have believed that the PCI was not far from taking power, or even inaugurat-ing an era of 'proletarian hegemony'. However, the price demanded by the DC, and passed on by the PCI's leadership to its members, remained high.

The stresses and contradictions of this period are reflected in the party's changing framing strategies. The decline of the 'ultra-left adventurist' framing, firstly, can be related to the PCI's growing reluctance to stress its own posi-tion on the Left; the only political enemies which can be recognised as such are neo-fascists. The 'provocateur' framing, secondly, is modified during the period as well as being applied to broader groups. Initially the PCI empha-sises its own class base, stressing that the working class in particular is unshakeable in its opposition to the provocateurs and readiness to work with other democratic forces. This is subsequently replaced by a commitment to legality and the Italian state. The provocateurs themselves are sometimes portrayed as neo-fascists, sometimes (as at Parco Lambro) as sheer nihilists. The 'disorganised lumpenproletariat' framing, finally, expresses an opposi-tion between a party which sees itself as embodying political rationality and a social movement it sees as neither political nor rational. The PCI would shortly be forced to give serious attention to the new movement; it was singularly ill-equipped to offer anything but hostility.

'A kind of homogeneous, impassable block': framing the phase of engagement, 1976–7

The 'engagement' phase is marked by an increasingly open confrontation between the movements of the second cycle and the PCI: the PCI adopts an uncompromising 'law and order' stance in opposition to social movements and armed struggle groups alike. There are five main developments in this period. First, the new movements' opposition to the PCI becomes explicit, ideologically and physically: the key event in this development was the 'rout of Lama' in February 1977. Second, between March and May a series of marches, demonstrations and riots is met with progressively less tolerance by the state (backed by the PCI). Third, as the movement begins to flag in the summer and autumn of 1977, both the BR and the smaller armed groups respond with an increased level of violent activity. Fourth, the PCI's insistent dissociation of its own programme from the new movements distances the party from its own supporters; the long-demanded isolation of the autonomists was finally achieved at the December 1977 FLM demonstration, which also registered union members' disaffection with the PCI. The marginalisation of the autonomist and youth movements, which closed the phase of engagement, required enduring changes to the party's broader orientations. It also tended to promote the diffusion of the armed struggle repertoire. The final major development of this period, marking the close of the engagement phase of the main cycle, is the PCI's official recognition of the armed groups as leftists rather than neo-fascist provocateurs; this development, marked publicly in December 1977, marks the opening of a hostile engagement with the armed groups.

There are three main framing strategies at work in this period. The 'provocateur' frame is applied consistently both to the autonomists and to the armed groups. The 'disorganised lumpenproletariat' framing continues to be applied to the proletarian youth movement and its successor, the 'movement of 1977'. Lastly, towards the end of the period an 'anti-democratic extremist' framing is applied to the armed groups, following the PCI's official acknowledgment that their left-wing allegiance was genuine.

Until this change of direction, the armed groups are uniformly labelled as provocateurs, or more specifically as neo-fascist provocateurs. The autonomists, by contrast, are often charged with provocateurism combined with both fascism and destructive nihilism, particularly in the earlier part of the period. In the wake of the 'rout of Lama' in February 1977, an anonymous commentator wrote:

> Who are these individuals who have been described over the last few years as the main actors – together with the fascists – in episodes of violence and hooliganism? . . . It's not a party, not even in an embryonic state: it's the

outright negation of all parties and all forms of organisation . . . Another fact
which characterises the action of these groups is the complete absence of political platforms (Anon. 1977d)[38]

This supposed ideological nihilism went along with an indiscriminate appe-
tite for destruction. Reporting the clashes at La Scala, the Milan edition of
l'Unità declared that 'The self-styled "Youth circles", sowing chaos and
destruction, took their latest provocative plan to the limit' (Anon. 1976m):

> What the self-styled 'Proletarian youth circles' carried out last night was
> revealed, from the outset, to be a provocation coolly worked out at a desk, in
> which the supposed 'protest' against the opening spectacle of the season at La
> Scala ended by showing itself to be a pure pretext. In fact, the real 'strategic'
> objective of the plan pre-arranged by the 'circles' became clear very early: the
> pure and simple pursuit of violence and . . . ideological or social motives were
> always entirely extraneous to the organisers of the provocation. (Anon.
> 1976n)[39]

As we have seen, provocateurs are assumed to have a double identity
('self-styled') as well as a plan worked out beforehand. The novelty of this
framing is that these are nihilist provocateurs, whose plan is for motiveless
violence. The circularity of the argument is also striking: the existence of a
plan 'coolly worked out at a desk' was apparently 'revealed' by the events
themselves.

The theme of nihilist provocateurism was also prominent in *l'Unità*'s
coverage of the March 1977 riots, with evocations of 'violent groups [who]
mingled with the demonstrators, groups of armed hooligans determined to
provoke incidents at any cost' (Criscuoli 1977).[40] Once again, the unlikely
combination of premeditation and random destructiveness is emphasised:

> hundreds of firebombs were handed out, having been assembled by groups of
> specialists . . . the climate of tension built up continually, eventually reaching
> paroxysms of hysteria . . . [from an ironmonger's] one group took chains, iron
> spikes, spanners and other objects useful for the destructive plan which would
> later unfold . . . some groups of citizens, who would not put up with such rash,
> indiscriminate violence towards everything and everyone, prevented further
> looting and arson (Scagliarini 1977a)[41]

On 12 May, Giorgiana Masi was shot by the police. For *l'Unità*, hooligan
provocateurs were to blame for the entire course of events, the death of Masi
herself not excluded:

> Clashes began after [sic] the first police charges against the demonstrators
> arriving in Piazza Navona; over the hours that followed, groups of armed and
> masked hooligans played a distinct role of criminal provocation . . . Giorgina
> [sic] Masi fell . . . while she was in the midst of a dense group of demonstrators
> which had clashed with the police a few minutes earlier. (Anon. 1977e)[42]

A more conventional version of the 'nihilist provocateur' frame associated neo-fascist provocateurs with acts of random destruction. Of the Bologna riots of 11 March, the PCI Secretariat wrote:

> A vast and obscure manoeuvre of anti-democratic provocation is under way in our nation; exploiting the state of unease of many groups of students, this develops by way of acts of intimidation, hooliganism and destruction, with the objective of sowing panic, overthrowing civilised life and striking at democratic institutions. These criminal acts are carried out by squaddist groups, supported and even given theoretical justification by certain extremist organisations, creating in this way tumultuous and violent demonstrations in which a determining part is played by out-and-out agents provocateurs and fascists. (Anon. 1977c)[43]

If this framing let the broader movement off the hook, its condemnation of the autonomists was all the more severe. In the Bologna context these 'out-and-out agents provocateurs' were identified, more or less explicitly, with the 'desiring' wing of Autonomia, symbolised by Radio Alice and Franco Berardi in particular.

> what is (or was) this Radio Alice? . . . There has been an alarming increase [in incitement to violence], with the transmission of hallucinatory messages, almost always aimed at a single objective: to fuel anti-Communism and bring union organisations and the public administration into as much discredit as possible. The language is irresponsible, defamatory and destructive – and it is passed off as the most effective means of fighting 'power and the regime'. In reality it is the ideal channel for exacerbating the anger of young people, driving them towards violence and the 'destruction of everything'. The station is completely in the hands of desperate 'autonomists', continually in search of new provocations so as to help to damage our institutions and democracy. It continually tries to raise the level of violence, with behaviour which recalls the role played by certain radio stations in the Chilean events. There is only one real question: who exactly is behind 'Alice'? (Buozzi 1977)[44]

On 18 March, the paper noted that police had not been able to arrest Berardi (he would be arrested in Paris on 7 July and released soon after; an extradition request was not granted (Del Bello 1997: 337)). *L'Unità*'s Scagliarini wrote:

> [Berardi] is believed to be one of the organisers and leaders of the subversion of recent days. . . . He is charged, among other things, with having made repeated appeals for armed struggle to the students . . . and having, so to speak, 'foreseen' the nihilistic violence which shook the city, even before it broke out . . . Berardi, in fact, had already printed . . . several thousand copies of an underground journal ('*Heaven has fallen to earth – Revolution – Journal in movement*') which celebrated the armed occupation of urban areas from which

police, carabinieri and PCI had been driven out. (Scagliarini 1977b; emphases in original)[45]

The paper was titled *La Rivoluzione*; the front page of its only issue carried the headline 'HEAVEN HAS FALLEN TO EARTH AT LAST. 12 MARCH: A GOOD DAY TO BEGIN' (Monti 1977).[46] At the time of the shooting, Scagliarini had suggested that blame for the 'tragedy' should be placed on the 'bomb-throwers' (*attentatori*) who provoked it (Scagliarini 1977c). Now he suggested that Berardi in particular was more directly culpable:

> The material which appeared in [*La Rivoluzione*] was sent to the printer . . . a week earlier by Francesco Berardi . . . 12 March: a good day to begin. But Pier Francesco Lorusso was killed the day before. By whom? . . . Tramontani, the carabiniere, has not changed a comma of what he said that Friday night: I only fired in the air, I never saw the young man who died. (Scagliarini 1977d)[47]

The accusation of provocateurism reaches its peak in the bizarre and offensive insinuation that Berardi himself was responsible for killing Lorusso and hence provoking the 12 March riots.

During this period the paper also stressed the argument that provocateurism aimed to disrupt Italian democracy and hence targeted the PCI (and Communist-governed Bologna): 'The plan was clear and perhaps prearranged: strike at democracy at the point where it appears strongest and most solid. For this reason Bologna has been, in the last few days, at the centre of extremely serious events' (Enriotti 1977b).[48] This theme was particularly insistent following the 'rout of Lama':

> at the end of the demonstration, an out and out assault of the squaddist variety broke out. . . . Workers and students were bombarded with balloons full of water, paint and gravel; and then with blows, bottles, stones, iron bars . . . Groups of 'autonomists' began to push against the union cordon and, as the workers closed ranks around the secretary general of the CGIL, who was leaving the university, they reached the lorry used as a platform for the speakers and destroyed it . . . Then the attacks on workers and democratic students, the beatings. (Botta 1977)[49]

> Shouts went up among the crowd: 'Look out – they're acting like fascists!' . . . Comrade Lama then concluded the meeting, calling on the crowd to disregard the serious provocation. A moment later [Bruno] Vettraino [of the CGIL] took the microphone . . . and shouted to the crowd, which was breaking up under the assault of the squaddists: 'Isolate the provocation! Form a march out of the university straight away!' (Anon. 1977f)[50]

Following the Rome confrontation, the autonomists were increasingly branded explicitly as Fascist:

There is nothing spontaneous or 'autonomous' about these groups. On the contrary, these groups are trained, organised and controlled. They can be judged by their actions, which are squaddist. But they can also be judged by the platform they adopt: against all the democratic institutions, against all the parties, against the unions, against the Communists. And in order to be 'against', they explicitly rely on violence. So what is the difference between these groups and the well-known positions which were at the origin of the Fascist movement? (Tortorella 1977a)[51]

This rhetorical question was echoed by Lama himself, interviewed by the *Corriere*:

For Lama, the 'new fascism' is not only revealed by the use of violence and bullying intolerance. Fascism itself, he says, had at the outset 'demagogic and irrational roots like these', particularly among young people. Then there is the right-wing populism of hostility to the parties, concrete politics, the mechanics of democracy. There's the attack on symbolism, stripping it of meaning, the nihilist derision typified by slogans such as 'Fewer holidays, more exploitation' or 'Dromedary power'. And, naturally, there's the choice of enemies: the unions, the Communists. 'How else do you recognise fascism?' (Tornabuoni 1977)[52]

(The slogan which mystified Lama was explained to the journalist Mario Monicelli by a Metropolitan Indian: 'We are tired . . . of obstinately repeating "Workers' power" over and over again, without a smile or a tear, while the workers continue not to get any power from anyone. So we say *"potere dromedario"*: it sounds like *"potere proletario"*, but it also raises a laugh' (Monicelli 1978: 97)[53].)

References to the autonomists in terms of fascist provocation, to be countered by the PCI's historic anti-fascism, could be multiplied. In March:

they shamelessly call out 'Freedom for Curcio, prison for Pajetta' – the latter being something which the Fascists supplied amply in their time. . . . History repeats itself; only those who are blinded by anti-Communism refuse to understand. (Anon. 1977g)[54]

(Renato Curcio was a founder member of the BR, arrested in 1976. Enrico Pajetta was a senior PCI member and former Partisan commander.) In April, following the shooting of Passamonti:

Thanks to a firm and united mass response, the openly fascist stage of the strategy of tension and massacre has failed; other forms of aggression are now being used to sow fear and disorientation, and to drive the workers' movement back from the positions it has conquered. All confusion must end, all attempts to find justifications have now crossed the line into complicity (Anon. 1977h)[55]

Pajetta's own views appeared in the *Corriere* in September, prior to the Bologna conference.

> 'For us, guaranteeing order means guaranteeing democratic life. I can remember a time when, in Italy, order was guaranteed in a different way . . . those who for so many years represented repression in Italy, the Fascists, began precisely by marching on Bologna, at the time when the city first had a Communist mayor.' (Moncalvo 1977)[56]

Berlinguer echoed Pajetta's anathema. Socialist intellectual Norberto Bobbio, former *azionista* and father of Lotta Continua's Luigi Bobbio, had called for dialogue between the institutional Left and the young people assembled at Bologna; Berlinguer's response was a front-page article in *l'Unità* headlined 'Those with whom no dialogue is possible' (Berlinguer 1977c). On the same day in the right-wing newspaper *La Stampa*, Berlinguer wrote: 'Facing the autonomists . . . it is our duty to be plain: we are dealing with irrational but clear-headed organisers of a new squaddism, who cannot be defined as anything other than "new fascists";[57] he further warned of the 'indulgence and weakness of many democrats towards Fascist squaddism, which we now ought not to repeat' (Berlinguer 1977a).[58]

The violence of the supposed autonomist provocateurs was also stressed. The opposition between the autonomists and the PCI, which frequently took physical form, was consistently presented as an opposition between the 'violence' and 'oppression' of the autonomists and the 'vigour' and 'firmness' with which the PCI defend democratic order. In March 1977, *L'Unità*'s report on the Turin clashes following protests against the Mamiani shooting ignored the demonstrators' attacks on right-wing targets:

> The strong, united, protest demonstration staged yesterday by Turin students against the fascist attack on the Roman students at the Mamiani was marred by a few squaddist acts carried out by a group of 'autonomists'. At the end of the demonstration, armed with 'Molotovs' and their faces covered with ski-masks, they attacked young Communists and democrats, boys and girls alike, assaulting them ferociously with clubs and spanners, demonstrating the violence and the cowardice which have always been characteristic of fascists. (Anon. 1977i)[59]

The 5 March edition of *l'Unità* returned to the incidents, although without mentioning the revenge attack on a group of Turin students by the PCI *servizio d'ordine* (Novaro 1991: 171). A report from a PCI-organised meeting in Turin tacitly endorsed the *servizio d'ordine*'s actions:

> The ever-present groups of organised provocateurs, led by individuals with an ambivalent and murky political past . . . make it impossible, for the moment, to initiate a democratic engagement between students and political and union

forces. A commitment to avoid falling into the trap of violence, set – as is now clear – by squads of fascist provocateurs, was the unanimous political decision which came out of the meeting held yesterday morning (Anon. 1977j)[60]

As an example of these 'individuals with an ambivalent and murky political past' the paper cited Riccardo d'Este, workerist, 'Comontist' and kidnapper: an early example of the abruptness with which the PCI's left-wing rivals could pass from political competitor to neo-fascist bandit.

This 'commitment to avoid falling into the trap of violence' does not signify pacifism so much as a redefinition of the PCI's use of physical force in terms of 'firmness' or 'discipline': the PCI is not proposing a rejection of violence so much as a forceful rejection of violent groups. On 16 March, the PCI organised a demonstration 'against violence' in Bologna. The PCI *servizio d'ordine* forcibly prevented a contingent of students from participating (Del Bello 1997: 316), a manoeuvre *servizi d'ordine* had repeatedly carried out earlier in the year (Del Bello 1997: 309, 312). As Kino Marzullo saw it in *l'Unità*, this was at once a physical and an ethical confrontation:

> the solidity of the crowd was such as to create around the platform . . . a kind of homogeneous, impassable block. . . . the groups of student hooligan-ism . . . repeatedly attempted to penetrate the demonstration and influence it with their pseudo-revolutionary politics, their extremism, their fundamental hatred for the workers and their organisations. But this solid, homogeneous, impassable block to which I referred earlier expelled them from its ranks: it demonstrated – as so often in its history – that the working class need not fear any kind of engagement and has the means to emerge victorious. Take note, this does not mean that the *servizio d'ordine* responded to the violence of the neo-squaddists with an equal and opposite violence: they did not even need to, because they were able to nip in the bud any attempt to turn this united mass presence into a new opportunity for conflict. (Marzullo 1977)[61]

A report in the *Corriere* gives a vivid portrayal of what this 'solidity' looked like in practice: '[in] the human wall of the *servizio d'ordine*, eight or more ranks of workers protect the piazza against any possible intrusion . . . Bags are opened and suspicious individuals searched' (Anon. 1977k).[62] The paper *Lotta Continua* asserted, ' "This isn't a party rally; it's a rally for a regime" ' (Anon. 1977l);[63] the PCI stood accused of lending a DC government its resources, including organisational (and physical) muscle. Undaunted, *l'Unità* embraced the charge: 'Yes! If by regime we mean our constitutional demo-cratic regime, the republican state formed out of the Resistance' (Anon. 1977l).[64]

Increasingly, the PCI's 'solidity' and imperviousness to critique was pre-sented as a virtue in itself. In April, an unsigned comment dismissed the idea that the PCI might have anything to learn about its violent opponents. Any such criticism weakened the party's unity and hence threatened the Italian republic:

> We have been told, as if this were a new discovery, that we need to be able to analyse the cultural roots [of the armed groups] . . . Fascism and Nazism had cultural roots, too . . . We have pointed out a precise distinguishing factor, and continue to do so: the factor of intolerance and bullyboy tactics – violence, in fact. . . . Facing the new, shameful attacks, the country and the masses need unity as never before. And so we strongly condemn those groups which, even now, are working with shameless disregard to introduce and exacerbate elements of division among the forces of the left. . . . Their efforts, we know, will be in vain. But there remains the fact that they are trying to erode, on any pretext, the firmest bulwark of the republican institutions. Let them think about that, if they are still capable of reasoning. (Anon. 1977m)[65]

In July, *l'Unità* published an anonymous piece emphasising the PCI's commitment to open debate while firmly rejecting unacceptable positions: 'The refusal to engage with opponents and the exaltation of intolerance are the ante-chamber to blind violence – and this must not be granted any space' (Anon. 1977n).[66] A few days later, Tortorella argued that freedom of thought could only be guaranteed by excluding certain groups and ideas from the debate: 'Even on the plane of ideas, there is a permanent battle to be waged for freedom: against intolerance, against fanaticism, against attempts to erect barriers, against new forms of division between manual workers and intellectuals, against those who preach alternatives to the terrain of democratic struggle. Communists must be able to stand in the front line in this battle, too' (Tortorella 1977b).[67] These arguments take the provocateur frame to its logical extreme. Provocateurs are, by definition, interested only in stirring up trouble, initiating violence and disrupting democratic politics; hence, anything a provocateur says or does can be assumed to be disruptive, violent and anti-democratic, and the only 'engagement' a provocateur should be offered is Marzullo's 'solid, homogeneous, impassable block'. *L'Unità* ended up calling for intolerance of intolerance, refusal to engage with those who refuse to engage.

This relish for confrontation also coloured *l'Unità*'s coverage of police action. On the occasion of the abortive attempts to protest against the abolition of the 19 May holiday, the paper recorded that 'throughout the city [of Rome] – around the University in particular, but also in the centre – a massive and omnipresent public order squad was deployed' (Palumbo 1977).[68] The characterisation of the police as a *servizio d'ordine pubblico*, likening the police to PCI stewards, underlines the PCI's self-identification with the 'democratic state' and its repressive actions against the autonomists. Ugo Pecchioli, a leading light of the PCI, had set out this position in March:

We certainly cannot exclude the possibility that there have been errors and excesses in the behaviour of this or that police unit. . . . However, the most important fact remains that we are facing subversive squads which use firearms and aim at guerrilla warfare. In these conditions the indispensable search for political and social solutions have one inseparable precondition: isolate and strike the men of violence. . . . The Italian police can and must be the police of our democratic state. There must be collaboration between the democratic institutions, the anti-fascist parties, the workers' organisations and the police forces. (Pecchioli 1977)[69]

We can see how far this identification took the PCI by comparing *l'Unità*'s coverage of the evacuation of Bologna University with the *Corriere*'s. The latter's story opened:

At dawn . . . the rumble of vehicles beneath the two towers [a Bologna landmark]. A fearful sound coming from far back, from the war years. At daybreak the people of Bologna open their windows, stunned: 'They've sent in the tanks!' The 'tanks' are in reality . . . armoured personnel carriers: 'panzers' without guns. . . . They are followed by light armoured cars. Behind them, moving slowly, very slowly, taking the utmost care, come armed men: police and carabinieri, on a war footing. (Monti 1977)[70]

By contrast, *l'Unità*'s correspondent (the dependable Scagliarini) wrote:

At dawn, with the support of carabinieri in armour-clad vehicles from which the machine guns had been removed, the university area was evacuated. The tension, however, remains extremely high . . . One concern is the fact that many pistols and rifles . . . are still in the hands of the groups who organised the vandalism, the thefts, the looting and the arson, precisely a plan for the 'criminalisation' of the student movement . . . The entrance into the university quarter was made with armour-clad vehicles owing to the fear of meeting with armed conflict. . . . The aim was to avoid giving the fomenters of disorder and looting an opportunity to embed themselves once more in the university. (Scagliarini 1977e)[71]

The difference in points of view is striking, with *l'Unità* taking the standpoint of the carabinieri carrying out the operation and the *Corriere* metaphorically standing with the 'stunned' residents of Bologna. Even the terminology is different: where the *Corriere*'s 'personnel carriers' are *corazzati*, suggesting armour-plate, *l'Unità*'s 'vehicles' are *blindati*, a term used of security vans.

Scagliarini's reference to 'criminalisation' is also noteworthy; this relates to contemporary allegations that the PCI's law-and-order stance amounted to 'criminalising' the movement. Scagliarini's logic was echoed, four months later, in an anonymous comment on critical reactions from the Left to the shooting of Lo Muscio:

> The movement isn't being criminalised, in point of fact, by those, like us, who
> conduct an open political battle against adventurist and irresponsible positions,
> unmasking them as foreign and hostile to the traditions of the workers' move-
> ment and deadly to Italian democracy. It's criminalised by those who flirt with
> these positions (Anon. 1977a)[72]

If the movement has been criminalised, the blame lies not with political forces
which treat its actions as criminal, but with its own sympathy for groups
whose actions are objectively criminal. What this argument overlooks (or
obscures) is that criminality is not an objective property, but depends on the
laws in force and the vigour with which they are implemented. These are
factors over which a major political party can have considerable influence,
as the 1970 amnesty for offences committed in the Hot Autumn had demonstrated. L'Unità's position amounts to a categorical assertion that certain acts
are inherently criminal, endorsing or even encouraging changes in the law to
address them; the effect of this argument is precisely the 'criminalisation' of
which the PCI was accused.

What went for the autonomists, naturally, also went for the armed groups,
at least until the end of 1977. Thus when, in June 1977, Prima Linea claimed
responsibility for arson attacks on two factories, l'Unità retorted: 'we know
not to give too much attention to which signature the attackers have chosen
to hide behind or which "colour" they have chosen to attribute to themselves . . . the masses have long learnt to see the only colour that counts: the
colour of the reactionary attack on democratic conquests' (Anon. 1977o).[73]
Given that the armed groups represented a fascist assault on the 'democratic
conquests' of the Italian Constitution, dissent from the PCI's hard line against
them betrayed confusion at best:

> the battle for the fate of our state is going on today within each one of us: it's
> the battle between the tendency to let ourselves be dominated and swept away
> by events and the will to understand them critically . . . Everyone knows about
> this struggle; we have testimony to it from Sciascia, Montale and a thousand
> others (Petruccioli 1977a)[74]

Leonardo Sciascia and Eugenio Montale were two of the PCI's more prominent intellectual critics. Both Sciascia and Montale had been critical of the
PCI's endorsement of the DC government's public order measures and its
intolerance of dissent; in particular, both had defended the abstention of
potential jurors in the Turin BR trial. Neither the substance of their arguments
nor their standing as intellectuals dented l'Unità's certainty that dissent from
the PCI line came only from 'those who are blinded by anti-Communism'.
The BR's shootings of journalists brought a particularly striking example of
this logic, when l'Unità chided the hospitalised Montanelli for fostering the
conditions that had led to his own shooting.

We don't know what has been going through Indro Montanelli's mind during these hours . . . or whether he will be brought to think again about the opportunities which a line of division and opposition, such as the one he has followed, creates for subversive forces. But we would be hypocrites . . . if we did not say to Indro Montanelli that this is our profound conviction: if we do not stand on the terrain of national solidarity, it will not only be the values and interests of the workers' movement that are threatened. (Anon. 1977p)[75]

Azione Rivoluzionaria's non-fatal shooting of *l'Unità* journalist Nino Ferrero in September 1977 provoked an emphatic restatement of the 'fascist provocateur' framing:

Responsibility for the attack on Nino Ferrero has been claimed by a group calling itself 'Azione Rivoluzionaria': one of the 120 signatures manipulated by those whose interest lies in provoking fear and tension in our nation. . . . In an insane statement, the criminals say that they intended to strike at 'the shameless campaign of lies and calumnies carried out by the regime's hired hacks [*pennivendoli*]'. '*Pennivendoli*' is a term dear to Franco Freda, the neo-Nazi brought to trial for the Piazza Fontana massacre. . . . The objective is always the same: to strike at democratic institutions and the organisations which are fighting intransigently in the defence of constitutional liberty. But when they reach the point of striking that political force which has always fought for a profound renovation of the political structures of the nation – when a comrade from *l'Unità* is defined as 'a bastard in the service of the regime' – then the game is finally up. . . . Condemnation cannot be enough. We need to flush out the dens of these bandits and find out who is behind them. The connections between terrorism and the centres of the secret services of this and other nations are no longer news. (Paolucci 1977a)[76]

The evocation of criminality and insanity is striking, marking an escalation in the paper's already elevated level of hostility to the armed groups. The precision of Paolucci's figure of 120 appears just as spurious as his association of Azione Rivoluzionaria with the neo-fascist Freda: the reasonably exhaustive list of armed groups given by Progetto Memoria (1994) includes 47 signatures, most of which were not active in 1977. Perhaps unsurprisingly, *l'Unità*'s correspondent at the September conference (Cavallini 1977a) records Azione Rivoluzionaria's leafleting but gives no sign of having read the leaflet, which (as we have seen) set out the group's aims with specific reference to its choice of targets associated with the PCI. The innovative nature of Azione Rivoluzionaria's actions and its self-presentation is lost on *l'Unità*, which had framed left-wing armed struggle groups as neo-fascist provocateurs five years ago and was now even more committed to that position.

Towards the end of the year, *l'Unità*'s certainty as to the nature of the armed groups, as well as its support for the state in combatting them, reached new heights. After the shooting of Casalegno in November 1977, *Corriere* journalist Enzo Biagi (like Casalegno, a former *azionista* and veteran of Giustizia e Libertà) wrote: '[the BR] accused him of being a "servant of the state". I don't know if this is an insult or not – whether this ramshackle republic . . . still deserves to be defended. . . . Carlo Casalegno, servant of the state, fell in a pool of blood for a boss, this state, which couldn't even guarantee him the right to think' (Biagi 1977).[77] Biagi's grief and doubt found no echo at *l'Unità*:

> Let them not fool themselves – the red brigadists [*brigatisti rossi*], their black [i.e. neo-fascist] allies and the forces which control them, here and abroad – about the possibility of finding weak points in the workers' movement. The new wave of terrorism marks them out, even more than before, as enemies of the workers. And let no one fool themselves that concerns for defending democracy can make us step back in the face of the need for decisive interventions and emergency measures. (Anon. 1977q)[78]

The paper now served notice that even its commitment to civil liberties was negotiable in defence of the Italian republic against the BR.

Casalegno died from his wounds later in the month. The day before he died, a group of neo-fascists in Bari stabbed to death a young Communist named Benedetto Petrone, who had been a sympathiser with the extreme left and an active anti-fascist (Rivera 1997: 175). The coincidence was too much for *l'Unità*: '[Petrone fought] against the subversive plot which threatens democratic life, and the fascists killed him. Exactly as other fascists, under the name of red brigadists [*brigatisti rossi*], killed Carlo Casalegno. They were the same hands, the same political thinkers, the same plan' (Anon. 1977r).[79] In both these pieces, the use of the lower-case 'b' in '*brigatisti rossi*' is striking. This dismissive rhetorical device had been abandoned after Sossi's release in 1974; the political importance of associating the armed groups with neo-fascism was now such as to revive it.

The autonomists, meanwhile, were being presented through a modified form of the 'autonomist provocateur' frame, replacing urgent condemnation with a relaxed, even amused contempt. *L'Unità*'s reports on the Bologna conference in September expressed relief at the relatively limited level of mayhem, tempered by ironic derision at the inability of the autonomist provocateurs to come up with anything worse. On 25 September, a report described a confrontation between autonomists and what it described as Lotta Continua militants (possibly members of the *Senza Tregua* area). The movement's violent tendencies are stressed, but its capacity for aggressive action is belittled:

> The 'armed party' thus achieved that military settling of scores on which it had been betting all along . . . the clash was resolved by the leader of the autono-

mists with the suggestive quip, 'Get lost, we can sort out these problems another time'. Then the speaker who had the platform resumed his speech, while once again paper aeroplanes flew quietly through the smoky atmosphere of the Palasport. . . . Of the 2000 shops in and around the centre of town, only about 40 had their shutters down. (Cavallini 1977b)[80]

The end of the PCI's engagement with the autonomists was marked by the FLM march on 2 December, which received three pages of coverage in *l'Unità*. The lead story stressed the diversity of the demonstration, then celebrated its unity and its closure to outsiders:

> workers, students, women, young people from the unemployed groups . . . part of 'Lotta Continua', PdUP-Manifesto, feminists, each with their own aims, ideas, watchwords, but all (with only a few exceptions) motivated by common aspirations . . . By 6.00 a.m., behind the fence put up in piazza San Giovanni as a defence against possible provocations and attacks (which did occur, but were kept within the narrowest possible bounds) there were already 4,000 members of the FLM *servizio d'ordine*. (Savioli 1977a)[81]

The 'organised' autonomists who had planned to mount an alternative march were bottled up in the university by police and carabinieri, just as the anti-Nixon demonstrators of February 1969 had been. The tone of *l'Unità*'s coverage was very different on this occasion.

> At the first attempt by the 'autonomists' to leave the university, around 9.30, the hint of a charge by the police made them retreat . . . At this point the university was completely surrounded by policemen and carabinieri. Anyone who attempted to leave was challenged and searched. . . . A little after 10.00 one group attempted to leave by via De Lollis . . . and on reaching il Verano formed a small march, which was then charged and dispersed with tear-gas grenades. Some of the young people later succeeded in reaching piazza San Giovanni, where they unleashed aggressive acts of hooliganism at the end of the union demonstration. . . . . the 'autonomists' abandoned the attempt to leave the university and staged a march within the campus, chanting provocative slogans . . . After midday the police dissolved their blockade and withdrew from the area of the university. A little later, a few thousand young people arrived at the university, returning from piazza San Giovanni. An assembly began, but was rapidly turned into a brawl by the 'autonomists'. The 'armed party' accused Lotta Continua of 'betrayal'. The atmosphere rapidly became tense and fists began to fly. Finally, around a hundred hooligans armed with clubs broke away and chased the other young people as far as piazzale delle Scienze. (Anon. 1977s)[82]

The autonomists are presented here as a menace in and of themselves, deserving only to be confined and controlled by the police. However, their identity as provocateurs is demonstrated mainly by their choice of slogans and their use of violence among themselves. There is only a passing reference to aggressive 'acts of hooliganism', whose impact is minimised; the insignificance of the autonomists is stressed. The description evokes elements of the 'disorganised lumpenproletariat' frame applied to the broader movement. This 'disorganised hooligan' framing, presenting the autonomist milieu as incoherent and relatively apolitical, reflects the closure of the PCI's engagement with the autonomists.

The 'disorganised lumpenproletariat' frame developed in the previous period is applied to the 'movement of 1977' throughout the year, with three different qualifications. Initially, the movement is characterised as a 'degenerate lumpenproletariat', combining disorganisation and political confusion with morally reprehensible qualities of self-indulgence; this reflects the temporary ascendancy of the policy of *austerità*. Thus a piece on the La Scala riots refers to the proletarian youth circles' role in *autoriduzione* at cinemas and concerts, noting that they were also responsible for 'a smaller-scale but no less frequent activity of attacks on shops and supermarkets, where, supposedly in the name of a action against the cost of living, they "expropriated" bottles of whisky and champagne. Indeed, "let's appropriate luxuries" is one of their slogans' (Anon. 1976o).[83] The slogan *'Riprendiamoci il lusso'* is quoted here less as a position statement than as an admission of guilt. A similar argument presented the demands raised by the Rome occupiers as wasteful, parasitic and (bizarrely) 'essentially reformist':

> while positive proposals and experiences have been produced in some universities, in others requests of an absurd and essentially reformist nature have come to the fore, such as the general payment of all students . . . These positions express a tendency to maintain the universities as they are . . . as an area of waste, parasitism and the avoidance of productive work. These student groups . . . end up fighting above all against the workers' movement and its rigorous politics of national renovation and development. (Anon. 1977t)[84]

This 'degenerate lumpenproletariat' framing was elaborated most fully in Asor Rosa's 'New forms of anti-Communism'. Asor Rosa's essay evinces the shock caused by the rout of Lama, the confrontation between the autonomists and the FGCI *servizio d'ordine* in particular.

> the struggle is no longer about imposing a *different* political programme on the *same* masses, but a struggle between two different *societies*. The political point is this: we must ask ourselves what we have done for this *second society*, which has grown up alongside the first and even at its expense, but without gaining significant advantages from it, without having outlets or any real roots in the 'first society'. . . . It doesn't seem accidental that worker–student unity, the dominant watchword of '68 – which rested on an expansive vision of society, even when it was dressed up in revolutionary terms – has now been abandoned

in favour of slogans based on alliance between different marginalised sectors . . . Together, these sectors *remove themselves* from the rest of society and counterpose themselves to it. In this context, beating up *organised workers* – which would in the past have appeared inconceivable and sacrilegious to the most extreme of protesters – becomes a logical step

. . .

What need is there to build communism . . . when you can appropriate right now, day by day, what you feel you need? The worst enemies of this perspective are thus precisely the people who don't accept this society but at the same time believe in transforming it. . . . We need to have the courage to recognise that, within this 'second society', some of our most authoritative watchwords don't have any purchase. Austerity, for example, depends for its meaning on being directed to the productive sectors of society – to the *workers* – who, being producers and consumers at the same time, can (if they want) calibrate a different balance between these two aspects of life. . . . [On 17 February] there was nothing except the union and the PCI (the PCI above all) standing between the system and student protest and representing the arguments of that 'first society' . . . We can't be surprised if, in those conditions, the new anti-Communism is fuelled by our being presented as the first line of defence of the system

. . .

Between the 'second society' and its theorists of 'need' and certain sectors of Italian political and economic life . . . there is today a convergence (objective? subjective?) on the need to strike *first of all at the presence of organised workers* in society . . . An alliance between social conservatism and fragmentation may appear strange, but it's not impossible (Asor Rosa 1977b; emphases in original)[85]

The 'second society' is defined here both by its immediatism and by its socioeconomic marginality; both factors lead it to oppose the status quo and to oppose the PCI, whose commitment to orderly reform makes it in practice a bulwark of the status quo. The PCI thus faces not a political enemy but a problem of social exclusion: a framing which suggests an increased attention to the problems of the 'second society', but also removes any possibility of a political engagement. In the longer term, the PCI may be able to reintegrate the 'second society'; in the short term, it must be resisted.

The PCI leadership's appeals to 'austerity' were relatively short-lived; the party's framing of the student movement developed accordingly. Following the March riots, the PCI's Paolo Bufalini presented the movement in darker terms:

There are violent squaddist formations – the main one appears to be the group called 'Autonomi' [sic] – which operate on a national level; they are solidly

organised and directed coolly and skilfully; their main area of action is the
confused student movements and demonstrations, where their guerrilla actions
provoke the most serious disorder. . . . this tactic has until now been made possible by the mass shelter provided by confused movements, by an infantile
maximalism and extremism itself fuelled by the state of profound unease of
large groups of students, the unemployed, the excluded

. . .

these subversive forces use certain free radio stations, which incite and direct
violent demonstrations . . . this is another problem which must be immediately
confronted and resolved using existing laws or, if need be, with new legislative
provisions. . . . the most important and the most serious novelty . . . is that these
subversive forces are using weapons; and not only makeshift weapons but true
weapons, among which we can count Molotov cocktails: they use guns, and
they shoot.

. . .

The police, for us, has never been the enemy, even in the years in which it was
used to defend class privileges and we clashed with it . . . even then, we called
on the police – who were also sons of the people, in the words of Di Vittorio
[the first leader of the CGIL], and southern peasants in particular – to understand what other workers, their brothers, were fighting for . . . The police force
which defends democratic order is defending our heritage, the heritage of the
working class and the nation.

. . .

Nor must we lose sight of the fact that, around the active nucleus of squaddism
and provocation, there is a fairly wide area of extremism built on intolerance,
sterile and inconclusive rebelliousness, the refusal of rationality, adventurism,
or a dark ideology inspired by a decrepit mechanistic deformation of
Marxism . . . the young people who, in good faith, follow extremist groups,
believing that it makes them revolutionaries . . . must isolate the men of violence and the provocateurs; they must repudiate all forms of intolerance and
bullyboy tactics . . . If they don't do this, abandoning themselves instead to a
confused and inconclusive rebelliousness and 'movementism', then without
knowing it they will be playing the game of reactionary and conservative
forces . . . just those forces which now oppose the political turning which is
ever more necessary and urgent. (Bufalini 1977)[86]

Asor Rosa's characterisation of the clashes with the FGCI *servizio d'ordine*
as 'beating up organised workers' recalled Pasolini's contempt for the students who fought the police at Valle Giulia ('the cops come from poor fami-
lies'). Bufalini went further, explicitly extending Communist solidarity to the
police who defended the Italian state. Against them stood a 'second society'
whose degeneracy found expression, not in the immediatism of the *autoridut-*

tori, but in a confused and adventurist version of radicalism, tending to offer 'shelter' to the provocation of the autonomists; this in turn gave aid and comfort to the right of the DC, thus postponing the PCI's entry to government. The reference to 'new legislative provisions' is also significant, suggesting (as noted above in reference to 'criminalisation') that the PCI aspired to set the boundary of legality. Similar overtones are carried by the reference to the autonomists using both 'makeshift weapons' (*armi improprie*) and 'true weapons' (*armi proprie*), and in particular the abrupt decision to place Molotov cocktails in the latter category. The Italian penal code at this time imposed heavy penalties for the use of 'weapons of war' (*armi di guerra*). A 1970 court case involving Potere Operaio had established that Molotov cocktails were not true bombs, and hence were not classifiable as *armi di guerra*, on the basis that their detonation was the result of a physical rather than a chemical process (Grandi 2003: 168).)

This framing replaces the moralistic denunciation of the 'degenerate lumpenproletariat' frame with a demand for reform: the 'adventurist lumpenproletariat' must overcome its own confusions and dissociate itself from the autonomists, to the satisfaction of the PCI. In the changed circumstances of the 19 May protests, two writers in *l'Unità* developed these demands further, setting the movement beyond any political dialogue unless and until it renounces its 'programme':

> after the repudiation and condemnation of bloody acts of terrorism, it is still difficult for some to make a clean and definitive break with the 'party of the P.38', to reject and isolate, once and for all, the provocateurs and hooligans of the area of 'autonomy' (Palumbo 1977)[87]

> leading groups [of the movement of 1977] are now trying to take their distance from the gunmen. But, while their decision to disown the men of violence must be considered a step forward, the fact remains that this decision was taken late, equivocally and opportunistically. This is precisely because these people have not abandoned either the profoundly negative and sterile substance of the political analysis from which they began, which hinges on the so-called 'opposition to the system', or the absolute void which they offer to the left . . . They have dissociated themselves from the men of violence. Good: but if they still believe that republican democracy is a farce and that the parties and the unions are only servants of the bosses, and that the state is for defeating and not for changing, why have they dissociated themselves? (Ghiara 1977)[88]

Ostensibly, the movement is defined by the presence of autonomist 'provocateurs' within it. Whether it is endorsed or opposed depends less on its own politics than on whether it repudiates 'all forms of intolerance and bullyboy tactics'. However, faced with signs of dissociation, *l'Unità*'s writers raise the stakes: 'a clean and definitive break' is needed rather than a decision 'taken late, equivocally and opportunistically'; even this cannot be trusted unless the movement also abandons 'the profoundly negative and sterile substance of [its] political analysis'. The movement was indelibly guilty by association; what was being demanded was not dissociation but dissolution.

A third variant on the 'disorganised lumpenproletariat' framing emerged in September 1977, on the occasion of the Bologna conference, when the heat of *l'Unità*'s attacks on the autonomists was beginning to subside. The contrast between a broader movement and a minority of violent (but ineffectual) provocateurs was developed in surprisingly favourable terms:

> the advocates of the 'armed party' were isolated inside the Palazzo dello sport, which they took by force and held for three days as a stronghold. The others tried instead to conduct a debate, expressing positions which we don't share and which we fight on the political and ideological level, but remaining on the terrain of political struggle and engagement. (Enriotti 1977c)[89]

As the conference drew to a close, this (by recent standards) conciliatory stance developed further, notably in a second report from the front line by Cavallini.

> There has been some small-scale *autoriduzione*. A barman in via Zamboni told me, 'Some of them came in, drank and then left without a "by your leave", even taking the odd bottle of mineral water with them. But what can you say, these things happen during climbers' meetings as well.' . . . What we have had before us has been, for good and ill, the image of the central contradiction of our society, the reflection of a deep-seated historic crisis of old and outmoded models of civilisation, culture and productive work . . . the workers' movement cannot leave the confused demands which emerged from the conference unanswered. The experience of Bologna, in this sense, was a precious one. (Cavallini 1977a)[90]

With regard to the broader movement represented at Bologna, a flurry of comment pieces printed on 27 September completed the reversal of *l'Unità*'s earlier position:

> What is being experienced and mediated by the younger generations has the qualities of an outright crisis of civilisation . . . From this point on we propose to take young people on in open debate, with only one condition: the refusal of, and open struggle against, subversive [*eversiva*] violence. (Petruccioli 1977b)[91]

> Setting aside the adventurist and violent fringe, with their elitist and anti-popular strategy of 'the worse, the better', and setting aside the 'creative' and folkloric fringe, the movement contains a mass of young people who are certainly driven by a piercing hatred for the regime which has ruled the country

for thirty years, but whose inclination towards democratic and socialist change it would be senseless to doubt. (Maldonado 1977)[92]

The student movement faces an important phase of clarification and engagement . . . The words are confused, but this only reflects the difficulties and problems which affect us *all*. In their gestures and actions something new is identifiable, something new is under way. (Veca 1977; emphasis in original)[93]

This superficially favourable 'misguided lumpenproletariat' framing in fact reflects the end of the PCI's engagement with the movement. Despite the contrast between *l'Unità*'s dismissal of the autonomists and its proclaimed willingness to 'take young people on in open debate', the movement did not in fact receive more favourable attention after September 1977. This may have been because the supposed opposition between a violent minority and a constructive, law-abiding majority did not exist: Petruccioli's single condition was precisely what no element of the movement could accept. (Even the dissident autonomists of 'the 11', who opposed the recourse to violence, did so not because it was *eversiva* (a word which suggests right-wing subversion) but because it was self-defeating (Mordenti 1997: 24–31).) Moreover, after ten months of street clashes, political denunciations and internal dissension, the movement was faltering. The Bologna conference was the last moment at which the movement made itself felt in a unified form and on a mass scale. *L'Unità*'s change of emphasis marks, not the emergence of a challenging but law-abiding movement, but the decline of a previously challenging movement into irrelevance.

With the autonomists dismissed as an ineffectual rabble and 'proletarian youth' demoted to the status of a challenging social problem, the closure of the PCI's engagement with the mass movements of the cycle left the party with no significant rivals to its Left. This in turn enabled the party to move decisively to the Right by recognising the BR and other armed groups as genuine leftists, while continuing to demand that they be given no quarter. The key framing, introduced in December 1977, is 'anti-democratic extremist': the PCI's long-proclaimed commitment to the Italian republic now openly took precedence over its revolutionary politics. This shift began earlier in the year, with the re-reading (if not rewriting) of recent history. On 5 May Paolucci wrote:

who are these famous Red Brigades? Is there really anyone who still believes that this is the same organisation which was born, years ago, in the Sociology department at Trento? Then its policies were crazy; now assassination is its policy. (Paolucci 1977b)[94]

On 21 June Massimo Cavallini reported from the shop floor:

'At the beginning,' explains Giovannini of the [SIT-Siemens] factory council, 'the BR used, so to speak, "combined" tactics: their terrorist actions were always accompanied by the attempt to gain the support of groups of workers. . . . They were very active in the union, some of them even managed to get nominated as delegates.' This phase has been over for some time. Clandestine with regard to the law, the brigadists – assuming that there are still some of them left at Siemens – are clandestine twice over with regard to the workers: isolated and despised, in their actions they have descended to the logic of pure provocation. They kill, they set fires, they shoot people in the legs, and that's all. The messages which follow seem ever more to be elements of a tired ritual, the relics of a founding illusion. This sad trajectory probably reflects the process of transformation rapidly undergone by the Red Brigades: from an organisation of insane ideologues of 'armed struggle' to a docile instrument of the strategy of tension, the repository of every type of infiltration in a dark entanglement with the criminal underworld (Cavallini 1977c)[95]

These articles evince an uneasy combination of contradictory interpretations, loosely bridged by the image of a 'trajectory' which had taken the BR from genuine extreme leftism to isolation and 'pure provocation'. Perhaps needless to say, this speculative narrative bears no resemblance to *l'Unità*'s own reporting of earlier BR actions ('Idalgo Macchiarini was kidnapped by an unknown group which defined itself as "red brigades", but which was clearly fascist and in the service of the bosses' provocations' (Anon. 1972b)[96]). Significantly, both articles refer to episodes in the BR's history which had been reported in the *Corriere* (e.g. Sposito 1973) but had been excluded from *l'Unità*.

In November, a more comprehensive process of rethinking began, with meetings around the country and a formal investigation led by Pecchioli. On 14 December *l'Unità* published an interview with Pecchioli laying out the party's new line on terrorism.

> Italy [is] at an extremely advanced phase of renewal, a phase to which the working class, standing on the threshold of government, gives a hegemonic imprint. Terrorism, subversion, violence are one of the games which the enemies of democracy play to prevent a positive outcome to the crisis. But we must make some distinctions. An error into which many people fall is to confuse the 'black' and the 'red', arguing (incontrovertibly) that, whatever their intentions, both groups are enemies of democracy and of the working class . . . The 'black' and the 'red' groups both want to overthrow the democratic regime and open the way to an authoritarian regime. But the 'black' stop there. The 'red', by contrast, proclaim a second objective: to provoke the 'rebellion of the proletariat' with the establishment of an authoritarian regime (Savioli 1977b)[97]

The 'red' doctrine described echoes the German RAF's outlook (della Porta 1995: 131), but had few if any followers within the Italian armed milieu. However, this framing of the armed groups as anti-democratic extremists allowed Pecchioli to acknowledge them as left-wing while maintaining that

terrorism was intrinsically a phenomenon of the extreme right. Pecchioli
further argued that the groups' actions were exploited by enemies of the PCI:

> there is an area of 'political' solidarity, made up of those extremist organisa-
> tions within which criticism, distancing, dissociation from the armed groups
> has only begun to flourish recently. . . . Close to this 'political' area . . . or
> inside it, or partly within its leadership, forces and people are at work who are
> not at all subject to 'suggestions' or 'visions' but, on the contrary, are con-
> sciously intent on using extremism instrumentally for quite concrete aims of
> political struggle. This is the explanation for certain 'flirtations', certain 'court-
> ships', certain 'sponsorships' embarked upon by this or that politician, this or
> that union leader, this or that organisation associated even with parties with
> governmental responsibilities. The target to strike is, of course, the PCI. . . .
> Finally, let us not forget the use which state forces wishing to defeat the
> democratic movement have made of extremism and of terrorism. Certain
> compromises are already well-known to everyone; others, less so. The passivity
> at certain points of this or that civil servant, this or that judge, often seems
> rather suspicious, unless it can be explained by fear. (Savioli 1977b)[98]

Pecchioli concluded by restating the party's support for the forces of order
and its disdain for civil libertarian arguments:

> 'if an individual citizen or a member of a democratic workers' organisation,
> rank-and-file member or leader, learns that a serious crime is being prepared,
> is he or she supposed to keep silent, respecting who knows what code of
> silence? Do the hard-line civil libertarians perhaps want to spread the scourge
> which is the Mafia's code of silence to the whole of Italy? . . . the struggle
> against terrorism . . . is a *national* duty of the utmost importance. This duty also
> includes collaboration with the police and the judiciary, by democratic organi-
> sations and by individuals.' (Savioli 1977b; emphasis in original)[99]

Having acknowledged the armed groups as left-wing, the PCI is more
rather than less aggressive in its guardianship of the 'democratic regime'.
Any party whose stand against terrorism was unclear, any judge who passed
lenient sentences, any inflexible civil libertarian could be painted as irresponsible and motivated by anti-Communism – or, more straightforwardly, as a
coward. In Hellman's words, '[the PCI's] behaviour in this second phase,
which began late in 1977, was a conscious policy, in its leaders' own words,
of 'scorching the earth' around the terrorists. Whoever failed utterly and
unequivocally to condemn terrorism with an enthusiasm equal to the PCI's
was viewed as insufficiently committed to democracy and perhaps even sus-
pected of harbouring sympathies for the Red Brigades' (Hellman 1988: 36).
This final rhetorical shift marked the opening of the PCI's engagement with
the armed struggle milieu – a long and hostile interaction which lies outside
the scope of this study.

The period of engagement was dominated by the 'disorganised lumpen-proletariat' and 'provocateur' framings, applied to the youth movements and the autonomists respectively. The armed groups are framed as provocateurs throughout 1977, until the change of direction at the end of the year intro-duces the 'anti-democratic extremist' framing.

Throughout the year, organised autonomists were alternately condemned as neo-fascist and charged with lacking a political identity. The youth move-ment is condemned first as a morally reprehensible 'degenerate lumpen-proletariat', then (following Asor Rosa and Bufalini's statements) as an 'adventurist lumpenproletariat'. Against both the 'squaddist' autonomists and this confused and extremist movement, the PCI stood for the workers, legal-ity, democracy, the national interest and the police force. The 'adventurist lumpenproletariat' framing was repeatedly reiterated in the form of demands on the movement, which was called on to break with the autonomists on the levels of repertoire, organisation and ideology. Henceforth the movement would be forced to define itself in terms of a choice between an orderly and subordinate alignment with the PCI and outright illegality. Either alternative would be fatal to it.

Prior to the Bologna conference, the double provocateur/lumpenproletariat framing was reiterated by Berlinguer, labelling the autonomists as 'the new Fascists' and the movement as *'poveri untorelli'*. In the more positive framing which emerged during the conference, the movement was presented as a disorganised force which could yet move towards dialogue with the PCI. This 'misguided lumpenproletariat' framing reflected the PCI's confidence that the movement, reintegrated or not, was no longer a threat. The autonomists were also reduced to a disorderly fringe, who could be framed, dismissively, as 'disorganised hooligans'.

One final shift remained. Throughout 1977, the paper's coverage of the BR and the other armed groups had been marked by an emphatic and reiterated conviction that the phenomenon was essentially neo-fascist and aimed against the PCI. Pecchioli's December interview repeated the long-running stress on provocateurism, but his central point was entirely new: his warning against confusing 'the "black" and the "red"' silently invalidates almost everything *l'Unità* had printed about the armed groups. Concluding with an exhortation to collaboration with the police and a derisive reference to 'hard-line civil libertarians', Pecchioli's interview marks the end of the party's engagement with the mass movements of the second cycle and the beginning of its engagement with the 'anti-democratic extrem-ists' of the armed groups: a phase which would find the PCI, in the name of Italian democracy, calling for the suppression of a left-wing rival by any means necessary.

Framing, engagement and the closing of the cycle

The PCI's engagement with the movements of the second cycle of contention is dominated by two framings. Participants in movement events are presented overwhelmingly in terms of two characterisations: the presumptively neo-fascist 'provocateur' and the threateningly aimless 'lumpenproletariat'. Both of these framings had been applied to political rivals of the PCI in earlier periods. Autonomists had regularly been denounced as provocateurs, whether carrying out arson attacks ('provocative techniques such as firebombing') or organising *spese proletarie* ('a group of provocateurs . . . made a disgraceful scene'). Similarly, the armed groups had consistently been presented as provocateurs, from Segrate onwards. The 'lumpenproletariat' framing was of more recent vintage, dating to the November 1976 'Proletarian youth happening'.

Both of these framings developed and changed in the course of the PCI's engagement with the movements. The 'provocateur' framing initially carried strong overtones of nihilism, coexisting uneasily with an unchanged imputation of neo-fascism. After the rout of Lama in February 1977, the 'nihilist provocateur' theme disappeared, to be replaced by a stronger and more insistent restatement of the 'neo-fascist provocateur' framing. February 1977 also saw a change in the 'lumpenproletariat' framing: the relatively neutral 'disorganised lumpenproletariat' frame, used to characterise the supposedly confused and directionless proletarian youth movement, was replaced by an explicitly condemnatory 'degenerate lumpenproletariat' frame.

Between February and September 1977, the 'neo-fascist provocateur' framing was applied both to the autonomists and, with mounting intensity, to the armed groups. The concept of violence, together with related concepts such as 'intolerance' and 'bullying' (*sopraffazione*), was insistently associated with the autonomists; by contrast, the coercive physical force exerted by the PCI's own *servizio d'ordine* was described, and even celebrated, under the name of 'firmness' or 'solidity'. Meanwhile the 'degenerate lumpenproletariat' framing (associated with the unpopular 'austerity' theme) gave way to an 'adventurist lumpenproletariat' frame: in effect, the young people of the 'movement of 1977' were presented as misguided idealists whose juvenile extremism led them to harbour the much more dangerous autonomist provocateurs.

September 1977 and the Bologna Convegno saw a significant shift in both these framing strategies: the autonomists were dismissed with contempt and the movement of 1977 recognised (belatedly) as a significant social phenomenon. As in the previous phase, these two rhetorical moves went together: the PCI was effectively offering the movement the benefit of its leadership, on condition that it dissociated itself from the waning forces of Autonomia. In December, finally, with the autonomists framed as an ineffectual rabble, the other cohort of neo-fascist provocateurs – the armed groups – could be reframed as dangerously anti-democratic but genuinely left-wing extremists. This shift, the most abrupt and startling of all, is testimony to the effectiveness with which the PCI had cleared the ground to its Left, delegitimising the autonomists and depoliticising the movement of 1977. Engagement with the armed groups lay ahead – but, as far as the mass movements were concerned, the second cycle of contention had been brought to a close.

Notes

1 'ROMA IN PIAZZA MANIFESTA/Scatenata la violenza poliziesca nelle strade per stroncare la possente protesta antimperialista'.

2 'La violenza invece della soluzione dei problemi . . . la disgregazione della democrazia che apre il varco alle iniziative autoritarie ed eccita la repressione, la prepotenza del bastone al posto della politica. Non lo permettiamo. Non possono permetterlo lavoratori, studenti, democratici.'

3 'Una manifestazione appassionata, vibrante, ma composta, controllata dagli stessi giovani. . . . i dimostranti hanno dimostrato la loro determinazione di evitare lo scontro . . . Intanto le cariche continuavano: per difendersi i giovani avevano sbarrato con auto via della Panetteria e via dei Crociferi. Alcune auto sono rimaste incendiate . . . Ripetutamente, infatti, gli studenti hanno effettuato delle sortite dall'Università accerchiata ed ogni volta hanno dovuto affrontare la violenza poliziesca. In serata, per proteggersi dalle cariche delle jeep, gli studenti avevano sbarrato con ostacoli di fortuna tutte le strade adiacenti all'università: le cariche, infatti, si svolgevano in tutta la zona'.

4 'la tattica è sempre la stessa. Una volta infiltrati, i fascisti svolgono il doppio ruolo di informatori per i loro "camerati" e di provocatori, attuando attentati la cui responsabilità possa ricadere sui "gruppetti" o cercando, ad ogni occasione, di causare incidenti con la polizia. . . . si presentano alla manifestazione contro la visita di Nixon con tanto di fazzoletti rossi e non perdono occasione, durante le cariche poliziesche, di creare ancor più confusione e compiere atti di vandalismo'.

5 'Una banditesca provocazione è avvenuta nel tardo pomeriggio a Milano'.

6 'una fantomatica organizzazione che si fa viva in momenti di particolare tensione sindacale con gravi atti provocatori nel tentativo di far ricadere sui lavoratori e i sindacati la responsabilità di atti ed iniziative che nulla hanno a che vedere con il movimento operaio e le sue lotte'.

7 'Idalgo Macchiarini era stato sequestrato da un gruppo di ignoti autodefinitosi "brigate rosse", ma di chiara marca fascista al servizio della provocazione padronale.'

8 'un incredibile e delirante comunicato in cui si giustifica e si esalta l'episodio teppistico'.

9 'Tutto, nella tragica vicenda di Segrate che ha avuto a protagonista Giangiacomo Feltrinelli, è profondamente oscuro. . . . Una sola cosa appare invece chiara come la luce del sole: e cio è che l'episodio giunge nel momento più opportuno e adatto per le forze reazionarie e conservatrici, per le classi dominanti, per tutti coloro che vogliono ancora una volta distrarre l'opinione pubblica dai reali problemi del paese e creare un clima torbido, di paura, di violenze, di tensione.'

10 'Occorre non dimenticare mai che l'Italia è il paese "occidentale" in cui è, oggi, più avanzato il sistema democratico, più forte e unitario il movimento operaio e popolare, più forte il Partitio Comunista. Contro tutto ciò è scattata la macchina della provocazione. Ed è perciò che la nostra polemica è così dura contro le posizioni estreme che a questa macchina provocatoria possono fornire alibi e vittime.'

11 'Ci risiamo. Ancora una volta nel pieno di una vertenza sindacale alla FIAT, puntuale come un cronometro svizzero, è arrivata la grossa provocazione. . . . La storia di questi ultimi anni di vita politica e sindacale nel nostro Paese è ricca di episodi che hanno avuto come protagoniste le sedicenti "brigate rosse". . . . Quali che siano le verniciature che questa organizzazione assume, la sua azione si è venuta intrecciando, con assoluta sincronia . . . con le trame eversive dei gruppi neofascisti.'

12 'essi hanno in pratico attribuito la qualifica di "lotta armata" a una serie di azioni sconnesse, irresponsabili, provocatorie, che si inquadrano perfettamente nella strategia delle forze più reazionarie, condotte da gruppi che costituiscono un vero e proprio terreno di colutra per ogni tipo di avventurieri, di spie, di agenti provocatori'.

13 'È ovvio che questa frase verrà colta come alibi dalle forze della peggiore destra per avvalorare le proprie tesi. Ma non è neppure questo il male peggiore. Il male peggiore è nell'assoluto vuoto culturale, ideale e politico che queste posizioni esprimono, un vuoto che ne fa strumenti pericolosi di natura antioperaia, antipopolare e controrivoluzionaria. Coloro che sostengono queste posizioni spacciandosi per ultrasinistri non sono soltanto, in realtà, nemici acerrimi del nostro Partito: essi sono, prima di ogni altra cosa, avversari di tutto il cammino in avanti compiuto dal movimento operaio e comunista'.

14 'La motivazione "politica" del gesto sarebbe che la scelta di oggi dovrebbe essere tra "compromesso storico e potere proletario armato" poiché "le vie di mezzo sono state bruciate" e che "una divisione si impone in seno al movimento operaio" poiché da "questa divisione nasce la unità di un fronte rivoluzionario". . . . Il tentativo di spezzare il fronte di lotta dei lavoratori . . . è la testimonianza di una volontà provocatoria. Poco conta, a questo punto, se si tratta di frasi dettate a un delirio frenetico o da calcolata opera di professionisti: il risultato è il medesimo. Esso è quello di chi, in sostanza, si fa complice e protagonista delle torbide mene eversive che tendono ad ostacolare il cammino della classe operaia e dei lavoratori e a minare le conquiste democratiche del Paese.'

15 'Si tratta di un'azione che non ha niente a che vedere con il movimento sindacale. La nostra è una lotta democratica. Chiunque si mette contro la legge, da qualunque parte pretenda di essere – ha aggiunto Lama – deve essere rapidamente colpito e punito'.

16 'Chiunque siano gli esecutori materiali, è del tutto evidente che questa strategia è voluta da chi vuol attentare alla democrazia italiana . . . da chi vuole terrorizzare il Paese per cercare di far passare una svolta reazionaria.'

17 'Con assoluta e purtroppo prevedibile puntualità, proprio mentre la destra sta giocando le sue carte per attaccare il Parlamento e accrescere la confusione nel Paese, è scattata la provocazione presentata sotto una maschera "di sinistra". . . . Più difficile è comprendere se si tratta di veri e propri fascisti che agiscono in prima persona e poi si nascondono dietro fraseologie e messinscena "rivoluzionarie", oppure di folli esaltati che hanno perso ogni contatto con la realtà e sono ormai affondati in pieno nel pantano dell'irresponsabilità antioperaia e antidemocratica. Il fatto stesso che tale interrogativo si possa fondatamente porre bolla, chiunque siano, gli autori dell'impresa.'

18 'Si tratta di un vasto e criminale piano provocatorio'.

19 'Non saremmo certo noi ad avere la pur minima indulgenza verso iniziative condotte con lo stile del commando e con tecniche provocatorie quale il lancio di bottiglie incendiarie. E poi, che erano i protagonisti della bravata, non annunciata e non rivendicata da nessuno, neanche dai più arrabbiati gruppi estremisti?'

20 'Un gruppo di provocatori, prendendo a pretesto l'aumento dei prezzi ha inscenato ieri sera una gazzarra davanti all'ingresso del negozio Coop del quartiere Cantalupo a Monza, tentando di impedire il regolare accesso degli acquirenti. Sul posto sono intervenuti numerosi iscritti della locale sezione del PCI che hanno respinto con energia i ripetuti tentativi dei teppisti di provocare la rissa'.

21 'Domenica pomeriggio gruppi dei cosiddetti "autonomi" si erano limitati a "prelevare" polli congelati senza pagare il conto . . . ed a contestare in modo "vivace" i prezzi della "Capanna del zio Tom", il locale che ha avuto la sventura di trovarsi nel cuore del festival. . . . Il vero intento di alcuni gruppi di giovani, giunti al Parco Lambro con il passamontagna nello zainetto, assieme alle chiavi inglesi ed alle bottiglie di benzina, si è rivelato nel pomeriggio di ieri. . . . Episodi di provocazione nei confronti dell'istituto tecnico industriale si erano già verificata nella notte di sabato, quando, con il pretesto del temporale, alcuni fra i molti che si erano andati a rifugiare sotto le pensiline dell'edificio, ne avevano approfittato per forzare numerose porte e finestre, entrare e commettare atti di vandalismo. Ieri pomeriggio si è avuta, invece, la sensazione di una vera e propria manovra preordinata e l'intervento della polizia è stato inevitabile: lancio di sassi da una parte e di candelotti lacrimogeni dall'altra. . . . La polizia ha evitato fino in fondo lo scontro ed ha atteso che fosse lo stesso servizio d'ordine a bloccare l'ennesima sortita di questi "autonomi" al cui presenza in manifestazioni pubbliche corrisponde regolarmente alle piu gravi provocazioni. Funzionari di polizia ed organizzatori della manifestazione stavano decidendo insieme sul da farsi, quando un "commando" si e staccato dal gruppo degli "autonomi" . . . Ancora una volta l'intervento della polizia è stato inevitabile. Questa volta ai candelotti lacrimogeni si è risposto con il lancio di due bottiglie incendiarie e . . . a quanto pare anche con alcuni colpi di pistola.'

22 'l'oscuro duplice omicidio di Padova era ed è episodio che si inquadra senz'ombra di dubbio nel clima di tensione e di losche manovre che rappresentano una con-

tinua minaccia e un pericolo per la vita democratica e della città veneta e dell'intero Paese. . . . questi messaggi delle sedicenti "Brigate rosse" hanno la medesima logica nazi-fascista: non solo per il tentativo – del tutto impossibile – di confondere, in qualche modo, le piste, ma per l'idea stessa della vendetta, della faida, dell'assassinio che è idea, appunto, che ha origine nel bagaglio infame delle dottrine naziste.'

23 'tenta di parlare in nome della classe che prima e più di ogni altro ha bollato questi metodi e azioni fascistiche.'

24 'sconvolgere l'ordinato e civile svolgimento della campagna elettorale . . . per colpire il regime democratico e impedire che il popolo italiano compia, nella libertà, nuove scelte che facciano uscire il Paese dalla crisi e dal disordine.'

25 'Ai rapitori Coco aveva risposto negativamente con la "voce dello Stato": "ritengo che . . . i poteri sono assolutamente indisponibili per ogni uso radicalmente diverso da quello cui sono ordinati (anzi incompatibile e opposto) . . ." Questo forte "senso dello Stato", che non deve e non può capitolare, è sempre stato presente nella attività di Francesco Coco.'

26 '"Noi lottiamo per difendere i posti di lavoro – diceva un operaio – e chi fa queste cose li vuole distruggere." "Nel 1945 – ricordava un altro – sono stati gli operai a salvare le fabbriche che i tedeschi volevano distruggere. Oggi i lavoratori hanno lo stesso compito".'

27 'Queste manifestazioni di violenza gratuita . . . non hanno nulla a che vedere con la lotta politica unitaria e democratica espressasi in questi giorni per condannare l'infame assassinio dei cinque giovani patrioti spagnoli. Qualunque sia la loro ispirazione, essi possono oggettivamente portare solo a un alleggerimento dell'isolamento che circonda il boia fascista e a gravi incrinature nel vasto fronte di solidarietà antifascista'.

28 'All'appuntamento, davanti alla stazione di Lambrate, stamani erano anche i diversi gruppi di extraparlamentari. . . . si sono diretti verso l'Innocenti-Leyland e hanno varcato i cancelli. . . . Molti avevano il viso macherato da fazzoletti, molti armati di aste nodose. La risposta operaia è stata dura: gli estranei sono stati scaraventati fuori dai cancelli. Poco più tardi tutti i lavoratori dell'Innocenti Leyland si riunivano in assemblea generale, ribadivano la volontà di confermare le proprie scelte di lotta, rifiutando ogni avventurismo e ogni trappola provocatoria, chiedevano il ritiro delle tessere sindacali ai tre operai che avevano giudato il precedente "assalto" alla fabbrica.'

29 'Il rientro in fabbrica dei lavoratori dello stabilimento di Lambrate . . . è stato però contrassegnato di alcuni incidenti. Un gruppo di giovani ha superato i cancelli della fabbrica ed ha compiuto un giro tra i reparti di lavorazione. Ad allontanare gli "intrusi" sono stati gli stessi operai dell'Innocenti intervenuti a bloccare le portinerie dello stabilimento. Durante questa azione sono sorti dei tafferugli ed alcuni lavoratori sono rimasti contusi.'

30 'gli episodi provocatori di ciu sono stati costellati gli ultimi mesi di lotta alla FIAT (macchine di capisquadra bruciate, attentati a capireparto, sabotaggi, diffusione di materiale dal tono delirante, incendi e tentati incendi di origine dolosa) hanno trovato sempre i lavoratori, e loro movimento sindacale unitario in primo

luogo . . . occorre andare oltre la sola denuncia . . . per costruire concretamente all'interno dei reparti e delle officine una rete di controllo democratico permanente che renda i lavoratori protagonisti della battaglia in difesa della democrazia.'

31 'gruppi che, fino all'altro ieri, l'*esproprio* lo avevano se non teorizzato per lo meno tacitamente approvato'.

32 'senza soffermarsi sulla matrice politica che questi gruppi amano darsi, diciamo ancora una volta che queste azioni sono caratteristiche della violenza fascista. Altresì condanniamo tutte quelle forze politiche che, pur dissociandosi da questi gruppi, troppo spesso danno spazio ad elementi che con le loro azioni si mettono in netta antitesi con il movimento operaio.'

33 'Forse il fatto di avere rappresentanti in parlamento demotiva i ragazzi che sono venuti ad accamparsi in questo polverosissimo parco milanese'.

34 ' "Ci annientano, vogliono sterminarci, ci confinano nelle riserve," dice un giovane con la camicia a fiori e un gran cappellone. Le riserve sono i quartieri dormitorio, le bidonville della periferia nebbiosa e ostile. . . . C'è una rabbia che cova sotto una massa profondamente differenziata che tenta di presentarsi unita autodefinendosi con il termine "giovane". . . . Nell'illegalità si continuerà a danzare intorno al totem della rivoluzione; si scaglieranno le frecce degli espropri contro la propria apatia.'

35 'I circa duemila ragazzi, molti dei quali giovanissimi . . . hanno dato vita ad una sorta di parco Lambro in formato ridotto di cui pochi sono rimasti soddisfatti. Si è discusso poco e in modo troppo confuso dei problemi della gioventù, si è rifiutato ogni discorso sull'organizzazione, non si sapeva bene cosa dire. . . . Gli interventi dei rappresentanti dei "circoli giovanili", seguiti con scarsa convinzione da un pubblico che cambiava rapidamente, sono rimasti in superficie testimoniando di una drammatica confusione di idee. . . . Non è un caso che in questo guazzabuglio, in cui una serie di aspirazioni pur giuste non riescono a oltrepassare il limite della protesta, abbiano avuto un largo spazio i temi dell'autoriduzione e dell'appropriazione non solo in teoria.'

36 'Non vi sono state violenze anche se in qualche caso la reazione dei proprietari dei locali è servita ad attenuare il danno ottenendo dagli estremisti qualche cosa di più di quanto loro pretendeva di pagare. . . . diciassette giovani sono entrati . . . hanno occupato tutti i posti liberi, hanno mangiato 17 pizze e bevato 19 birre, quindi si sono alzati e stavano per andarsene quando il proprietario ha presentato loro il conto; 48 mila lire. "Siamo studenti – hanno risposto – possiamo pagare solo ottomila lire". Deposto su un tavolo il denaro, prima che il gestore potesse riaversi dalla sorpresa, sono tutti fuggiti.'

37 'un gruppo di una trentina di giovani ha fatto irruzione nella salumeria-rosticceria di Giuseppe Vecchi . . . Dopo aver gridato: "Questo è un esproprio proletario, nessuno si muova", i giovani si sono impadroniti di generi alimentari. Il proprietario del negozio, dal retrobottega, ha avvertito la polizia e sul posto si sono recate numerose pattuglie dell'ufficio politico e della squadra "volante" della questura. Nove giovani che si trovavano ancora nei pressi del negozio sono stati fermati e condotti in questura. I nove sono stati successivamente rilasciati dopo

che hanno rimborsato al titolare della salumeria una parte del costo degli oggetti rubati.'

38 'Chi sono dunque questi individui che la cronaca degli ultimi anni descrive – assieme ai fascisti – come protagonisti della maggior parte degli episodi di violenza e teppismo? . . . Non è un partito, nemmeno allo stato embrionale: è la negazione aperta di tutti i partiti, e di ogni forma di organizzazione. . . . Un altro dato infatti che caratterizza l'azione di questi gruppi, è l'assenza completa di piattaforme politiche'.

39 'Quella compiuta ieri sera dai sedicenti "Circoli proletari giovanili" si è rivelata, sin dall'inizio, come una provocazione freddamente studiata a tavolino ed in cui l'asserita "contestazione" dello spettacolo di apertura della stagione scaligera ha finito per rivelarsi un puro pretesto. Quello che, in effetti, è apparso ben presto il vero obiettivo "strategico" del piano preordinato dai "circoli" è stato la ricerca pura e semplice . . . della violenza e dei vandalismi . . . motivazioni ideali o sociali sono state sempre del tutto estranee agli organizzatori della provocazione.'

40 'ai manifestanti si sono mescolati gruppi di violenti, di teppisti armati e decisi di provocare incidenti ad ogni costo'.

41 'sono state distribuite centinaia di bottiglie incendiarie costruite da bande di artificieri . . . il clima di tensione andava aumentando fino a raggiungere espressioni parossistiche di isterismo . . . si sono impadroniti di catene antifurto, paletti di ferro, chiavi inglesi e altri oggetti utili per il disegno devastante che si sarebbe dispiegato più tardi. . . . alcuni gruppi di cittadini, che non si capacitavano di tanta inconsulta, indiscriminata violenza verso tutto e tutti, hanno impedito ulteriori saccheggi e incendi.'

42 'Gli scontri sono dunque cominciati dopo le prime cariche della polizia contro i manifestanti che affluivano in piazza Navona, e nelle ore a seguire hanno svolto un ruolo preciso di criminale provocazione gruppi di teppisti armati e mascherati. . . . Giorgina [sic] Masi è caduta . . . mentre era mescolata ad un folto gruppo di manifestanti che si erano scontrati da pochi minuti con le forze di polizia.'

43 'È in atto nel Paese una vasta e torbida manovra di provocazione antidemocratica, che – facendo leva strumentalmente sullo stato di disagio di larghi strati studenteschi – si sviluppi attraverso atti di intimidazione, di teppismo e di devastazione, con l'obiettivo di seminare panico, di sconvolgere la vita civile e di colpire le istituzione democratiche. Tali atti criminosi sono compiuti da gruppi squadristici e sono assecondati e persino teorizzati da talune formazioni estremiste, dando in tal modo vita a tumultuose e violente manifestazioni in cui determinante diviene il ruolo di veri e propri agenti provocatori e di fascisti.'

44 'chi è (o chi era) questa radio Alice? . . . In questa direzione vi è stato un crescendo pauroso, con l'irradiazione di messaggi allucinanti e quasi sempre miranti ad un unico obiettivo: alimentare l'anticomunismo, gettare il massimo discredito sulle organizzazioni sindacali e sugli amministratori pubblici. Con un linguaggio irresponsabile, diffamatorio, distruttivo e che si cerca di far passare come il mezzo più efficace di lotta "al potere e al regime". È, invece, il canale scelto per contribuire ad esasperare giovani, a spingerli alla violenza, alla "distruzione di tutto".

L'emittente è completamente nelle mani di "autonomi" disperati, alla continua caccia di nuove provocazioni per contribuire così ad intaccare le istituzioni e la democrazia. Si tenta di alimentare continuamente la violenza, con un comportamento che richiama alla memoria il ruolo che nella vicenda cilena hanno avuto alcune emittenti. Un interrogativo per tutto: chi c'è esattamente dietro "Alice"?'

45 '[Berardi] è ritenuto uno dei promotori e cappeggiatori dell'eversione dei giorni scorsi. . . . Gli si fa carico, tra l'altro, di avere lanciato ripetuti appelli agli studenti per lo scontro armato . . . e di avere, per così dire, "previsto" le violenze nichilistiche che hanno squassato la città, già prima che esplodessero . . . Berardi, infatti, aveva stampato in anticipo . . . alcune migliaia di copie di un giornale "underground" (*"Il cielo è caduto sulla terra – Rivoluzione – Giornale in movimento"*) in cui veniva caldeggiata l'occupazione armata di aree metropolitane da cui fossero stati scacciati polizia, carabinieri e PCI.'

46 'FINALMENTE IL CIELO È CADUTO SULLA TERRA. 12 MARZO: UN BEL GIORNO PER COMINCIARE'.

47 'Il materiale per comporre il foglio era stato consegnato in tipografia . . . una settimana prima da Francesco Berardi . . . Dodici marzo: un bel giorno per cominciare. Invece Pier Francesco Lorusso fu ucciso il giorno prima. Da chi? . . . il carabiniere Tramontani non ha cambiato una virgola a quel che aveva detto venerdì notte: ho sparato soltanto in aria, non ho visto il giovane che è morto.'

48 'Il piano era chiaro e forse preordinato: colpire la democrazia nel punto dove essa si presenta più forte e più compatta. Per questo Bologna è stata in questi giorni al centro di eventi estremamente gravi'.

49 'alla fine della manifestazione, è scattato un vero e proprio assalto di stampo squadristico. . . . Contro lavoratori e studenti sono stati lanciati palloncini pieni di acqua, di vernice, di calce; e poi bastoni, bottiglie, sassi, bulloni . . . Gruppi di "autonomi" hanno iniziato di premere contro il cordone sindacale, e, mentre i lavoratori si stringevano attorno al segretario generale della CGIL, lasciando l'ateneo, il camion usato come palco per gli oratori è stato raggiunto e distrutto . . . E poi le aggressioni ai lavoratori e agli studenti democratici, i pestaggi.'

50 'Le esclamazioni tra la folla si ripetono: "Ma guardateli: fanno come i fascisti!" . . . Intanto il compagno Lama ha concluso il comizio, invitando la folla a non raccogliere la gravissima provocazione. Un attimo dopo impugna il microfono Vettraino . . . e grida alla folla che si divide sotto l'assalto degli squadristi: "Isoliamo la provocazione! Formiamo subito un corteo che si diriga fuori dell'università"!'

51 'Questi gruppi non hanno nulla di spontaneo o di "autonomo". Al contrario, essi sono formazioni esperte, organizzate e dirette. Essi vanno giudicati per i loro atti, che sono squadristici. Ma vanno giudicati anche per la piattaforma che adottano: contro tutte le istituzioni democratiche, contro tutti i partiti, contro i sindacati, contro i comunisti. E questo essere "contro" esplicitamente si affida alla violenza. Dove sta la differenza tra questi gruppi, dunque, e le posizioni, ben note, dell'origine dei movimenti fascisti?'

52 'Il "nuovo fascismo" Lama non lo identifica soltanto nella violenza e intolleranza sopraffatrice. Anche il fascismo storico, dice, ebbe all'inizio, specie tra i giovani,

"radici demagogiche e irrazionali simili a queste". Poi c'è il qualunquismo dell'ostilità ai partiti, alla politica concreta, ai meccanismi della democrazia. C'è lo svuotamento dei simboli, la irrisione nichilista esemplificati da slogan quali "Meno ferie, più sfruttamento" o "Potere dromedario". E, naturalmente, c'è la scelta del nemico: i sindacati, i comunisti. "Da cos'altro si riconosce, il fascismo"?'

53 'Siamo stanchi . . . di ripetere duri duri senza un pianto né un sorriso "Potere operaio", mentre all'operaio il potere continua a non darglielo nessuno. Per questo diciamo "potere dromedario": suona come "potere proletario" ma in più far ridere.'

54 'costoro che non si vergognavano di urlare "Curcio libero, Pajetta in galera", cosa quest'ultima alla quale provvidero ampiamente, a suo tempo, i fascisti. . . . La storia si ripete, e solo chi si lascia accecare dall'anticomunismo si rifiuta di capire.'

55 'Fallita – grazie alla ferma risposta unitaria di massa – la fase apertamente fascista della strategia della tensione e della strage, si ricorre ad altre forme di aggressione per seminare paura e disorientamento, e per ricacciare indietro il movimento operaio e democratico dalle sue conquiste. Ogni confusione deve finire, ogni tentativo di ricercare giustificazione sconfina ormai nella complicità.'

56 '"Garantire l'ordine per noi vuol dire garantire la vita democratica. Ricordo quando in Italia l'ordine era garantito in modo diverso. . . . quelli che rappresentarono per tanti anni la repressione in Italia, i fascisti, avevano cominciato proprio marciando su Bologna quando la città ebbe per la prima volta un sindaco comunista".'

57 'Di fronte agli "autonomi" . . . abbiamo il dovere di essere netti: si tratta di irrazionali ma lucidi organizzatori di un nuovo squadrismo, e non sono definibili con alcun altro termine se non quello di "nuovi fascisti"'.

58 'indulgenze e debolezze che molti democratici ebbero (verso lo squadrismo fascista), che oggi dovrebbero non essere ripetute'.

59 'La forte, unitaria, manifestazione di protesta degli studenti torinesi per l'aggressione fascista agli studenti romani del "Mamiani" è stata ieri turbata da alcune azioni squadristiche di un gruppo di "autonomi" che, muniti di "molotov", i volti coperti da passamontagna, a manifestazione finita hanno aggredito giovani comunisti e democratici – ragazzi e ragazze – infierendo su di essi con bastoni e chiavi inglesi, ostentando la violenza e la vigliaccheria che è sempre stata caratteristica dei fascisti'.

60 'La presenza costante di gruppi organizzati di provocatori capeggiati da personaggi dall'ambiguo e losco passato politico . . . rendono, per il momento, impossibile l'avvio di un confronto democratico fra studenti e forze politiche e sindacali. La scelta di non cadere nella trappola della violenza, ormai chiaramente innescata da squadre di provocatori fascisti, è emersa come scelta politica unanime dalla riunione che si è svolta ieri mattina'.

61 'la compattezza della partecipazione è stata tale da creare attorno al palco . . . una specie di blocco omogeneo, invalicabile. . . . i gruppi del teppismo studentesco . . . hanno invece tentato ripetutamente di penetrare nella manifestazione, di

condizionarla col loro pseudo-rivoluzionarismo, col loro estremismo, con il loro sostanziale odio verso i lavoratori e le loro organizzazioni. Ma questo blocco compatto, omogeneo, invalicabile di cui si parlava prima li ha espulsi dal proprio corpo: ha dimostrato – come già tante volte nella sua storia – che la classe operaia non ha paura di nessun tipo di confronto ed ha i mezzi per uscirne vittoriosa. Questo non significa, si badi, che alla violenza dei neo-squadristi il servizio d'ordine . . . abbia risposto con una violenza eguale e contraria: non ne ha avuto neppure bisogno, perchè è riuscito ad isolare sul nascere ogni tentativo di trasformare questa presenza unitaria di massa in una nuova occasione di conflitto.'

62 'il muro umano del servizio d'ordine: almeno otto file di lavoratori proteggono la piazza da eventuali incursioni . . . Le borse vengono aperte, le persone sospette perquisite.'

63 ' "Quella di oggi non è una manifestazione di partito. È una manifestazione di regime".'

64 'Si! se per regime si intende il nostro regime democratico, e costituzionale, lo Stato repubblicano formato dalla Resistenza'.

65 'Ci è stato risposto, quasi si trattasse di chissà quale scoperta, che occorre saper analizzare le radici culturali . . . Anche il fascismo e il nazismo hanno avuto le loro radici culturali. . . . Noi abbiamo indicato e continuiamo a indicare una dis- criminante precisa: ed è la discriminante della intollerenza, della sopraffazione, della violenza appunto. . . . Mai come in questo momento, dinanzi alla nuova infame aggressione, il paese e le masse hanno bisogno di unità. Condanniamo dunque con forza quei gruppi che, ancora in questi giorni, operano con vergog- nosa incoscienza per introdurre e acutizzare elementi di divisione tra le forze della sinistra . . . I loro sforzi, lo sappiamo, saranno vani. Ma resta il fatto che essi stanno cercando di intaccare con ogni pretesto quello che è il baluardo più saldo delle istituzioni repubblicane. Meditino su questo, se sono ancora capaci di ragionevolezza.'

66 'Il rifiuto del confronto, l'esaltazione dell'intollerenza sono la anticamera della violenza cieca. E a questo non può essere concesso alcuno spazio.'

67 'Anche sul piano delle idee, dunque, una permanente battaglia di libertà va com- battuta: contro l'intollerenza, contro il fanatismo, contro i tentativi di elevare barriere, contro nuove forme di divisione tra lavoratori manuali e intellettuali, contro chi predica di uscire dal terreno della lotta democratica. I comunisti devono sapere stare in prima file anche in questa lotta.'

68 'in tutta la città – in particolare nella zona intorno all'Università ma anche in centro – era stato predisposto un massiccio e capillare servizio d'ordine pubblico.'

69 'Non si può certo escludere che errori ed eccessi vi siano stati nel comportamento di questo o quel reparto di polizia. . . . Resta tuttavia il fatto preeminente che ci si trova in presenza di squadre eversive che usano armi da fuoco e puntano alla guerriglia. In queste condizioni l'indispensabile ricerca delle soluzioni sul piano politico e sociale non può prescindere da una premessa: isolare e colpire i violenti. . . . La polizia italiana può e deve essere la polizia del nostro Stato demo-

cratico. Ci deve essere collaborazione tra le istituzioni democratiche, i partiti antifascisti, le organizzazioni dei lavoratori e le forze di polizia.'

70 'All'alba ... lo sferragliare dei mezzi sotto le due torri. Un rumore temuto, che viene da lontano, gli anni della guerra. I bolognesi, alla prima luce, aprono le finestre sbigottiti: "Ci sono i carri armati!" I "carri armati" in realtà sono ... veicoli corazzati per trasportare truppo. Sono "panzer" senza il cannone. ... Poi ci sono le autoblinde. E dietro, lenti, molto lenti, attentissimi, gli uomini armati. Polizia e carabinieri in assetto di guerra.'

71 'All'alba con l'appoggio di mezzi blindati dei carabinieri a cui erano state tolte le mitragliatrici, il quartiere universitario è stato disoccupato. La tensione, tuttavia, resta elevatissima. ... C'è preoccupazione perchè molte pistole e carabine ... sono ancora nelle mani di quei gruppi che avevano organizzato i vandalismi, le ruberie, i saccheggi e gli incendi giusto un disegno di "criminalizzazione" del movimento studentesco ... L'ingresso nel quartiere universitario era stato fatto con i mezzi blindati perchè si temeva il verificarsi di conflitti a fuoco. ... Non si voleva, infatti, dare l'opportunità ai fomentatori dei disordini e dei saccheggi di annidarsi nuovamente nell'ateneo.'

72 'Criminalizza il movimento, infatti, non chi, come noi, combatte una battaglia politica aperto contro le posizioni avventuriste, irresponsabili, smascherandole come estranee e avverse alla tradizione del movimento operaio, e come nefaste per la democrazia italiana. Criminalizza chi civetta con queste posizioni'.

73 'assai scarso rilievo abbia sapere dietro quale sigla gli attentatori abbiano scelto di coprirsi o quale "colore" abbiano scelto di attribuirsi. ... le masse hanno da tempo imparato a vedere l'unico colore che conta: quello della reazione e dell'attacco alle conquiste democratiche'.

74 'la battaglia che riguarda la sorte del nostro Stato si svolge oggi dentro ciascuno di noi: ed è la battaglia fra la tendenza a lasciarci dominare e travolgere dagli avvenimenti e la volontà di comprenderli criticamente ... Le testimonianze di questo travaglio che ciascuno avverte le abbiamo, da Sciascia, da Montale e da mille altri'.

75 'Noi non sappiamo quali siano in queste ore le riflessioni di Indro Montanelli ... e se egli sarà indotto a qualche ripensamento sugli spazi che una linea di divisione e di contrapposizione, quale quella da lui perseguita, ha offerto all'eversione. Saremmo però degli ipocriti se ... non dicessimo anche a Indro Montanelli che questa è la nostra profonda convinzione: se non ci si pone sul terreno della solidarietà nazionale, ad essere minacciati non saranno solo i valori e gli interessi del movimento operaio.'

76 'L'attentato contro Nino Ferrero è stato rivendicato da un gruppo che si definisce "Azione rivoluzionaria", una delle 120 sigle terroristiche manovrate da chi ha interesse a provocare paura e tensione nel Paese. ... In un farneticante comunicato, i criminali dicono di avere inteso colpire "la spudorata campagna di bugie e di calunnie portata avanti dai pennivendoli del regime". "Pennivendoli" è un termine caro a Franco Freda, il neo-nazista rinviato a giudizio per la strage di piazza Fontana. ... L'obiettivo è sempre lo stesso: colpire le istituzioni democratiche e le organizzazioni che si battono con intransigenza per la difesa della

legalità costituzionale. Ma quando si arriva a colpire quella forza politica che, da sempre, si batte per rinnovare profondamente le strutture del Paese, quando un compagno dell'*Unità* viene definito "un bastardo al servizio del regime", il gioco diventa fin troppo scoperto. . . . la condanna non può bastare. Occore snidare i covi di questi banditi, accertare chi sta dietro alla loro spalle. Gli intrecci fra il terrorismo e le centrali di servizi segreti del nostro e di altri Paesi non costituiscono più elemento di novità.'

77 'l'accusavano di essere "servo dello Stato". Non so se questa è una infamia, se questa sgangherata repubblica . . . merita ancora di essere difesa . . . Il servo dello Stato Carlo Casalegno è caduto in una pozza di sangue per un padrone, questo Stato, che non gli assicurava neppure il diritto di pensare.'

78 'Non si illudano, i brigatisti rossi, i loro alleati neri e le forze che li muovono, all'interno e all'estero, di trovare delle debolezze nel movimento operaio. La nuova ondata di terrorismo li qualifica ancor più di prima come nemici dei lavoratori. Di più: non si illuda nessuno che la preoccupazione di difendere la democrazia possa farci indietreggiare di fronte alla necessità di interventi decisi e di misure chieste dall'emergenzia'.

79 'contro la trama eversiva che minaccia la vita democratica e i fascisti lo hanno ucciso. Esattamente come altri fascisti, sotto il nome di brigatisti rossi, hanno ucciso Carlo Casalegno. Si tratta delle stesse mani, delle stesse menti politiche, dello stesso disegno.'

80 'Il "partito armato" è dunque arrivato a quella resa dei conti militare sulla quale aveva fin dall'inizio puntato le proprie carte. . . . lo scontro. . . è stato risolto dal capo degli autonomi con un'indicativa battuta: "Lasciate perdere, questi problemini possiamo risolverli in altri momenti". Poi, mentre l'oratore di turno riprendeva il suo discorso, gli aeroplanini di carta tornavano tranquillamente ad incrociarsi nell'aria fumosa del Palasport. . . . Dei 2000 negozi circa del centro storico, non più di una quarantina hanno abbassato le saracinesche.'

81 'lavoratori, studenti, donne, giovani delle leghe di disoccupati . . . di una parte di "Lotta continua", del PdUP-Manifesto, delle femministe, ciascuno con le sue parole d'ordine, le sue idee, le sue intenzioni, ma tutti (o quasi, con qualche eccezione) mossi da aspirazioni unitarie . . . Alle sette, dentro il recinto eretto in piazza San Giovanni a difesa contro possibili provocazioni ed attacchi (che non sono mancati, ma che sono stati contenuti entro limiti riducissimi) vi erano già quattromila membri del servizio d'ordine della FLM.'

82 'Ma appena gli "autonomi" tentano di uscire dall'ateneo, verso le 9,30, basta un accenno di carica da parte degli agenti e tutti rifluiscono . . . A questo punto l'ateneo viene completamente circondato da agenti e carabinieri. Chiunque tenti di uscire viene identificato e perquisito.. . . Poco dopo le 10 un gruppo tenta una sortita in via De Lollis . . . e forma, al Verano, un piccolo corteo che viene caricato e disperso con lancio di lacrimogeni. Alcuni dei giovani riuscivano poi a raggiungere San Giovanni, dove scatenavano l'aggressione teppistica alla fine della manifestazione sindacale. . . . Gli "autonomi", a questo punto, desistono dal tentativo di uscire dall'ateneo, fanno un corteo all'interno della città universitaria scandendo slogan provocatori. . . . Dopo mezzogiorno la polizia scioglie il presi-

dio e si allontana dalla zona dell'ateneo. Poco più tardi arrivano all'università alcune miglaia di givovani, di ritorno da San Giovanni. Ha inizio un'assemblea che subito dopo gli "autonomi" trasformano in rissa. Il "Partito armato" accusa "Lotta continua" di "tradimento". L'atmosfera si fa subito tesa. Volano i primi pugni e alla fine un centinaio di teppisti armati di bastoni si scatenano e inseguono fino a piazzale delle Scienze gli altri giovani.'

83 'un'azione più minuta, ma non meno frequente, di assalto a negozi e supermercati dove, in nome di una pretesa azione di lotta al carovita, hanno "espropriato" bottiglie di whisky e champagne. Del resto "appropriamoci del lusso" è una delle loro parole d'ordine.'

84 'mentre in alcuni Atenei si sono prodotte esperienze e proposte positive, in altri sono venute avanti richieste assurde e di natura corporativa quali quella della retribuzione generalizzata di tutti gli studenti . . . Si esprime in queste posizioni una tendenza a mantenere l'attuale Università . . . come luogo dello spreco, del parassitismo e della fuga dal lavoro produttivo. Questi gruppi studenteschi . . . finiscono per indirizzare la loro battaglia soprattutto contro il movimento operaio e la sua politica di rigore, di risanamento e di sviluppo del Paese.'

85 'la lotta non è più per imporre una *diversa* ipotesi politica alla *stesse* masse, ma è tra due diverse *società*. Il punto politico è questo: dobbiamo chiederci che cosa abbiamo fatto per questa *seconda società*, che è cresciuta accanto alla prima, e magari a carico di questa, ma senza trarne rilevanti vantaggi, senza avere uno sbocco e senza un radicamento reale nella "prima società". . . . Non sembra fortuito che la parola d'ordine dominante del '68 – l'alleanza fra classe operaia e studenti – la quale, anche quando si presentava rivestitia di forme rivoluzionarie, poggiava su di una ipotesi espansiva della società, sia oggi abbandonata a favore di parole d'ordine che puntano sulla saldatura tra i diversi settori dell'emarginazi one . . . Il complesso di questi settori *si stacca* dal resto della società e gli si contrappone. In questo senso, picchiare *operai organizzati* – cosa che in passato sarebbe apparsa inconcepibile e sacrilega ai contestatori più estremi – diventa un fatto logico . . . Che necessità c'è di costruire il comunismo . . . quando si ha la possibilità di appropriarsi oggi, giorno per giorno, di ciò di cui si prova il bisogno? Il peggior nemico di questa prospettiva diventa dunque proprio chi non accetta questa società ma al tempo stesso pensa di poterla trasformare. . . . Bisogna riconoscere coraggiosamente che all'interno di questa "seconda società" alcune delle nostre parole d'ordine più autorevoli non mordono. L'austerità, per esempio, ha un senso in quanto è rivolta ai settori produttivi della società – ai *lavoratori* – i quali, in quanto produttori e consumatori al tempo stesso, possono, se vogliono, calibrare un rapporto diverso tra questi due aspetti della vita. . . . Fra il sistema e le forze della contestazione studentesca non c'erano che il sindacato e il PCI (ma soprattutto il PCI) a rappresentare le ragioni di quella "prima società" . . . Non c'è da stupirsi se in quelle condizioni l'anticomunismo nuovo abbia trovato alimento nel nostro essere presentati come antemurale del sistema . . . Fra i teorici del bisogno della "seconda società" e certi settori del mondo politico ed economico italiano . . . c'è oggi una convergenza (oggettiva? soggettiva?) sulla necessità di colpire *in primo lugo la presenza operaia organizzata* nella società.

L'alleanza fra conservazione e disgregazione sociale può apparire strana, ma non è impossibile'.

86 'Vi sono formazioni squadristiche violente – la principale delle quali sembra essere quella denominata "Autonomi" – che operano su scala nazionale, sono saldamente organizzate ed abilmente e freddamente dirette, si inseriscono soprattutto nei confusi movimenti studenteschi e nelle loro manifestazioni, e con azioni di guerriglia provocano gravissimi disordini. . . . questa tattica è stata finora resa possibile dalla copertura di massa fornita da movimenti confusi, da un massimalismo ed estremismo infantile alimentato dallo stato di disagio profondo di larghi strati di studenti, di discoccupati, di emarginati . . . le forze sovversive utilizzano alcune radio libere, le quali incitano alle manifestazioni violente e le guidano . . . è questo un altro problema che deve essere subito affrontato e risolto, utilizzando le leggi esistenti, o, se occorre, con nuovo provvedimenti legislativi. . . . il fatto nuovo più importante e grave . . . è che queste forze eversive fanno uso delle armi; e non solo delle armi improprie, ma delle armi proprie (e tra queste mettiamo anche le bottiglie incendiarie): delle armi da fuoco; e sparano. . . . La polizia, per noi, non è mai stata il nemico, neppure negli anni in cui veniva impiegata a difesa dei privilegi di classe e ci scontravamo con essa. . . . anche allora, invitavamo i poliziotti – anche essi, come diceva Di Vittorio, figli del popolo, e in particolare contadini meridionali – a comprendere le ragioni delle lotte degli altri lavoratori, dei loro fratelli. . . . La polizia che difende l'ordine democratico difende un patrimonio nostro, della classe operaia e della nazione. . . . Nè deve sfuggire il fatto che, attorno al nucleo attivo dello squadrismo e della provocazione, vi è un'area abbastanza ampia di estremismo fatto di intolleranza, di sterile e inconcludente ribellismo, di rifiuto della ragione, di avventurismo, o di una cupa ideologia ispirata alla decrepita deformazione meccanicistica del marxismo . . . i giovani che, in buona fede, seguono le formazioni estremistiche, credendo di essere così rivoluzionari . . . devono isolare i violenti, i provocatori; devono ripudiare ogni forma di intolleranza e di sopraffazione . . . Se non faranno questo, abbandonandosi ad un confuso ed inconcludente ribellismo e movimentismo, senza saperlo faranno il gioco delle forze reazionarie e conservatrici . . . proprio di quelle forze che oggi si oppongono alla svolta politica che è sempre più necessaria e urgente.'

87 'resta, dopo il ripudio e le condanne dei sanguinosi gesti terroristici, la difficoltà di rompere definitivamente e nettamente con il "partito della P.38", di respingere e isolare una volta per tutte i provocatori e i teppisti dell'area della "autonomia"'.

88 'gruppi dirigenti cercano oggi di prendere le distanze dai pistoleri. Infatti, se la loro decisione di sconfessare i violenti deve considerarsi un fatto positivo, resta che si è trattato di una decisione tardiva, equivoca, opportunistica. E ciò perchè resta la sostanza, profondamente sterile e negativa, dell'analisi politica da cui essi partono, tutta imperniata sulla cosiddetta "contrapposizione al sistema", e resta il nulla assoluto che essi propongono alla sinistra . . . Si sono dissociati dai violenti. Bene, ma se continuano a pensare che la democrazia repubblicana è una farsa e che i sindacati e i partiti operai sono soltanto servi dei padroni, e che lo Stato si abbatte e non si cambia, perché si sono dissociati?'

89 'i fautori del "partito armato" sono rimasti isolati all'interno del Palazzo dello sport, conquistato con la forza e mantenuto per tre giorni come una roccaforte. Gli altri cercavano invece di intessere un dibattito esprimendo tesi che non condividiamo e che combattiamo sul piano politico e ideale, ma mantenendosi sul terreno del confronto e delle lotte politiche.'

90 'C'è stata anche qualche autoriduzione individuale. "Alcuni – ci dice un barista di via Zamboni – entravano, bevevano e se ne andavano all'inglese, magari portandosi dietro anche qualche bottiglia di acqua minerale. Ma che vuole, queste cose succedono anche durante i raduni degli alpini." . . . Quello che abbiamo avuto sotto gli occhi è stata, nel bene e nel male, l'immagine della contraddizione centrale della nostra società, il riflessione di una crisi profonda, storica di vecchi e non più proponibili modelli civili, culturali, produttivi. . . . il movimento operaio non può lasciare senza risposta le domande confusamente emerse dal convegno. Quella di Bologna, in questo senso, è stata una preziosa esperienza.'

91 'Quella che appare alle nuove generazioni, e attraverso le nuove generazioni, ha i tratti di una vera e propria crisi di civiltà. . . . A partire di qui noi ci proponiamo di dialogare e misurarci con i giovani, con una sola discriminante: quella del rifiuto e della lotta aperta alla violenza eversiva.'

92 'Lasciando da parte le frange della violenza avventuristiche, del disegno elitario e antipopolo del "tanto peggio tanto meglio", lasciando anche da parte le frange di folklorismo "creativo", c'è nel movimento una massa di giovani che è certamente spinta da un odio lacerante contro il regime che ha governato il Paese per trent'anni, ma la cui tensione verso un mutamento democratio e socialista sarebbe insensato mettere in dubbio'.

93 'Il movimento degli studenti ha affrontato una importante fase di chiarificazione, di confronto . . . Le parole sono confuse: ma questo esprime solo le difficoltà e i problemi che ci riguardano *tutti*. Nei gesti e nelle pratiche qualcosa di nuova è rintracciabile, è in marcia.'

94 'Chi sono . . . queste famose Brigate rosse? C'è davvero qualcuno che può ancora credere che questa organizzazione sia la stessa di quella, anni fa, nacque a Trento, nella sede della Facoltà di sociologia? Allora i suoi programmi erano farneticanti, ma oggi ciò che viene programmato è l'assassinio.'

95 '"All'inizio – spiega Giovannini del consiglio di fabbrica – quella delle BR era una tattica – come dire? – 'combinata'. Alle loro azioni terroristiche si univa sempre il tentativo di trovare il consenso di settori di lavoratori. . . . Erano molto attivi sindacalmente, tanto che qualcuno riuscì a farsi nominare delegato." Questa fase si è chiusa da tempo. Clandestini rispetto alla legge, i brigatisti – ammesso che alla Siemens ve ne sia ancora qualcuno – sono clandestini due volte rispetto ai lavoratori. Isolati e disprezzati hanno riportato la propria azione alla logica della pura provocazione. Uccidono, incendiano, sparano alle gambe e basta. I messaggi che seguono appaiono sempre più aspetti di uno stanco rituale, i relitti di un'originaria illusione. E in questa triste parabola si riflette, probabilmente, anche il processo di trasformazione rapidamente subito dalle Brigate rosse: da organizzazione di deliranti ideologhi della "lotta armata", a docile strumento della

strategia della tensione, ricettacolo di ogni infiltrazione in un torbido intreccio con la malavita comune.'

96 'Idalgo Macchiarini era stato sequestrato da un gruppo di ignoti autodefinitosi "brigate rosse", ma di chiara marca fascistica al servizio della provocazione padronale.'

97 'l'Italia . . . [è] ad una fase avanzatissima del rinnovamento, a cui la classe operaia, giunta alle soglie del governo dà un'impronta egemonica. Il terrorismo, l'eversione, la violenza, sono "uno dei tavoli" su cui i nemici della democrazia giocano le loro carte per impedire lo sbocco positivo della crisi. Però bisogna distinguere. È un errore, in cui molti cadono, fare confusione fra "neri" e "rossi" con l'argomento (in sé inconfutabile) che gli uni e gli altri, a prescindere dalle intenzioni, sono nemici della democrazia e della classe operaia. . . I "neri" e i "rossi" vogliono entrambi abbattere il regime democratico ed aprire la strada ad un regime autoritario. Ma i "neri" si fermano qui. I "rossi", invece, proclamano un secondo obiettivo: quello di provocare, con la nascita di un regime autoritario, la "ribellione del proletariato"'.

98 'c'è un'area di solidarietà "politica", composta da quelle organizzazioni estremistiche, al cui interno solo di recente hanno cominciato ad affiorare atteggiamenti di critica, di presa di distanza, di dissociazione . . . Accanto a quest'area "politica" . . . o dentro di essa, o in parte al vertice di essa, agiscono forze, uomini, niente affatto vittime di "suggestioni" e di "allucinazioni", ma, al contrario, consapevolmente intenti ad impiegare strumentalmente l'estremismo per scopi di lotta politica assai concreta. Si spiegano così certe "civetterie", certe "corteggiamenti", certi "patrocinii" a cui si dedicano questo o quell'uomo politico, questo o quel sindacalista, questa o quell'organizzazione periferica di partiti che pure hanno responsabilità nazionali. L'obiettivo da colpire è, naturalmente, il PCI. . . . Infine, non va dimenticato l'uso che dell'estremismo (e del terrorismo) è stato fatto da forze dello Stato interessate a battere il movimento democratico. Certe compromissioni sono ormai note a tutti. Altre lo sono meno. Certe passività, di questo o quel funzionario, di questo o quel magistrato, appaiono spesso assai sospette, a meno che non si spieghino con la paura.'

99 'se il singolo cittadino, se il membro o il dirigente di una organizzazione operaia e democratica, viene a sapere che un grave reato è in preparazione, deve forse tacere? Deve forse rispettare non si sa bene quali principii di "omertà"? I "garantisti" esasperati vorrebbero forse estendere la piaga dell'omertà mafiosa a tutta l'Italia? . . . la lotta contro il terrorismo . . . è un dovere *nazionale*, di primissimo piano. E in questo dovere rientra anche la collaborazione delle organizzazioni democratiche e dei singoli cittadini con la polizia e la magistratura.'

6

A cycle and its aftermath

The framing interactions traced through the previous chapter have been presented as the record of a political party's hostile engagement with contentious movements, designed to deny them political space and exclude their innovations from mainstream political repertoires. This reading requires us to assume that these contentious movements existed in their own right, rather than as the after-effect of a previous cycle; and that they had the potential to occupy the legitimate political space that the PCI denied them, rather than being inherently and pathologically violent.

Both of these positions are contested. My reading of the second cycle of contention builds on Sidney Tarrow's model of the first, early 1970s cycle. However, as I noted in chapter 2, Tarrow reads the entire period of the second cycle as an extended aftermath to the first. '[V]iolence was the product of the *end* of a period of mass mobilisation, when protest in most social and economic sectors was being institutionalised' (Tarrow 1989: 324; emphasis in original): the armed groups grew out of stranded activist minorities who adopted extreme tactics in an effort to win their constituencies back from the PCI. The autonomist groups of the late 1970s were 'practically *born* in clandestinity'; 'the only way for them to gain the attention of the workers was through violence' (Tarrow 1991: 60; emphasis in original). Meanwhile, the innovations of the first cycle were absorbed and Italian democracy reaped the benefit: 'As the Italian cycle ended in violence and demobilisation, the forced entries, obstructions and symbolic actions of the peak of the cycle were gone, but the factory assemblies, the public marches and meetings, and the lobbying campaigns remained' (Tarrow 1989: 347).

Tarrow's model can be broken down into five propositions:

A1 The 1970s were characterised by a single cycle of contention, which peaked with the absorption of social movement innovations by the institutional Left.
A2 The repertoire of democratic protest was enriched by the cycle, with an enduringly heightened level of activity.

A3 The mass demobilisation which followed the waning of the cycle prompted minorities to engage in violent actions.
A4 As the cycle ended, these groups' actions developed into outright terrorism.
A5 Terrorist actions themselves grew progressively more violent, sustained by 'outbidding' between rival groups.

An alternative model of the period, supporting the analysis given in the previous chapter, would offer the following propositions:

B1 The 1970s were characterised by two successive cycles of contention; the first of these peaked with the institutionalisation of social movement innovations, while the second was met with hostility by the mainstream Left.
B2 The repertoire of democratic protest was impoverished by the second, hostile engagement process, leading to decreased levels of protest activity.
B3 Actions stigmatised as illegal and violent were central to the repertoire of this second cycle, and were carried out on a mass scale.
B4 Armed violence accompanied this second cycle from the outset and became a large-scale phenomenon at the time of the Left's hostile engagement with the cycle.
B5 'Outbidding' between rival groups only became a significant factor when the armed milieu itself was in decline.

Testing these propositions, accordingly, involves answering five questions:

Q1 *Cycles of contention*: can two successive cycles be identified, or only one?
Q2 *Level of democratic protest*: at the end of the 1970s, is it elevated or depressed?
Q3 *Violent acts*: were these carried out minorities left isolated by the ebb of a cycle of contention, or by large groups whose actions formed part of a second cycle?
Q4 *Terrorism*: was this the last resort of isolated groups in a period of declining activity, or a minority practice which spread more widely in response to the blockage of a mass movement?
Q5 *Terrorist 'outbidding'*: at what point is this process observable, if at all?

A cycle in review, 1: mass movements

In order to test these propositions, I have used the chronology compiled by Vinciguerra and Cipriani (Vinciguerra and Cipriani 1999). This extraordinary resource, initially developed by an imprisoned (and unrepentant) member of the neo-fascist terrorist group Ordine Nuovo, amounts to an almanac of Italian political unrest throughout the period and beyond. While not an academic source, the chronology is fuller and more detailed than any other single source; I have no reason to doubt its broad accuracy.

In the following analysis I have used the period from 1970 to 1981 as a frame of reference. While this is considerably longer than the period of the second cycle of contention, it allows for comparison with the peak years of the first cycle of contention. It also corresponds to the life span of the BR and, with a very few exceptions, of the armed milieu. (No armed group predated 1970; only two armed groups, other than successor groups to the BR or PL, survived beyond 1981, and both of these disbanded in 1982.) The extended time frame also makes it possible to consider the after-effects of the cycle and the PCI's engagement with it; I shall review the 'aftermath' of the cycle as it affected the mass movements, the armed groups and the PCI.

Table 6.1 and figure 6.1 give an overview of this period in the 'mass' perspective; the activities of the armed groups are covered separately. Events have been categorised under the headings of 'Demonstration', 'Strike', 'Occupation' and '*Autoriduzione*'. 'Occupation' refers to workplace and university occupations, including events such as permanent assemblies and *cortei interni*; '*Autoriduzione*' includes housing occupations and *mercatini rossi* as well as more direct forms of action against the cost of living. Strikes and demonstrations held in support of the government, against the autonomists or against 'violence' have been excluded; with this exception, the figures include PCI-endorsed as well as autonomist strikes and demonstrations. The figures refer not to individual actions but to the number of days on which an action took place or began (with exceptions noted below); multiple events called on a single day are only counted once per category.

The figures in the '*Autoriduzione*' category may be incomplete, particularly for the years 1976–8: Vinciguerra and Cipriani record few incidents of *autoriduzione* associated with the 'proletarian youth circles' and the 'move-

Table 6.1 Days including demonstrations, strikes, occupations and *autoriduzione* actions, 1970–81

	1970	1971	1972	1973	1974	1975	1976	1977	1978	1979	1980	1981
Demonstration	124	129	92	76	98	140	111	132	87	48	14	59
Strike	100	96	132	79	81	84	79	73	58	47	16	15
Occupation	26	56	29	17	39	57	28	36	27	5	2	1
Autoriduzione	7	49	16	4	39	52	64	36	18	3	1	6

Source: Vinciguerra and Cipriani (1999)

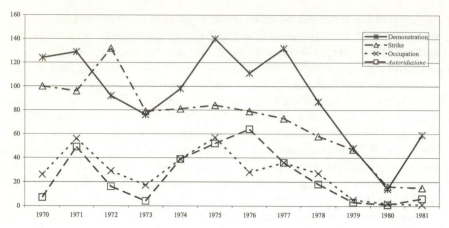

Figure 6.1 Days including demonstrations, strikes, occupations and *autoriduzione* actions, 1970–81
Source: Vinciguerra and Cipriani 1999

ment of 1977'. That said, Del Bello's chronology for 1977 (Del Bello 1997: 305–60), which features numerous *autoriduzione* actions associated with the 'movement', gives the same total number of incidents for the year (36); a composite figure, including all incidents recorded in either source, might be around 45 or 50. The figure for 1978, on the other hand, is inflated by the fact that many occupations of empty property are only reported at the time of their evacuation; 10 of the 18 incidents listed for 1978 are police evacuations of properties, many of which were almost certainly occupied before 1978. Similar factors will probably have depressed the figures for 1976 and 1977. Taking both these distortions into account, we can speculate that accurate figures for 1976, 1977 and 1978 might be around 80, 60 and 10 respectively. The figures may also give a misleading impression of the health of contentious movements towards the end of the period, since abortive as well as successful actions are recorded; the single episode of *autoriduzione* recorded in 1980, for instance, took place when a group of CAO activists attempted to pay their electricity bills at a reduced rate and were arrested on the spot.

With these caveats, table 6.1 allows us to give a sketch of the course of the second cycle in its 'mass' form. The high level of strike activity in 1972 and the sharp drop in 1973 mark the close of the first cycle of contention; 1973 also shows the lowest figure for workplace occupations of the 1970–8 period. The relatively high strike figures for 1974 and 1975 may reflect a successful, if temporary, institutionalisation of workplace militancy. Alternatively, these figures may represent a contradictory trend, with pressures for workplace pacification being countered by the influence of the autonomists.

Support for the latter interpretation comes from the level of workplace occupations, which rose substantially in 1974 and reached a peak in 1975. Set against a relatively small increase in strike activity, this suggests that a large and growing proportion of workplace activism was taking disorderly forms. As the bosses and unions reasserted control within the factories, the level of occupations declined sharply between 1975 and 1976, while the level of strike activity fell less dramatically. The resurgence in occupations in 1977, against a continuing fall in the level of strike activity, reflects the spread of university occupations and of the 'movement of 1977'. Thereafter, the trend for both strikes and workplace occupations is downwards, with particularly sharp drops between 1978 and 1979 (occupations), and between 1979 and 1980 (strikes).

There were numerous occurrences of organised squatting and other forms of *autoriduzione* in 1971, at the peak of the first cycle. This type of protest was widespread in the first cycle of contention, declined sharply after 1971 but returned to prominence from 1974 onwards. The high and rising figures for *autoriduzione* between 1974 and 1976 reflect the continuing incidence of older forms of action, from rent strikes to *mercatini rossi*, together with a rise in *autoriduzione* in its new, luxury-oriented forms. Heavily policed, *autoriduzione* declined steadily after 1976, showing only a slight revival in 1981. Demonstrations, lastly, share with the other forms of action a low point in 1973, at the close of the first cycle. Subsequently, figures for demonstrations rise to a peak in 1975, drop in 1976 (the peak year for *autoriduzione*), then rise again in 1977, before falling continuously until 1980. Alone of all these forms of action, demonstrations rise substantially in 1981; in part, this reflects the contemporary Europe-wide mobilisation for nuclear disarmament (see table 6.2).

Vinciguerra and Cipriani's chronology thus supports the thesis that a second cycle of contention began after the trough of 1973. The figures suggest a progressive diffusion of new forms of protest, increasingly dissociated from the industrial activism of the first phase. The new forms of action began

Table 6.2 Days including feminist and anti-nuclear demonstrations, 1970–81

	1970	1971	1972	1973	1974	1975	1976	1977	1978	1979	1980	1981
Feminist		1	1	3	2	14	17	12	14	9	3	3
% of total		0.8	1.1	3.9	2.0	10.0	15.3	9.1	16.1	18.8	21.4	5.1
Anti-nuclear								8	6	6	2	18
% of total								6.1	6.9	12.5	14.3	30.5
All others	124	128	91	73	96	126	94	112	67	33	9	38
% of total	100.0	99.2	98.9	96.1	98.0	90.0	84.7	84.8	77.0	68.7	64.3	64.4

Source: Vinciguerra and Cipriani (1999)

in and around the factory: demonstrations and workplace occupations peaked in 1975. As Autonomia declined in the factory, community-based activism took its place: *autoriduzione* peaked in 1976. The new vocabulary of protest was then adopted by the 'proletarian youth movement' and the 'movement of 1977': hence the second peak for demonstrations in 1977, alongside reduced levels of activity in all other categories. The figures also show that each of these forms of activism declined between 1978 and 1980, particularly steeply in the case of workplace occupations and *autoriduzione* actions: the two forms most closely associated with the second cycle of contention.

In short, Vinciguerra and Cipriani's data are consistent with the model of the second cycle of contention presented in the previous chapter, and tend to bear out propositions B1 and B3 above. Two cycles can be identified rather than one; and the illegal, confrontational and often violent repertoire of direct action associated with Autonomia was central to the growth and spread of this cycle, rather than an effect of its decline.

Into the aftermath, 1: mass movements

in '78 everything was still standing [. . .] Summer '78, after Moro, found us in our thousands at Nova Siri in Basilicata, closing down the CNEN nuclear waste dump. Right after 7 April 1979 the anti-nuclear movement mobilised to block-ade Caorso, with tens of thousands of people filling the Piacenza stadium. In '80, the year of the earthquake, despite hundreds of people getting arrested or taking flight . . . the movement found itself in the solidarity of local people . . . creating the conditions for regrouping. '83, the year of recovery. (Miliucci 1997: 18)[1]

The figures shown only offer limited support for proposition B2: conten-tious activity declined after the 'engagement' of 1977 but did so relatively slowly, with a revival of some forms of activity in 1981. Miliucci's account suggests two explanations. Firstly, faced with a choice between demobilisa-tion and illegality, many activists appear to have responded with a defiant commitment to activism: this impression is also borne out by the diffusion of armed struggle tactics in 1978–9. In 1978 the CPV, who had kept their distance from the 'area' until the previous year, began joint work with the autonomists of *Rosso*, significantly renamed *Rosso: Per il potere operaio* (Progetto Memoria 1994: 116). In the same period, the CPV collaborated with autonomists close to Negri on another journal, *Autonomia* (Piazza 1987: 266). Both joint initiatives were short-lived.

Miliucci's reference to anti-nuclear activism is also significant. Vinciguerra and Cipriani's data suggest that, in the 'aftermath', a significant role was played by feminist and anti-nuclear mobilisations.

As table 6.2 shows, feminist events occurred during the 'innovation' phase of the second cycle and were a significant presence during the 'diffusion' phase; activism directed against nuclear power and nuclear weaponry first appeared during the 'engagement' phase. After 1977, feminist and anti-nuclear activity accounted for an increasingly significant proportion of a greatly reduced number of events.

Cohen and Arato's analysis of 'new social movements' is germane here. They associate this type of movement (typically understood to include the women's and anti-nuclear movements) with 'self-limiting radicalism': 'a self-understanding that abandons revolutionary dreams in favour of radical reform that is not necessarily and primarily oriented to the state' (Cohen and Arato 1992: 493). For Cohen and Arato, 'self-limitation' represents a reaction against revolutionary socialism; they argue that the historical experience of Communism showed that 'these fundamentalist projects lead to the breakdown of societal steering and the suppression of social plurality' (Cohen and Arato 1992: 16). In the Italian context, the increasing prominence of 'new social movement' activism in the 'aftermath' phase of the second cycle seems to derive not from a ideological stance such as this, but from a strategic decision to avoid engagement with a hostile gatekeeper. In other words, 'self-limiting radicalism' appears to be less the result of a decision to abandon 'revolutionary dreams', more an after-effect of defeat.

A cycle in review, 2: 'armed struggle' groups

We [the BR] came out of '77 in good shape . . . At the same time, we could see that those people who had made different choices didn't know what the hell to do any more; from the first of January 1978, they didn't know what to do. ('Andrea' 1997: 200)[2]

The fourth and fifth propositions to be tested relate to the armed struggle milieu. Propositions A4 and A5 above would lead us to expect a three-stage chronology: first the adoption of violent and illegal tactics by small groups, then terrorism, then 'outbidding' and higher levels of terrorist violence. By contrast, propositions B4 and B5 suggest that armed activity ran alongside the second cycle, which was characterised by mass illegality; that armed activity spread and gained in intensity following the political exclusion of the mass movements of the second cycle; and that violent 'outbidding' only appeared when this large-scale armed milieu was itself in decline. The next two figures and tables address these issues. Table 6.3 and figure 6.2 show the distribution, year by year, of the 472 actions claimed by or attributed to the BR between 1970 and 1981, together with the recruitment dates of the 426 people known to have joined the BR.

Table 6.3 BR actions and recruitment figures, 1970–81

	1970	1971	1972	1973	1974	1975	1976	1977	1978	1979	1980	1981	Total
BR actions	4	6	28	7	25	30	53	56	106	65	61	31	472
% of total	0.8	1.3	5.9	1.5	5.3	6.4	11.2	11.9	22.5	13.8	12.9	6.6	100.0
BR recruits	10	32	4	1	10	10	33	48	138	92	34	14	426
% of total	2.3	7.5	0.9	0.2	2.3	2.3	7.7	11.3	32.4	21.6	8.0	3.3	100.0

Source: Moss (1989: 67)

Note: Actions include actions claimed by by BR-WA. Moss's recruitment figures only account for 252 of the BR's 426 members; 'The remaining 176 [sic] would be distributed through the period 1978–82' (Moss 1989: 67). His figures also exclude the group's founder members. I have assumed a founding membership of 10 and distributed the remaining 164 unaccounted recruits over the period 1978–81, in proportion to Moss's figures for those years

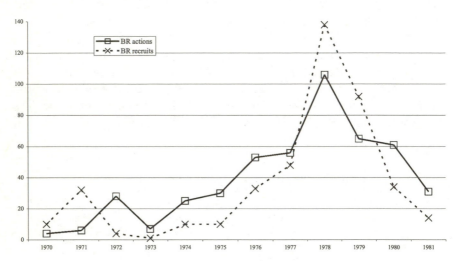

Figure 6.2 BR actions and recruitment figures, 1970–81
Source: Moss 1989: 67

BR actions were relatively sporadic and showed no particular trend until 1975. Thereafter the group had what was effectively a five-year peak period: over 70 per cent of actions took place between 1976 and 1980. The curve for BR recruitment rises later and falls more steeply; over 65 per cent of recruits joined the group in the three years from 1977 to 1979. This suggests that, as the mass movements faced institutional hostility and went into decline, militant activists gravitated towards the BR in particular, as well as the armed milieu in general. The figures for BR actions, on the other hand, suggest that the group responded to and capitalised on the success of the mass movements rather than their decline.

Table 6.4 and figure 6.3 show the 2,841 actions claimed by or attributed to left-wing armed groups other than the BR, together with the dates of formation and dissolution of the 44 significant non-BR armed groups formed in the period and the 40 groups dissolved in the period.

Armed activity outside the BR was sporadic between 1970 and 1976; after this it rose rapidly for two years, then declined more slowly over the next three.

Table 6.4 Non-BR armed groups: groups formed, groups dissolved and actions, 1970–81

	1970	1971	1972	1973	1974	1975	1976	1977	1978	1979	1980	1981	Total
Actions	1	17	42	24	72	62	116	404	1004	737	197	110	2786
% of total	0.0	0.6	1.5	0.9	2.6	2.2	4.2	14.5	36.0	26.5	7.1	3.9	100.0
Groups formed	2	0	3	2	3	1	7	8	6	8	2	2	44
% of total	4.5	0.0	6.8	4.5	6.8	2.3	15.9	18.2	13.6	18.2	4.5	4.5	100.0
Groups dissolved	0	0	3	0	3	1	3	4	2	9	11	4	40
% of total	0.0	0.0	6.8	0.0	6.8	2.3	6.8	9.1	4.5	20.5	25.0	9.1	90.9

Sources: Moss (1989: 37, 67); Progetto Memoria (1994)

Note: The total of 44 is based on Progetto Memoria (1994), which gives a total figure of 47 groups. I have excluded the BR, seven BR successor groups and two BR spinoff groups, but added to the total seven groups which are described as operating in their own right, but are assimilated to a parent group in the main listing. The total of 40 groups dissolved in the period excludes two small autonomist groups which dissolved in 1982 and two Prima Linea splinters which dissolved in 1983 and 1984. Percentages have been calculated to include these, i.e. out of 44.

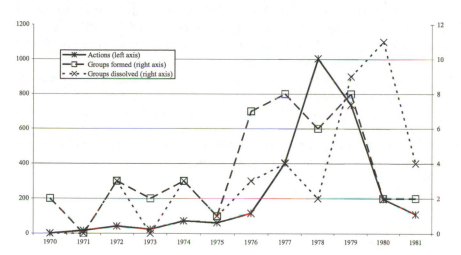

Figure 6.3 Non-BR armed groups: groups formed, groups dissolved and actions, 1970–81
Source: Moss 1989: 37, 67; Progetto Memoria 1994

While the figures for actions and group formation follow a similar curve to those relating to the BR, small-group actions were concentrated into a narrower space of time than those of the BR: 77 per cent of actions between 1970 and 1981 took place between 1977 and 1979, with 11 per cent taking place in the next two years and 12 per cent in the entire 1970–6 period. The difference reflects the greater 'professionalism' of the BR, and in particular its greater autonomy from the (increasingly barren) mass movement terrain. Unlike the figures for BR membership, the number of groups in the milieu grows more slowly in 1978–9 than in 1974–7; taken together, these two trends suggest that the 'engagement' phase promoted consolidation of the armed milieu around the BR. The figures for group formation both rise and peak earlier than the figures for BR membership: 29 groups out of 44 were formed in the four years from 1976 to 1979. Eleven groups (one in four) formed in the six years before 1976; four formed in 1980–1. The figures for group dissolution echo this trend. 20 groups (over 45 per cent) dissolved in 1979 and 1980: a period which immediately followed, and overlapped with, the peak period for group formation.

Both these sets of data suggest, firstly, that armed activity accompanied the second cycle from the outset; secondly, that the armed groups at their peak represented a widespread and relatively large-scale phenomenon in their own right; and, thirdly, that the peak period for armed activity directly followed the peak in mass movement activity, and was followed by a rapid decline. Rather than an obstinate and wrong-headed reaction to the closure of a cycle, the armed milieu is better seen, in accordance with proposition B4, as a junior partner of the mass movements of the cycle: a partner whose greater 'militarisation' enabled it initially to profit from the discomfiture of the mass movements, but which, with the exception of the BR, only had a very limited capacity for autonomous survival. This relationship is vividly illustrated in table 6.5 and figure 6.4, below.

The figures bear out neither Tarrow's model of a complete divorce between the two spheres nor the idealistic model of *doppia militanza*. What remains is a complex and evolving relationship between two distinct but overlapping milieux. During the mass movements' period of diffusion, there was a similar diffusion of armed tactics. In the 'engagement' period a more contradictory relationship prevailed: the armed groups offered to build on the successes of

Table 6.5 Mass events and armed actions, 1970–81

	1970	1971	1972	1973	1974	1975	1976	1977	1978	1979	1980	1981
Mass events	257	330	269	176	257	333	282	277	190	103	33	81
Armed actions	5	23	70	31	97	92	169	460	1110	802	258	141
Total	262	353	339	207	354	425	451	737	1300	905	291	222

Sources: Moss (1989: 37, 67); Vinciguerra and Cipriani (1999)

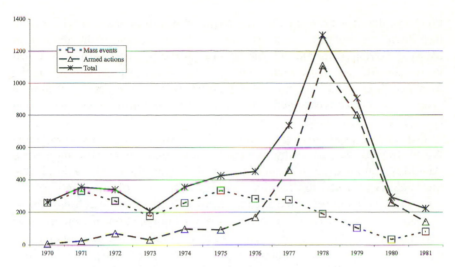

Figure 6.4 Mass events and armed actions, 1970–81
Source: Vinciguerra and Cipriani 1999

the movement, defend its gains and recover its losses, subject to the move-ment's acceptance of the armed groups' leadership. Viewed from a pure 'movementist' standpoint, this was an inherently unacceptable demand. The movement could not meet the PCI's demands and renounce 'violence' without losing much of its identity; neither could it abandon the principle of equality among all participants in an action, violent actions included. That way lay the PCI's own framing of the movement as divided into 'men of violence' and their naive followers: in the metropolitan Indians' mocking account, 'we followed 50 autonomists using this technique: 200 of us behind each one of them . . . These 50 squaddists then persuaded us to throw bottles at the police jeeps, which to our amazement burst into flames' (Del Bello 1997: 315).[3]

However, in practice the principle of equal participation in violent actions, like that of *doppia militanza,* was more honoured in the breach than the observance. The constituency of the movement, from which the participants in large-scale actions were drawn, was a patchwork of *gruppusculo* veterans, autonomist activists and unorganised protesters. Within the movement the armed groups and the 'hard' autonomists had considerable prestige as profes-sionals of violence – all the more so in a period when policing was becoming increasingly militarised. Consequently the question of 'militarisation' was not confined to the armed groups and their sympathisers, but caused constant and divisive debate within the movement: different positions were held by different groups (e.g. the 'hard' autonomists of the CAO as against the Bolog-nese 'creative wing') and by factions within groups (with a group's *servizio d'ordine* typically taking a 'harder' view than its political leadership). In 1978

Piperno called for the armed groups to put themselves at the service of the movement, adding the 'geometric firepower' displayed in the murder of Moro's bodyguards to the 'terrible beauty' of the March 1977 riots (quoted in Wright 2002: 214; translation modified). More prosaically, prior to the demonstration of 12 March, one BR member recalls being approached by a group of young activists, who asked him to take them to the demonstration and organise them (Piccioni 1997: 131–2).

During 1977, the developing relationship between the armed groups and the movement was driven by two contradictory dynamics. The movement could not submit itself to the leadership of the 'professionals' while it had the strength to assert itself in its own right; but the 'professionals' of the armed milieu could only take a leadership role while there was a movement to lead. The intensification of debate around the question of militarisation was a product of the repression which tended to reduce the numbers participating in movement actions, however public. Ironically, the 'professionalisation' of violence did not counter this trend but entrenched it.

That said, at no point between 1973 and 1978 is there a simple progression from lower to higher levels of violence, larger to smaller groups, mass participation to isolation. Indeed, as figure 6.4 illustrates, before 1979 there is no point where the total number of events falls from year to year. Rather, the years 1975–7 see a succession of peaks: workplace autonomist activism; *autoriduzione*; the movement of 1977; and armed activity, a fourth peak in 1978. Given the scale of the armed milieu at this stage, as well as the close relationship between the armed groups and the mass movements of the second cycle, it is reasonable to view this as a specialised case of repertoire innovation. Effectively, we can qualify proposition B4 by understanding the armed milieu as a movement in its own right: a subordinate actor in the earlier phases of the cycle, coming to dominate it in 1978.

Initially, the armed milieu profited from the suppression of the mass movements: in the conditions of 1978 and 1979, relatively small groups planning actions in relative clandestinity were considerably more viable than the mass public activism of earlier years. However, once deprived of a dependable milieu of movement sympathisers (the 'locals' of Moss's analysis (Moss 1989)) the armed groups were thrown back on their own support structures, whose carrying capacity was necessarily limited. These conditions also cut into the ideological basis of armed activism, which could no longer be situated within a broader revolutionary project; for many, the result was a dogged determination to keep going for as long as possible. For the more organised groups, the BR's successor groups in particular, this could amount to several years. The last murder by a group unrelated to the BR was carried out in January 1982; the last murder claimed by a BR successor group, in April 1988.

In this context, it's worth revisiting Tarrow's observation on the association between violent tactics and clandestinity: 'Once repression is triggered, the group has no alternative but to go underground, where the only tactical alternatives left to it are violent' (Tarrow 1991: 58). After the initial (and not insignificant) innovation represented by the choice of the armed route, a high proportion of the armed groups' actions fell into familiar categories of criminal activity: bank robbery, kidnapping and extortion, gun battles with the police. For some groups, the NAP in particular, this choice of terrain was itself a statement of intent, heralding the politicisation of the career criminal milieu. Many others, particularly in the later stages of the cycle, found this choice forced on them by the decline of the mass movements and the demands of clandestine operation; an emblematic case was the formation in 1979, by militants unwilling to abandon the armed struggle, of a group calling itself 'Rapinatori Comunisti' ('Communist Robbers') (Progetto Memoria 1994: 89, 139). Tarrow's observation is suggestive but misdirected. The change of tactics necessitated by the isolation of the armed groups was not from peaceful to violent actions, but from actions answering (however distantly) to the demands of a broader movement to actions whose only point of reference was the group itself.

Tables 6.6 and 6.7 address the question of violence and 'outbidding', reviewing the relationship between the progress of the cycle, the number of actions

Table 6.6 BR actions, woundings and killings, by year and by period, 1970–81

a. By year

	1970	1971	1972	1973	1974	1975	1976	1977	1978	1979	1980	1981
Total actions	4	6	28	7	25	30	53	56	106	65	61	31
Killings	0	0	0	0	3	2	6	2	15	10	13	6
% of total	0.0	0.0	0.0	0.0	12.0	6.7	11.3	3.6	14.2	15.4	21.3	19.4
Woundings	0	0	0	0	0	3	2	19	18	14	11	5
% of total	0.0	0.0	0.0	0.0	0.0	10.0	3.8	33.9	17.0	21.5	18.0	16.1
% non-violent	100.0	100.0	100.0	100.0	88.0	83.3	84.9	62.5	68.9	63.1	60.7	64.5

b. By period

	Innovation	Diffusion	Engagement	Aftermath	
	1970–3	1974–7	1978–9	1980–1	Total
Total actions	45	164	171	92	472
Killings	0	13	25	19	57
% of total	0.0	7.9	14.6	20.7	12.1
Woundings	0	24	32	16	72
% of total	0.0	14.6	18.7	17.4	15.3
% non-violent	100.0	77.5	66.7	62.0	72.7

Sources: Moss (1989: 67); Progetto Memoria (1994)
Note: As in table 6.3, figures for 1980 and 1981 include actions by BR-WA

Table 6.7 Non-BR armed groups: actions and killings by year and by period, 1970–81

a. By year

	1970	1971	1972	1973	1974	1975	1976	1977	1978	1979	1980	1981
Total actions	1	17	42	24	72	62	116	404	1004	737	197	110
Killings	0	1	0	0	1	1	2	3	13	11	11	7
% of total	0.0	5.9	0.0	0.0	1.4	1.6	1.7	0.7	1.3	1.5	5.6	6.4
% non-lethal	100.0	94.1	100.0	100.0	98.6	98.4	98.3	99.3	98.7	98.5	94.4	93.6

b. By period

	Innovation 1970–3	Diffusion 1974–7	Engagement 1978–9	Aftermath 1980–1	Total
Total actions	84	654	1741	307	2786
Killings	1	7	24	18	50
% of total	1.2	1.1	1.4	5.9	1.8
% non-lethal	98.8	98.9	98.6	94.1	98.2

Sources: Moss (1989: 37, 67); Progetto Memoria (1994)

carried out by the BR and other groups in any given year, and the proportion of these actions which involved violence against the person. The period has been broken down into four phases: 'Innovation' (1970–3), 'Diffusion' (1974–7), 'Engagement' (1978–9) and 'Aftermath' (1980–1). These phases broadly follow the course of the second cycle until 1977; the armed groups' 'Engagement' and 'Aftermath' phases, following from the PCI's change of course in December 1977, were not examined in detail in earlier chapters.

Between 1970 and 1973, the BR's sporadic actions were all directed against property. Actions quadrupled over the period 1974–7 as compared with the previous four years; in the next two years, the average number of actions per year doubled again, before halving in the last two years of the group's existence. Meanwhile, the BR's use of personal violence rose sharply before falling more slowly. Between 1974 and 1977, 24 woundings and 13 killings made up 22.5 per cent of the group's total actions. The proportion rose to over 30 per cent during 1978 and 1979, with woundings accounting for slightly more than half of all violent actions. After 1979 the group's level of activity ebbed, but the proportion of actions involving personal violence increased: in 1980 and 1981 violent actions accounted for nearly 40 per cent of the group's actions, while the majority of actions in the 'violent' category involved murder. The BR carried out five killings in the first six years of its existence but six in 1981, the year in which it ceased to exist as a unitary organisation; these figures amounted respectively to 5 per cent and over 20 per cent of its total actions in the two periods. The figures for 1977 represent a slight departure from this pattern, with over a third of actions involving non-lethal violence: the 19 woundings and two murders recorded in 1977 contrast with five and 11 respectively committed in the whole of the previous three years. It has been suggested that several demonstrative woundings carried out in 1977, epitomised by the wounding of three journalists in different cities on successive days in June, were primarily intended to enhance the prestige of the BR; the audience was less the general public than the area of Autonomia (Caselli and della Porta 1991: 98).

The curve described by the figures shown for non-BR groups (table 6.7) is similar but steeper: an eightfold increase in the level of actions between 1970–3 and 1974–7 is followed in the next two years by a further fivefold increase in the average number of actions per year. The drop between the 'engagement' and 'aftermath' phases is also steeper, in line with the looser organisational structures of the diffuse milieu. As with the BR, the proportion of actions involving killing rises sharply in the aftermath phase, although over 90 per cent of actions are still non-lethal.

As table 6.8 suggests, the BR stood out in its commitment to the use of personal violence. The BR accounts for 20 per cent of actions in the diffusion phase, less than 10 per cent in the period of engagement and nearly 25 per cent in the aftermath. However, the BR alone accounts for 65 per cent of the murders carried out in the phase of diffusion, and 50 per cent of those in the phases of engagement and aftermath. (The 'innovation' phase is omitted from this table: the Gruppo XXII ottobre's 1971 killing of Alessandro Floris was the only relevant murder before 1974.) Of the 44 non-BR armed groups active between 1970 and 1981, 23 carried out no killings, while another 13 carried out one. Prima Linea, founded in emulation of the BR's 'military' organisation, carried out another 19 killings, a third of the BR's total of 57. The BR's preparedness to kill was a defining feature of the organisation, central to its standing within a milieu whose own actions, if not non-violent, were almost exclusively non-lethal. Figure 6.5 also illustrates the contrast between the 1978–9 period and the previous seven years. This suggests that the wide-

Table 6.8 Armed groups by number of murder victims, 1974–81

	1974	1975	1976	1977	1978	1979	1980	1981
BR (and splinters)	3	2	6	2	15	10	13	6
Prima Linea	0	0	1	1	2	6	7	2
Other groups (>1 killing)	0	0	1	1	9	3	0	4
Other groups (1 killing)	1	1	0	1	2	2	4	1

Source: Progetto Memoria (1994)

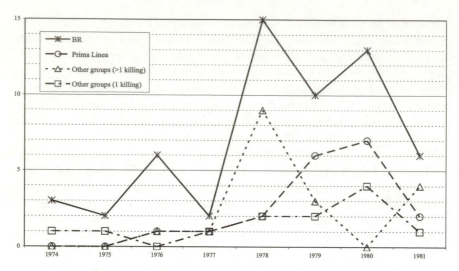

Figure 6.5 Armed groups by number of murder victims, 1974–81
Source: Progetto Memoria 1994

spread recourse to lethal violence was, like the upsurge in armed activity more generally, a product of the closure of engagement with the mass movements of the cycle.

Into the aftermath, 2: engaging with the armed struggle

At the end of 1977, the PCI finally acknowledged the existence of armed struggle groups which were genuinely on the Left. However, '[t]he basic goal of terrorism was still viewed as the thwarting of the PCI's efforts to be accepted as a legitimate partner in a national coalition' (Hellman 1988: 84). Three months after Pecchioli's exposition of the new line had heralded the 'engagement' phase, the BR launched their greatest single 'attack on the heart of the state'. Aldo Moro was kidnapped and his five bodyguards murdered on 16 March 1978; Moro himself was killed 55 days later. During the kidnap, the PCI played a leading role in the *partito di fermezza* ('resolute party'). Extending the refusal to negotiate which had previously been set out by Francesco Coco and endorsed by *l'Unità*, the party now argued that it was inappropriate for any constitutional party to negotiate with terrorists. This position was not universal within the *arco costituzionale*: Craxi advocated negotiation with the BR and made some attempts to contact them, exploiting the Potere Operaio background shared by BR members such as Valerio Morucci and prominent autonomists such as Franco Piperno.

The state's intransigence, bolstered by the PCI, cost Moro his life but prevented the BR from profiting from his death. The outcome fostered dissent within the BR and prompted a search for new forms of action by smaller armed groups. The milieu continued to expand until mid-1979; what could be called 'grass-roots armed struggle' briefly became a reality. Morucci and Adriana Faranda left the BR in February 1979 to form the Movimento Comunista Rivoluzionario (MCR; 'Revolutionary Communist Movement'). Faranda recalled, 'We thought it was necessary to go on fighting, but fighting in a completely different way from that of the Red Brigades. . . . The armed struggle was to be internal to what people really wanted to do, rather than drag them along behind it. Of course, in the end people rejected the armed struggle. It didn't take us long to find that out!' (quoted in Jamieson 1989: 282).

The hostility of the PCI towards the armed groups and the remnants of Autonomia reached its peak in April 1979. On 7 April the Communist-aligned judge Pietro Calogero issued a warrant for the arrest of Negri, Scalzone, Piperno and nine other autonomists, who were accused of involvement with the BR. According to the 'Calogero theorem', the BR, the smaller armed groups and the area of Autonomia made up a single subversive organisation, operating on overt and clandestine levels. Successive waves of arrests, and a series of qualifications to Calogero's highly coloured model, followed in June, July and December 1979 (Piazza 1987: 2–8). December 1979 also saw the passage of a new law which introduced mandatory prison sentences for members of organisations engaged in violence for subversive ends, as well as mandating reduced sentences for 'penitents' and enhanced sentences for crimes committed for subversive ends. The Calogero operation suppressed what remained of the area of Autonomia and deterred disorderly activism: 1980 was the year of Miliucci's 'hundreds of people getting arrested or taking flight', and the year in which (according to Vinciguerra and Cipriani 1999) only 14 days saw any kind of demonstration taking place.

The Calogero arrests also undermined the 'diffuse' armed groups which had been rooted in Autonomia; a faltering milieu now went into decline. As table 6.4 illustrates, 1979 saw the first overall drop in the number of active armed groups; a steeper drop followed in 1980. If successor groups to the BR and Prima Linea are discounted, the last new armed group was formed in 1980, while the last to dissolve did so in 1982. The sharpest decline in armed activity followed the Calogero arrests but predated the enactment of the December 1979 legislation, suggesting that a hostile engagement was already taking its toll. Moss notes: 'the most dramatic decline in the volume of violence . . . can be traced with some precision to mid-1979, between the semesters with the highest and lowest incidence of clandestine attacks recorded for any six-month period since 1976. The sharpest fall thus anticipated, rather than followed, the State's most innovative legislative initiatives' (Moss 1989: 77).

However, the remnants of the armed milieu were slow to disappear; the splintering BR alone carried out as many as 92 actions in the 1980–1 period, including 19 murders (a third of the total for which the group was responsible). For the most committed activists of the armed groups, the closure forced by Calogero seems, like the 1977 closure of engagement with the mass movements, to have prompted a renewed commitment to yet more confrontational repertoires. Table 6.9 demonstrates that the years after 1979 saw some of the worst excesses of the 'years of lead', with a dwindling number of groups carrying out more violent actions. This table includes both the BR and its successor groups.

After 1979 some elements of the increasingly factionalised BR returned to a focus on factory-based targets, but most victims came, as before, from the police and prison system (Centro di Documentazione 'Fausto e Jaio' 1995). By 1981 the BR had lost its presence in Milan, its original base, with the departure of BR-Walter Alasia (BR-WA), a Milan group which split from the BR at the end of 1980. The group that remained was divided between rival factions, which competed bitterly both before and after the formal dissolution of the organisation in October 1981. Table 6.10 suggests, in line with proposition B5, that Tarrow's model of violent 'outbidding' between rival groups maps most fully onto the last days of the BR in 1980–2, with small and isolated groups raising the level of confrontation so as to maintain their status. However, this took place within an armed milieu which had not entirely disappeared, but was weak enough to be dominated by the remnants of the BR. 'Outbidding' in this sense began in 1980 and ended in 1982; it was essentially a BR affair, a product of the independence and paramilitary organisation which it had cultivated since its founding, and which had enabled its successor groups to outlive the close of the second cycle.

Table 6.9 Armed groups active and responsible for killings by period, 1970–88

	Innovation	Diffusion	Engagement	Aftermath	Post-BR
	1970–3	1974–7	1978–9	1980–1	1982–8
Groups active during period	8	24	28	25	12
Groups responsible for killings	1	6	9	11	6
Killings in period	1	20	49	37	21
Killings per year	0.3	5	24.5	18.5	3

Source: Progetto Memoria (1994)

Table 6.10 Formation and dissolution of BR successor groups and killings carried out, 1980–8

	1980	1981	1982	1983	1984	1985	1986	1987	1988
BR successors formed	1	3	2	0	0	1	0	0	1
BR successors dissolved	0	0	2	3	0	0	0	2	1
Killings									
BR	8	3							
non-BR groups	11	7	3						
BR successors	5	3	10	1	1	1	1	3	1

Source: Progetto Memoria (1994)

The figures given in table 6.9 above for the 1978–9 and 1980–1 periods make a stark contrast with the progressive demobilisation recorded by table 6.1. After the peaceful demobilisation of the first cycle of contention in the early 1970s, the autonomists and the *servizi d'ordine* were still able to go in search of new repertoires. By 1979, the activists of the second cycle had been comprehensively excluded from the workplace, from working-class communities and from the streets; there was almost no one left standing, apart from the BR. As a result, significant numbers of activists moved on to the terrain which the BR had prepared. It was the ideological and physical exclusion of a strong movement, rather than the absorption of a movement in decline, which gave a brief period of mass support to armed struggle tactics, as well as helping the more organised armed groups to gain an extended lease of life.

The discussion of the 'aftermath' period in this chapter makes it possible to return to, and extend, the schematic representation of the 1966–77 period presented in chapter 2.

Table 6.11 does not show the 'one-cycle' model given in table 2.1, as the entire period would fall into that model's 'aftermath' phase. The table shows how innovation of both mass and 'armed struggle' tactics, in 1971–2, was followed by a phase of diffusion between 1973 and 1976. The table also shows how the diffusion of armed tactics continued during the mass movements' engagement with the PCI and the political sphere; the peak of armed activity, and the armed groups' own (exclusive) engagement with the PCI, took place in the mass movements' 'aftermath' period. Only in the early stages of the cycle did the interests of the two milieux coincide; in the post-1977 'aftermath' period they diverged completely, with the armed groups capitalising on the discomfiture of the mass movements. The 'outbidding' process, hypothesised by Tarrow as the missing link between autonomist activism and the rise of armed struggle tactics, can in fact only be identified

Table 6.11 Key events in the second cycle of contention, mass movement and armed milieu, 1971–82

Year	Event	Mass	Armed
		Phase	
1971	'Lavoro illegale' group set up within Potere operaio		I
	First actions by Brigate Rosse		I
1972	First autonomous committees	I	
1973	First national meetings of Autonomia	D	
1974	Housing occupations, rent strikes	D	
	Formation of NAP		D
1975	Organised shoplifting	D	
1976	Emergence of proletarian youth movement	D	
	Formation of Prima Linea		D
1977	Confrontation between PCI and 'movement of 1977'	E	
	Widespread adoption of 'armed struggle' tactics		D
1978	Moro kidnap: PCI advocates *fermezza*	A	E
1979	Calogero arrests	A	E
1980	Intensification of BR actions	A	A
1981	Dissolution of BR	A	A
1982	'Outbidding' between BR and successor groups	A	A

I = Innovation, D = Diffusion, E = Engagement, A = Aftermath

in the early 1980s aftermath phase of the second cycle, as a phenomenon of the declining armed milieu.

Into the aftermath, 3: the decline and fall of the PCI

The PCI's stance in the second cycle was closely linked with the 'historic compromise' project. The party's status as an informal ally of the DC, the high-water mark of the 'historic compromise', was confirmed on 16 March 1978; Aldo Moro was on his way to the opening of parliament when he was kidnapped by the BR. Subsequently, the PCI's unqualified and uncomprehending hostility, to the armed groups and to the remnants of the mass movements, shut the second cycle of contention down. The costs were partly borne by the PCI itself. After the local elections in May 1978, which saw a large drop in the PCI vote, Berlinguer criticised the single-minded pursuit of alliances with the DC by Communists in local government. The criticism was apt but, coming from the architect of the alliance policy, less than fair.

The 'historic compromise' strategy was subsequently revised to allow for the possibility of 'alternation' in government. This was precisely the possibility against which the lessons of Chile had originally been cited and the 'historic compromise' formulated. Now, however, 'alternation was no longer viewed as necessarily leading to a dangerous polarisation of society' (Hellman 1988: 33). In January 1979 the PCI demanded full inclusion in government, rejecting previous subtleties with the slogan 'Either in the government or in the opposition'; the result was the fall of the government and a new election, in which the PCI vote fell by 4 per cent as compared to 1976. 1979 and 1980 saw the PCI consigned to the opposition by old-style centre-left and centre-right governments. In November 1980, Berlinguer revived the old slogan of the 'democratic alternative', now defined as an alternative to the historic compromise: the objective was a broad alliance excluding the DC. Within the PCI this reversion to pre-1972 positions was greeted with relief and hyperbole: its announcement at a press conference in Salerno allowed it to be hailed as a *seconda svolta di Salerno* (Hellman 1988: 110). The 'democratic alternative' now bore some resemblance to the 'left alternative' favoured by Amendola's right wing of the PCI and De Martino's PSI. Under Craxi, however, the PSI's openness to the Right and closure to the Left had hardened into an increasingly cynical alliance with the DC; the party would be in government continuously from 1980 until the fall of the DC system in 1994.

For the PCI, DC indifference meant that a continuation of the 'historic compromise' was not an option: Berlinguer's alliance policy had failed. However, given the depth of Berlinguer's commitment to the 'historic compromise', as well as the policy's genuine (if heavily qualified) roots in the *via italiana*, the *seconda svolta* risked appearing superficial and opportunistic. What was effectively a new programme called either for a new leader or, at least, for theoretical underpinnings as comprehensive as those of the 'historic compromise'. Berlinguer supplied neither.

Under Berlinguer's leadership the PCI had effectively remade itself, foregrounding its beliefs in order and national unity and articulating them within a conservative and authoritarian framework. Despite early appearances of success, the longer-term results of this shift were disastrous. In 1976 the PCI had over 1.8 million members; in that year's general election it received 34.4 per cent of the votes cast. (Membership and voting figures from Istituto Carlo Cattaneo (2005) and Ginsborg (1990: 442) respectively.) These were the highest membership the party had had since the end of the 1950s and the highest national vote it had ever achieved. Neither would ever reach these levels again. Between 1978 and 1990, Italy had 14 governments; the DC was represented in all of them and Craxi's PSI in all but three. Corruption charges were laid against DC and PSI politicians as early as 1983, although party leaders dismissed them as politically motivated. This was a political system in need of renewal. However, the PCI had lost the capacity to benefit from

its 'gatekeeper' position. Instead, its engagement with the second cycle isolated the PCI from sources of innovation and ultimately from much of its
own constituency: 'the PCI and the [CGIL] . . . had sawn through the branch
on which, despite everything, they were still sitting' (Virno 1997: 647).[4]

At the 1987 general election the party took 26.6 per cent of the vote, its
lowest share at any general election since 1963. In 1988, the party's membership dropped below the post-war low of 1.5 million: a figure set in 1968,
before the party's engagement with the first cycle. In 1990 the party split to
form the Partito Democratico della Sinistra ('Democratic Party of the Left')
and Partito di Rifondazione Comunista ('Party of Communist Refounda-
tion'); the combined membership of the two successor parties fell from 1.1
million in 1991 to 800,000 in 1995.

The PCI's hostility to the second cycle of contention had a crushing impact
on the mass movements of the cycle, although it briefly (and indirectly)
fostered the diffusion of armed struggle tactics. The outcome of the cycle
was hardly any less disastrous for the party itself. 'Instead of riding the wave
of the 1970s, the PCI was flattened by it' (Hellman 1988: 218).

Notes

1 'nel '78 è ancora tutto in piedi . . . L'estate '78, quella del dopo Moro, ci trova in
   migliaia a Nova Siri, in Basilicata, a chiudere il deposito di scorie nucleari del
   CNEN. In pieno 7 aprile del '79 il movimento antinucleare si mobilita per bloccare
   Caorso con decine di migliaia di persone che rimpiono la stadio di Piacenza.
   Nell'80, al tempo del terremoto, nonostante centinaia di arresti, di fughe . . . il
   movimento si ritrova nella solidarietà alle popolazioni . . . gettando le basi per
   riconoscersi. L'83, l'anno della ripresa.'
2 'Noi siamo usciti bene dal '77 . . . Mentre invece vedevamo che chi aveva fatto
   scelte diverse poi non sapeva più che cazzo fare; dal 1° gennaio '78, non sapevano
   cosa fare.'
3 'abbiamo seguito 50 autonomi con la seguenti tecnica: 200 di noi dietro ognuno
   di loro. . . . Questi 50 squadristi ci hanno poi convinti a tirare delle bottiglie contro
   le autoblinde che con nostro stupore si incendiavano.'
4 'il Pci e il sindacato . . . hanno segato il rame sul quale essi pure, nonostante tutto,
   erano seduti'.

7

Do you remember revolution?

a crushing campaign to criminalise the entire movement was set in motion I read the paper in the morning any paper there was no difference from the latest hack to the illustrious intellectual sociologist philosopher psychologist historian novelist etcetera they all wrote that the movement was nothing but a convulsive uprising of displaced adventurists Fascists schizophrenics delinquents who needed to be got rid of as quickly as possible in order to save democracy and civilised coexistence we had a sense of powerlessness in the face of this systematic falsification of everything but we believed that there was no choice but to accept the challenge somehow on the terrain of communication and so we decided to set up a movement radio station[1]

. . .

I asked about the radio station how it had gone with the radio station Ortica started to laugh again the station was ready to go we had everything we had a waveband we even had a telephone we'd done all the voice tests with Kina's voice one two three testing he laughed that's all we managed to say one two three testing it was all there ready to go we only had to press a button and speak but we didn't have anything to say any more nobody was going to the centre any more and every day there was a new disaster someone got arrested someone went mad someone shot somebody someone committed suicide everyone had disappeared there was nothing to say any more and so it all sat there gathering dust the transmitter the tape deck the amplifier the microphone and Kina's voice (Balestrini 1987: 211–12, 258)[2]

Memory, history, forgetting

This book has two distinct goals, each of which depends to some extent on the other. One is to tell the story of the movements of the second cycle. Between 1972 to 1977, tens of thousands of people were active in the different movement milieux: they demonstrated, occupied factories, read radical literature, withheld the rent, trained with weapons, went shoplifting, formed groups, went to conferences, smashed shop windows, wrote radical literature, planted home-made bombs, left restaurants without paying, fought with neo-fascists, gatecrashed cinemas, wrote on walls and hung out in social centres. Balestrini and Moroni's phrase '*L'orda d'oro*' – 'The Golden Horde' – is apt. The movements of the period were confrontational and lawless at best; their actions, at worst, were tragic and vile. But they represent an experience – or rather, a panoply of experiences – which was creative and innovative on all levels: tactical, organisational, ideological. Perhaps most striking of all was the dominant mood of these movements: an unyielding, rebellious playfulness, combining intransigent anger at the old world with a good-humoured confidence that they could build a new one – or have fun trying.

The movements described in this book were a sociological phenomenon worthy of study. Their seemingly paradoxical politics – combining pluralism with class analysis, achievable material goals with revolutionary ambitions – set them apart from the 'new social movement' template, which dominates study of European social movements in the 1970s. They also represent a major element in the family tree of contemporary radical activism, as well as a significant episode in the history of Italian Marxism. The armed struggle milieu, in particular, deserves to be accorded much greater prominence in discussions of political violence, terrorism and counter-terrorism. There are references to the movements in studies by Moss (1989), Jamieson (1989), Lumley (1990), Della Porta (1995) and Wright (2002), but until now no comprehensive account of their history has been available to English-speaking readers. This book brings into the light an important group of radical movements, which had been threatened not so much with the condescension of posterity as with being forgotten outright.

The name missing from the previous paragraph is Tarrow, who has touched on this area on a number of occasions (Tarrow 1983, 1989, 1991, 1996, 1998). My second purpose in writing this book is to engage with Tarrow's model of the cycle of contention and to demonstrate that it is in need of modification and extension. In this respect the 1972–7 period, and the second cycle of contention, illustrates how Tarrow's approach, unmodified, produces inadequate and misleading conclusions. More specifically, I have tried to remove the normative assumptions which limit the reach of Tarrow's model. Tarrow begins from the assumption that the outcome of a cycle of contention is positive, in the sense of increasing the available range of forms of political participation: 'Cycles of protest are the crucibles within which the repertoire of collective action expands' (Tarrow 1989: 20). From this unexamined assumption, it follows that the engagement process follows an immanent logic which is essentially benign, leading all the valuable innovations of the cycle to be absorbed into the political mainstream. A related assumption is that violence must be a pathological symptom of the decline of a previously healthy social movement; this assumption underlies formulations such as

Tarrow's reference to 'extremists . . . adopting increasingly violent tactics' in a 'spiral of violence' (Tarrow 1989: 320).

The history of the 1972–7 cycle of contention demonstrates that processes of innovation, diffusion and engagement can be driven by illegal and violent tactics, as well as by protest tactics which are no more than rowdy. The events of 1977, in particular, also demonstrate that the engagement phase is a contingent political process, whose outcome depends on the actions of the gatekeeper rather than on the nature of the innovations of the cycle. We have seen how movement innovations were labelled as unacceptable as part of the process of being rejected, rather than being rejected because they were unacceptable in themselves.

The two goals of this study are thus interdependent, in the sense that a full account of the period is necessary to demonstrate the shortcomings of Tarrow's model (and, it should be said, the strength of the same model once a few modifications have been made). However, interdependence runs both ways: a full account of the period is only possible once the normative assumptions described have been discarded. Tarrow's own brief account of the period is written on the basis of these assumptions: that violent activism is a symptom of social movement decline, and that movement innovations rejected as criminal must in fact be inherently criminal. A history of the period written on that basis would systematically neglect, ignore and forget the experiences of the second cycle of contention: experiences which, I believe, deserve to be remembered.

Closure: the PCI, the Historic Compromise and the end of the cycle

To remember the second cycle of contention is also to remember the actions of the gatekeeper which brought it to an unsatisfactory close. The effects of the PCI's hostility to the second cycle of contention were vast. No recognition, however qualified, was granted to any element of Autonomia or the movement of 1977. The 'big names' of Autonomia were all veterans of the first cycle, when relations with the political mainstream were more open: Potere Operaio was a reference point for autonomists ranging from Negri (who was 44 in 1977) to Berardi (who was 27). The younger generation represented by the 'movement of 1977' seems never to have had a public face. One partial exception is Turquet/'Gandalf', briefly celebrated as a figurehead of the 'metropolitan Indians'. However, Turquet now believes that the group had little real substance: 'my opinion is that it was all a bluff fed by the papers and TV looking for/making up news; the nice thing is that we believed in it ourselves' (personal communication).[3]

The PCI's view of the activities of the movements of the second cycle is typified by Rossanda's patronising dismissal: 'I understand what has led many young people to break shop windows, but I don't consider it a stage in the Italian revolution' (quoted in Monicelli 1978: 168).[4] Ideologically, the denial of legitimacy to the movements was even more glaring. The dogmatic 'communism' of the 'hard' autonomists; the armed groups' doctrine of *doppia militanza*; the CPO's quest for 'a different way of being ourselves'; the worldviews of the *centri sociali* and the *autoriduttori*; the 'maodadaism' of Berardi; the 'wowdadaism' of the metropolitan Indians: a vast and complex ideological panorama was at best ignored, at worst derided. The BR was a partial exception to this rule, as parts of its policy statements were publicised. However, the BR's claim to attack 'the heart of the state' was the perfect counterpart to the PCI's dedication to the defence of the state: the prominence given to the BR underscored the inadmissibility of any disorderly group to the left of the PCI.

This ideological exclusion facilitated open repression. Police action against movement intellectuals, publications and *centri sociali* (or *covi*) stalled the movement's cultural and tactical development. The movement's larger organisational forms – occupations, assemblies, marches, rallies – were driven out of the universities and off the streets and squares; any localised use of force, in a *ronda* or a 'proletarian shopping' trip, could and increasingly would be met with superior force. A movement which celebrated loose and spontaneous organisation was ill-equipped to survive under these conditions. Even armed struggle activists were increasingly divided and isolated from any possible *doppia militanza*. Some responded with increased determination, often including a commitment to an increased use of force. As one participant recalled, 'to go right to the end [was] the only chance for redemption I had, from a moral point of view, both for the violence I produced and the violence I suffered' (quoted in della Porta 1995: 181).

By 1980 the autonomy, intransigence and creativity of the cycle could find expression in few areas other than the voluntaristic armed actions carried out by autonomous clandestine groups, bound together only by members' personal commitment. Returning to the passage from Balestrini's 1987 novel quoted earlier: 'they hadn't had any movement experience partly because by now the movement had been swept away their only experience was reading some document the clandestine distribution of some leaflet writing on the walls a banner across a flyover and then perhaps a murder straight away among the first actions' (Balestrini 1987: 270).[5] All the themes of the second cycle of contention could be seen here in degenerated form: disregard for legality, commitment to direct action, spontaneity, creativity, intransigence and autonomy. Their degeneration was the result of a long and hostile engagement with the institutional Left.

'Then the eighties began. The years of cynicism, opportunism and fear' (Balestrini and Moroni 1997: 669).[6] The longer-term legacy of the movements of the late 1970s, and of their suppression, was complex. Nanni Balestrini's extraordinary novels *Gli invisibili* ('The Unseen') and *L'editore* ('The Publisher') have been cited repeatedly in this book. Chapter 1 closed with a brief quotation from *L'editore*. The passage is worth quoting at greater length:

> the young people who were 15 or 20 years old when they faced that choice which develops between 71 and 72 and which in subsequent years becomes a general process in factories schools parishes neighbourhoods it's as if they had undergone an anthropological modification there's no other word for it an irreversible cultural self-modification and after this there's no turning back and so these individuals later after 79 when everything ends they go mad they kill themselves they drug themselves precisely because being reassimilated is impossible it's intolerable . . . they can't turn back from that train of events which breaks in 79 at that point everything breaks everything is broken but to break everything it takes the all-party alliance it takes the armed forces it takes the judiciary it takes the whole of the mass media it's never been known in a modern state for it to take this whole array of forces to put a stop to what was defined as a minority which was really a majority of society in the process of transformation one part of which had undergone a radical anthropological modification in terms of its perceptions of the world emotions sex culture the use of money (Balestrini 1989: 130)[7]

'Everything was broken' – but beneath it all there was still 'a majority of society in the process of transformation'. This kind of connection between the movements of the second cycle and broader structural processes had been suggested as early as 1977, with *A/traverso*'s quixotic declaration of victory ('*La rivoluzione è finito, abbiamo vinto*'). A corrective to this optimistic reading is provided by Virno.

> The truly decisive competences, when it comes to the optimal performance of post-Fordist work routines, are those formed outside production, in everyday life. . . . And so the movement of '77 gets *put to work*: its 'nomadism', distaste for predefined jobs, a certain self-reliant entrepreneurism, even the taste for experimentation and personal autonomy, all this meets the requirements of the organisation of capitalist production. We need only think, to take an example, of the massive development of 'autonomous work' in the 1980s in Italy: that is to say, the mass of micro-businesses, sometimes little more than family-based, which were set up by former factory workers. Right enough, this 'autonomous work' continues the migration away from the factory regime which began in '77, but it is tightly bound to the changing requirements of the big companies; to be precise, it's the specific method used by the major Italian industrial groups to externalise part of their costs of production. (Virno 1997: 648; emphasis in original)[8]

Rejected, marginalised and criminalised, the movements of the second cycle of contention succeeded nevertheless in fostering habits and attitudes which were useful to 'post-Fordist' capitalism. A particularly optimistic autonomist might argue that this in itself was an achievement: the development of post-Fordist capitalism had been shaped by the movements of the late 1970s, as workerist theory would predict ('Where capital is developed on the social scale, capitalist development is subordinate to workers' struggles' (Tronti 1964; quoted in Balestrini and Moroni 1988: 74)[9]). Nevertheless, this is a far cry from the engagement process described by Tarrow. In that process, activists develop new forms of resistance to capitalism, then prevail on established political forces to endorse their innovations. In this, businesses modify their organisation so as to exploit the energy which workers invest in 'the refusal of labour', turning points of strength for the workforce into assets of the business. The first is a qualified victory; the second, a qualified defeat.

The bitterest irony of all is that the preconditions for the PCI's hostile engagement with the second cycle – and its single-minded pursuit of a 'compromise' which benefited only the party's enemies – had been created by the party's successful engagement with the first cycle. The unstable conditions within the PCI under Longo had allowed an opening to the Left, enabling the party to acknowledge and exploit the first cycle of contention. The enhanced standing which the party enjoyed as a result was a major contributing factor to the ascendancy of Berlinguer, which entrenched the 'historic compromise' strategy and precluded any opening to the second cycle. The results, as we have seen, were disastrous for the party as well as the movements.

No alternative?

There are two possible counter-arguments to this critique. Firstly, it can be argued that the 'historic compromise' was not entirely unsuccessful. Arguably the strategy should not be judged for its effect on the PCI's capacity to renew itself, as its goal was not to facilitate party renewal but simply to bring the party closer to inclusion in the the polycentric but impermeable 'court' of Italian political power (see table 8.1). The doctrine of austerity, for example, can be seen as a calculated gamble with the party's support, aiming to conserve as much as possible of its mass base while repositioning the party into a moderate reformist institutional framework. Nor was this gamble entirely unsuccessful. While the PCI never entered government, from 1977 onwards the party built a base in Italy's nationalised industries and, crucially, broadcasting: the party's long 'occupation' of the third state television channel, Rai 3, dates from this period. Corrupt and stagnant though the DC regime was, it was in this period, thanks to Berlinguer's institutional strategy, that the PCI made the most effective progress towards gaining the right to participate in it – arguably a step towards rebuilding the post-war coalition.

Even so, the costs of the 'historic compromise' were crushing. The PCI's engagement with the second cycle both exhibited and entrenched the party's closure to potential sources of renewal. The PCI leadership decisively rejected challenges which were also opportunities: denying the movements any consequential political outlet, the party committed itself to an increasingly contentless institutional orientation, ultimately cutting itself off from much of its own ideological and tactical hinterland. If the movements had met a receptive gatekeeper, their encounter might have led to an expansion of the repertoire of radical and reformist politics. Equally, if the PCI had attempted its institutional shift without also moving decisively to the right, the party might have been able to gain a stake in the political system with its reformist credentials intact. The hostile engagement between the two was fatal to both, trapping each within its own sphere – anti-political movementism on one hand, self-referential institutional politics on the other. As late as 1977, Berlinguer's adviser Tatò could describe the 'historic compromise' as 'the transition period to the new [proletarian] hegemony' (quoted in Ruscoe 1982: 114). Hegelian to the point of mysticism, this perspective was quite as divorced from reality as anything the metropolitan Indians ever advanced, and attests just as eloquently to an absence of communication between institutional politics and movements within society.

Alternatively, it can be argued that it is not appropriate to judge the PCI's approaches to the two cycles of contention on the same criteria. In the first cycle, the interaction between the PCI and contentious movements echoed Charles Tilly's description of the emergence of the strike form: 'the antagonists created – in practice as well as in theory – a sharper distinction between the strike and other forms of action with which it had previously often been associated: sabotage, slowdown, absenteeism, the demonstration. A narrowed, contained strike entered the repertoire of workers' collective action' (Tilly 1979: 135). The first cycle of contention thus led to the definition of 'acceptable' forms of strike action and workplace organisation. Arguably an inclusive engagement with the movements of the second cycle was not possible; the PCI could not endorse a 'narrowed, contained' form of autonomist tactics because these tactics were inherently too violent and criminal for such a negotiation.

However, it can be shown that the PCI had both the means and the opportunity for a more inclusive approach. In the area of political values, firstly, the movements repeatedly gave the PCI (and other mainstream forces) the opportunity to engage with the new and redefined values which they were putting forward. A particularly clear and open invitation to dialogue appeared in the proletarian youth movement's 1976 document *Ribellarsi, è ora? Sì* ('Time to rebel? Yes'), cited earlier:

The bourgeois newspapers tell us: 'you don't want to work, you're on drugs, you're violent, immoral delinquents, young hippies and feminist guerrillas'. Let's look at these accusations one by one. . . . Working means living the life of our parents from an early age, eight hours a day on the production line or in an office, always having to answer to a boss, with the prospect for us young people of being oppressed and exploited for the rest of our lives. Looked at this way, how could anyone want to work? It's hard to imagine – but it might help if we were the ones who decided what we worked on, how and how much. . . . On drugs? . . . Who was it who built a society of millions of drug users: drugged with psychiatric drugs in order to sleep after eight hours of exploitation (tranquillisers) or to have the energy to work (stimulants, even coffee); drugged with tobacco to ease the nervous tension of daily social and human relations; drugged with television; drugged with alcohol . . . The accusation of being on drugs refers to our use of pleasing and harmless hashish cigarettes and tea, which relax inhibitions and help people communicate as well as a litre of wine . . . Delinquents? People without work, people who are short of money . . . may look for an individual solution and slip into what's called 'delinquency'. But the background of this choice (often unavoidable) was built and imposed by the bourgeoisie; it wasn't chosen by proletarians. . . . Are we violent? Yes, we bear on our backs all the violence which you have done to us and do to us every day. We have the memory of comrades killed by fascists and by the police, young people dead from heroin or killed in cold blood for carrying out a couple of robberies. But for us violence is an instrument at most, not an end in itself. We are pacific, because we want to go on living, but we are not pacifists, because we have learnt to understand power and how the bourgeoisie exercises it. (quoted in Balestrini and Moroni 1997: 514–16)[10]

A wide-ranging effort of rethinking and redefinition is apparent here, creating opportunities for any established political force prepared to enter an open-ended, exploratory dialogue. Perhaps the PCI of 1976 could not concede that to work for a living was to be 'oppressed and exploited'; that juvenile delinquency was a misguided response to an unjust society; that young people were more likely to suffer violent death than inflict it; or that wine, tobacco and even coffee were also drugs. But the party made no attempt to meet positions like these halfway, with a few isolated exceptions such as Bruno Trentin of the FLM (whose Partito d'Azione background put him outside the mainstream of PCI culture). Instead, the party responded to external pressure not only by reasserting its own values, but by presenting these in increasingly narrow and conservative forms, drawing in its ideological skirts to eliminate any common ground with the movements.

Perhaps more to the point, the PCI could have outflanked the movements by appropriating their material demands. The spread of *autoriduzione* and *spese proletarie* might have suggested a focus on limiting the effects of retail price inflation; the PCI could also have taken a lead from the youth movement's attacks on sweatshop employers and drug pushers. Despite the party's exclusion from government, the PCI and CGIL were in positions of consider-able power relative to the movements: much of what the movements tried to achieve for their constituency, the PCI could have offered its own, thereby legitimising the movements' demands while marginalising the movements themselves. From the outset, the movements combined workplace and com-munity activism, addressing their constituency both as workers and as con-sumers. The practical efficacy of this approach was demonstrated in Rome, where the CAO's presence at the state electricity company enabled members to reconnect households which had been disconnected for underpayment. An organisation of the size of the CGIL would, clearly, have been able to put an approach like this into much more widespread effect; indeed, some CGIL organisers did attempt to appropriate the tactic, albeit proposing a reduction of 50 per cent rather than 75 per cent (Wright 2002: 158). However, this approach never received central CGIL or PCI approval. Instead, the party's response to the inflation issue was to raise the banner of 'austerity', urging its own supporters to recalibrate the balance between production and con-sumption by doing more work or accepting less pay: 'Austerity . . . [is] directed to the productive sectors of society – to the *workers* – who, being producers and consumers at the same time, can (if they want) calibrate a dif-ferent balance between these two aspects of life' (Asor Rosa 1977b; emphasis in original).[11]

An even greater missed opportunity was created by the local elections of June 1975, which put the PCI in a strong position in local authorities through-out the country: council housing and public transport were key targets for *autoriduzione*. Municipal action against the cost of living was not unknown: in 1973, the Communist-run council in Bologna introduced free bus travel during the morning and evening rush hours, an experiment hailed by *l'Unità* as 'A major initiative by a democratic council' (Anon. 1973e). Now, however, any such action was ruled out, with *autoriduzione* criticised as harmful to working-class unity. In the words of an October 1975 *l'Unità* comment piece:

> Italian workers, as a whole, have shown that they are aware that forms of struggle such as the occupation of houses and *'autoriduzione'* . . . display, in general terms, the characteristic of preventing mass participation . . . isolating small vanguards, exposing them to reprisals and a swift defeat . . . what counts is a united mobilisation of all the forces which could in any way have an interest in a declared objective of greater social justice. (Fasola 1975)[12]

More bluntly, in 1978 one leading member of the Turin party argued that the party should tell its voters: 'Listen, comrades, some of the things (free rent, free transport) you are asking for are just stupid' (Hellman 1988: 97).

The reception of the proletarian youth movement and the *centri sociali* was equally hostile. The PCI's position was encapsulated by a piece headed 'How to respond to *autoriduzione'* which appeared in the *Corriere della Sera*'s 'Open Platform' guest comment slot on 28 November 1976. The guest columnist was Gennaro Barbarisi, lecturer at the Statale and president of the Cultural Commission of Milan's city council, to which he had been elected on a PCI list (personal communication). After referring briefly to *autoriduzione* of utility bills, with the tepid acknowledgment that this had 'enabled some people to resolve moments of uncertainty',[13] Barbarisi writes:

> its current extension to various areas of commerce (one leaflet even raves about the proletarian right to the luxuries and privileges of the bourgeoisie!) represents a watchword with absolutely no political content, almost an invitation to generalised consumerism (whose logic it thus accepts) . . . what we must ask for now . . . is not a drastic change of direction (the extreme example must be that offered by certain crazed representatives of 'youth circles' who asked me to redirect the funds earmarked for La Scala to their centres!) but the development and the constructive integration of cultural production and of all spare time activities (Barbarisi 1976)[14]

Nothing in Barbarisi's column is as telling as his use of exclamation marks: the demands of the new movement are not discussed or even attacked, but dismissed as self-evidently absurd.

Finally, both the armed groups and the movements posed an ideological and cultural challenge to the PCI, in their use of 'anti-fascist' and 'Resistance' themes. Responses might have included celebration of the radical elements of the Resistance or endorsement of the involvement of PCI *servizi d'ordine* in 'militant anti-fascism' (physical opposition to the neo-fascist MSI). Alternatively, the claim to offer armed resistance to neo-fascism could have been punctured by celebrating the PCI's success in keeping fascism at bay by constitutional means. The PCI's actual response can be gauged from the following *l'Unità* item, reporting on the court appearance of an armed group surprised while training in woodland outside Verbania, near the Swiss border:

> [The accused] maintain that they were on an ecological and cultural excursion: they wanted to revisit the wild and rocky places where the struggle against fascists and Nazis took place. So, no war with the democratic state which was inspired by that struggle? . . . As they left the court, around a hundred of their friends and relations staged a demonstration in solidarity, shouting, 'The only justice is proletarian justice'. What they mean by proletarian justice is hard to understand. Six of the accused work at Falck and Magneti Marelli, where, as far as we know, their ideas enjoy neither credit nor sympathy. They were isolated in the midst of the workers: on the political level, proletarian justice had

already condemned them. But if the opinion of the workers doesn't count, what is the proletarian justice they sing about? There's no doubt about the answer: their own. They are few, they count for nothing, but they have the arrogance and the violence to claim to pass sentences, to rule on what is just and unjust. Arrogance is what characterises them, as it did the Fascists. But in this country, the partisans and the people threw that arrogance in the lake back in April '45. (Anon. 1977u)[15]

For revolutionary socialists to hark back to the radicalism of the Resistance, outside the auspices of the PCI, is to be isolated; to persist despite this isolation is to be arrogant; to be arrogant is to be a fascist. The bizarrely strained logic of this piece suggests that the PCI was strongly committed to a hostile engagement, and that this hostility was not a necessary response to the facts.

Invisibility and violence

The title of Balestrini's 1987 novel, *Gli invisibili*, sums up a problem which confronts anyone studying the second cycle of contention. In most writing on the period, both the cycle itself and its component movements tend to be underestimated or ignored. It is symptomatic that Ginsborg's 1990 text – a comprehensive and invaluable source on the First Republic – hits one of its rare lacunae at this point, devoting fifty pages to the first cycle of contention but only two to the second (Ginsborg 1990: 298–347, 381–3).

In this approach, of course, Ginsborg followed Tarrow's dismissal of the second cycle. If we assume that the account given here is more adequate, this prompts the question of why writers on the period have overlooked the second cycle. Perhaps the simplest explanation turns on the nature of the engagement. As we have seen, engagement is a winnowing process, involving the acceptance of some movement innovations and the rejection of others. Those innovations which are rejected are redefined as deviant: quixotically idealistic, irrational or (above all) criminal. The engagement process as a whole can be seen as a means of regulating social disorder. During a cycle of contention, groups develop new forms of activity through which they can assert their own interests and challenge relationships of power; in the 'engagement' phase, some of these techniques are endorsed as elements of political practice, the remainder dismissed as disorder to be policed. Framing interactions, in this situation, can be seen as an extended and collective version of the 'labelling' operations through which deviancy is ascribed to individuals (cf. Becker 1973).

In this perspective, it is not difficult to see how an entire cycle could disappear from view. In the course of a negative engagement, the cycle's innovations are authoritatively labelled as phenomena of criminality and disorder.

Not only are these innovations not available to successive movements, as in Tarrow's optimistic conclusion ('new forms of collective action . . . [survive] as a legacy of disorder for the next, and inevitable, cycle of protest' (Tarrow 1989: 348)). Even in retrospect they tend to be lost to view, appearing as wild aberrations, episodes in the history of youth cults or popular delusions. Rossanda's aloof judgment anticipated the verdict of posterity on the second cycle: not 'a stage in the Italian revolution', just some young people smashing windows.

Perhaps the key manoeuvre in the framing of the second cycle was the evocation of violence. The theme of violence is prominent in retrospective accounts of the supposed degeneration of the movements of the period; it was also a prominent theme in contemporary accounts of the movement, although its rhetorical utility rapidly outstripped any consistent definition. As we have seen, the PCI's framing of the movements of the second cycle centred on the themes of provocateurism and nihilism. Both evoke destructive violence: in one case, it is caused by a small and isolated group, working in secret to divide the working class; in the other, it is the work of a mob of antisocial hooligans, driven by an irrational desire to destroy society. While superficially incompatible, both themes frame violent activism so as to exclude it from any possible identification.

Present-day critiques of violent activism have similar qualities. The assumption that violence can be explained by nihilist insanity remains available: Vite, quoting an evocation of 'the irrational explosion of deviant and marginal rage' in the street clashes of 1977 (Grispigni 1997: 43),[16] comments, 'It's curious how this type of analysis resembles those made by the PCI in those years' (Vite 2002: 46)).[17] The critique of provocateurism, with its roots in Communist history, is less prominent, although the assumption that violence is the work of an isolated and dedicated minority runs through Tarrow's discussion of Autonomia. Contemporary groups using violent tactics are also often criticised as 'elitist', as in Jean Cohen's insistence that protesters should 'avoid an elitist attitude' by ensuring that 'acts of protest have a symbolic character' (Cohen and Arato 1992: 601–2). The charge of elitism has distinct affinities with the PCI's critique of those who 'make the workers and the unions take the blame for acts and initiatives which have nothing to do with the workers' movement' (Anon. 1972a).[18]

These framings of irrationality and elitism, like their late 1970s precursors, are clearly inadequate. The movements' own understanding of the topic was both more consistent and more comprehensive. Many movement participants were actively involved in violence in the form of 'militant anti-fascism'. Indeed, one effect of the mass mobilisations of 1977 was, at least temporarily, to drive the MSI off the streets: one of Del Bello's interviewees recalls, 'We got rid of the fascists, in 1977 and afterwards; it was the culmination of an anti-fascist mobilisation which had lasted several years' ('Andrea' 1997: 197).[19] In this context, physical force was viewed neutrally or with approval, as an appropriate means to a commendable end. Much of the diffuse violence of the youth movement's *ronde*, as well as the more organised violence of the small armed groups which grew up after 1977, can be understood in these terms; as well as neo-fascists, targets included heroin pushers and sweatshop employers. Ethically, this amounts to saying that it is appropriate for certain groups to be informally constrained by violence or the threat of violence. The PCI's standpoint was hardly any different, as witness *l'Unità*'s celebration of the 'firmness' of PCI *servizi d'ordine*.

Secondly, both the armed groups and the movements habitually contrasted their own violent acts with the violence tolerated and legitimated by capitalist society. 'Anyone who says they are against violence is hypocritically repressing the fact that, in Italy, six thousand workers die at work every year,' Scalzone argued in 1977 (quoted in Monicelli 1978: 126).[20] The same year, Berardi took up the theme in 'creative' vein: 'When they write "Tomorrow, Monday, work resumes in the factories," they write a falsehood. Another linguistic version of the same event could be "Tomorrow, Monday, another twenty workers will be killed"' (quoted in Monicelli 1978: 104).[21] In 1978 a CAO member refused to denounce the BR's killings: 'if the BR shoot someone we won't cry for them. Four thousand workers die every year and nobody cries' (quoted in Monicelli 1978: 213).[22] More specifically, many movement participants saw themselves as victims, actual or potential, of disproportionate levels of violence: as victims of street violence, police shootings or drug addiction. The movements argued that these socially legitimated forms of violence should be named and criticised as such, and taken into account when the violence of the movement was in question. This position is difficult to dismiss, particularly for those who (like the PCI) are committed to reform of an unjust society.

Some forms of violence, although illegitimate, may be pragmatically acceptable as a proportionate means to a commendable end. Conversely, some forms of violence, although wantonly destructive and wasteful, may in practice be regarded as legitimate. Both these difficulties are reflected in the circularity of the PCI's portrayal of movement violence. What was unacceptable about the movements was that they used violence; what was unacceptable about the violence of the movements was that it was carried out by the movements. The PCI's critique of 'violence' and 'intolerance' can be understood as a form of scapegoating, loading the movements (and the Autonomists, above all) with all that was unruly and troubling about physical force tactics while associating the PCI itself with 'firmness' and 'discipline'. Framing transactions, driven by the PCI's tactical and organisational needs, thus promoted the exclusion of the movements from the political system. They also contributed to the movements' retrospective invisibility.

Coda: could it happen here?

Between 1966 and 1980, the PCI played the role of 'gatekeeper' to a relatively closed political system, admitting certain innovations to the sphere of political legitimacy and barring others. The movements of the second cycle were confronted by a hostile gatekeeper, which persistently framed their activities in terms which excluded them from political legitimacy. A key manoeuvre, as we have seen, was the evocation of violence: the movements were repeatedly denounced for the use of violence, toleration of violence, tardiness or insincerity in disowning those who used violence, and so on. The ultimate result was the repression of a broad area of social, cultural and intellectual ferment, accompanied by dozens of prison terms and a brief flourishing of openly illegal 'armed struggle' activity; the PCI itself also suffered, denying itself a source of much-needed ideological renewal.

As we have seen, the exclusiveness of the PCI's engagement was not a foregone conclusion until Berlinguer committed the party to the 'historic compromise' strategy – if then. The engagement was a missed opportunity which could have been taken. Similar choices could face other gatekeepers in other relatively closed systems. In Britain, where the electoral system excludes social movements from the national political system, the Labour Party remains the principal Left gatekeeper. Faced with a disorderly and uncontainable rival to its left, Labour would have the same options as the PCI. An inclusive engagement would require the party quietly to appropriate and absorb the demands and tactics of the new movement, while publicly denouncing its leadership as irresponsible extremists. An exclusive engagement, in contrast, would involve denunciations of violence, escalating demands for dissociation and emphatic assertions of the party's own commitment to democracy and the rule of law. Thirty years on, the Italian political system and the remains of the Italian Left still demonstrate how disastrous the effects of this approach could be.

Notes

1 'si è messa in moto una martellante campagna di criminalizzazione di tutto il movimento la mattina leggevo il giornale un giornale qualsiasi e non c'era nessuna differenza dall'ultimo scribacchino di cronaca fino all'illustre intellettuale sociologo filosofo psicologo storico romanziere eccetera tutti scrivevano che il movimento non era altro che un'agitazione convulsa di spostati avventuristi fascisti schizofrenici delinquenti che andavano spazzati via il più presto possibile per la

salvezza della democrazia e della civile convivenza c'era in noi un senso d'impotenza di fronte a quella falsificazione sistematica di tutto ma abbiamo creduto che non ci fosse altra scelta che accettare comunque la sfida sul terreno della comunicazione e così abbiamo deciso di costruire una radio di movimento'.

2 'ho chiesto della radio come aveva funzionato la radio Ortica si è rimesso a ridere la radio era tutto pronto c'era tutto il materiale c'era la frequenza c'era anche il telefono avevamo fatto tutte le prove di voce con la voce di China uno due tre prova rideva siamo riusciti a dire solo uno due tre prova c'era tutto lì pronto bastava schiacciare un pulsante e parlare ma non avevamo più niente da dire nella sede non ci andava più nessuno ormai ogni giorno capitava un disastro nuovo uno che arrestavano uno che impazziva uno che spariva uno che si suicidava tutti sono spariti non c'era più niente da dire e così tutto è rimasto lì a coprirsi di polvere il trasmettitore la piastra lo sterco l'amplificatore il microfono e la voce di China'.

3 'a mia opinione è che tutto fu un bluff alimentato da giornali e TV che cercavano/inventavano la notizia; la cosa simpatica è che ci credemmo anche noi'.

4 'Capisco quello che spinse molti giovani a spaccare le vetrine, ma non lo considero una tappa della rivoluzione italiana.'

5 'molti di questi nuovi venuti avevano storie assurde erano l'ultima generazione di combattenti tutti giovanissimi e avevano tutti una biografia simile non avevano avuto nessun percorso di movimento anche perché ormai il movimento era stato spazzato via per cui il percorso era stato la lettura di qualche documento la distribuzione clandestina di qualche volantino scritte sul muri uno striscione su un cavalcavia e poi magari un omicidio subito tra le prime azioni e poi l'arresto su dichiarazioni di qualche pentito'.

6 'Sono iniziati gli anni ottanta. Gli anni del cinismo, dell'opportunismo e della paura.'

7 'questi giovani che allora avevano 15 o 20 anni quando si trovano a fare questa scelta che matura tra il 71 e il 72 e che diventa negli anni successivi processo generale nelle fabbriche nelle scuole nelle parrocchie nei quartieri è come se avessero subito una modificazione antropologica non trovo altro termine una modificazione culturale di sé irreversibile da qui non puoi più tornare indietro per questo poi questi soggetti più tardi dopo il 79 quando tutto finisce impazziscono si suicidano si drogano proprio per l'impossibilità e l'insopportabilità di essere riomologati . . . non può più tornare indietro da quella vicenda che nel 79 si rompe allora tutto si rompe tutto si è rotto però per rompere tutto occorre l'unione di tutti i partiti occorrono le forze armate occorre la magistratura occorrono tutti i mass media non è mai successo in uno stato moderno che ci voglia tutto questo spiegamento di forze per far fuori quella che viene definita una minoranza che invece era una maggioranza sociale in movimento di trasformazione di cui una parte ha subito una radicale modificazione antropologica come percezione del mondo delle emozioni del sesso della cultura del rapporto col denaro'.

8 'Le competenze veramente decisive per eseguire al meglio le mansione lavorative postfordiste sono quelle che si formano al di fuori della produzione diretta, nel

"mondo della vita". . . . È così che il movimento del '77 viene *messo al lavoro*: il suo "nomadismo", il disamore per il posto fisso, una certa autoimprenditorialità, perfino il gusto per l'autonomia individuale e per la sperimentazione, tutto questo confluisce nell'organizzazione produttiva capitalistica. Basti pensare, a titolo di esempio, al grande sviluppo che, in Italia, durante gli anni ottanta, ha avuto il "lavoro autonomo", ossia l'insieme di microimprese, talvolta poco più che familiari, messe in piedi da ex lavoratori dipendenti. Questo "lavoro autonomo" è, sì, la prosecuzione della migrazione dal regime di fabbrica cominciata nel '77: ma esso è strettamente subordinato alle variabili esigenze delle grandi imprese; anzi, è il modo specifico con cui i maggiori gruppi industriali italiani scaricano parte dei loro costi di produzione all'esterno.'

9 'A livello di capitale socialmente sviluppato, lo sviluppo capitalistico è subordinato alle lotte operaie'.

10 'I giornali borghesi ci dicono: "non avete voglia di lavorare, siete drogati, siete delinquenti, violenti, di facili costumi, giovani hippies e femministe guerrigliere". Esaminiamo a una a una queste accuse. . . . Lavorare vuol dire iniziare fin da giovani a fare ancora la vita dei nostri padri, otto ore alla catena o in ufficio, sempre costretti a render conto a un capo, con la prospettiva per noi giovani di essere oppressi e sfruttati per tutta intera la nostra vita. Come è possibili quindi avere voglia di lavorare? Ci vuole molto sforzo e soltanto l'idea di essere noi a decidere come, quanto, cosa lavorare potrebbe ottenere qualche risultato. . . . Drogati? . . . Chi ha costruito una società di milioni di drogati, drogati di psicofarmaci per addormentarsi dopo otto ore di sfruttamento (tranquillanti); drogati di psicofarmaci per avere l'energia di lavorare (gli stimolanti, lo stesso caffè); drogati di tabacco per calmare la tensione nervosa dei rapporti sociali e umani quotidiani; drogati di televisione; drogati di alcoolici . . . L'accusa di essere drogati si riferisce all'uso di innocue e piacevoli sigarette o tè di hashish che fanno comunicare e "disinibiscono" come un litro di barbera . . . Delinquenti? Chi è senza lavoro, a chi i soldi non bastano perché sono pochi . . . è possibile che cerchi una soluzione individuale e scivoli nella cosiddetta "delinquenza". Ma il terreno di questa scelta, spesso obbligata, l'ha costruito e impostato la borghesia, non l'hanno scelto i proletari. . . . Siamo violenti? Sì, abbiamo addosso tutta la violenza che ci avete fatto e che ci fate ogni giorno. Abbiamo il ricordo dei compagni uccisi dai fascisti, dalla polizia, di giovani morti di eroina, uccisi a freddo per aver compiuto furtarelli. Ma per noi la violenza è al massimo uno strumento, non è la sostanza: siamo pacifici perché vogliamo vivere, ma non siamo pacifisti perché abbiamo imparato a conoscere il potere e come la borghesia lo esercita.'

11 'L'austerità . . . è rivolta ai settori produttivi della società – ai *lavoratori* – i quali, in quanto produttori e consumatori al tempo stesso, possono, se vogliono, calibrare un rapporto diverso tra questi due aspetti della vita.'

12 'I lavoratori italiani, nel loro insieme, dimostrano di aver coscienza che forme di lotta quale l'occupazione di case e l' "autoriduzione" . . . presentano in linea generale la caratteristica di eliminare preventivamente la partecipazione di massa di gran parte degli interessati . . . . di isolare ed esporre alla rappresaglia e ad una rapida sconfitta le singole avanguardie. . . . quello che conta è la mobilitazione

unitaria di tutte le forze che in qualche modo possono essere interessate ad un determinato obiettivo di maggiore giustizia.'

13 'l'autoriduzione ha potuto determinare momenti d'incertezza in una parte della popolazione'.

14 'la sua attuale estensione a vari settori del commercio (in un volantino si farnetica addirittura di diritto proletario ai lussi e ai privilegi della borghesia!) si presenta come una parola d'ordine assolutamente priva di contenuto politico, quasi un invito al consumismo generalizzato . . . la nuova richiesta . . . non deve portare a una drastica alternativa (l'esempio limite può esser offerto da alcuni dissennati rappresentanti di "circoli giovanili" che mi hanno chiesto di far dirottare sui loro centri i finanziamenti destinati alla Scala!) ma al potenziamento e alla proficua integrazione della produzione culturale e di ogni attività del tempo libero'.

15 'Erano – sostengono – in gita culturale ed ecologica: volevano rivisitare i luoghi aspri e selvaggi in cui si svolse la lotta contro fascisti e nazisti. Niente guerra allora contro lo Stato democratico che a quella lotta si ispira? . . . Un centinaio di loro amici e parenti . . . hanno inscenato all'uscita una manifestazione di solidarietà con gli imputati al grido di *"La unica giustizia è quella proletaria"*. Quale sia questa giustizia proletaria per loro è difficile capirlo. Sei degli imputati lavorano alla Falck e alla Magneti Marelli, dove, da quel che risulta, le loro idee non godevano nè credito nè simpatia. Erano, in mezzo agli operai, degli isolati. Il giudizio proletario li aveva, insomma, sul piano politico, già condannati. Ma se l'opinione degli operai non conta, qual è la *giustizia proletaria* di cui vanno cantando? Non ci sono dubbi: la loro. Sono pochi, non contano niente ma hanno tanta arroganza e tanta violenza da pretendere di decretare sentenze, di stabilire che cosa è giusto e ingiusto. L'arroganza è la loro caratteristica. Come per i fascisti. Ma qui partigiani e popolo nell'aprile del '45, questa arroganza l'hanno già buttata nel lago.'

16 'la rabbia deviante e marginale che esplode irrazionalmente'.

17 'È curioso quanto si somiglino questo tipo di analisi e quelle fatte del Pci in quegli anni.'

18 'far ricadere sui lavoratori e i sindacati la responsabilità di atti ed iniziative che nulla hanno a che vedere con il movimento operaio'.

19 'I fascisti vengono spazzati via nel '77 e dal '77, come punto d'arrivo di una mobilitazione antifascista durata alcuni anni.'

20 'Chi si dichiara contro la violenza rimuove ipocritamente il fatto che in Italia crepano di lavoro seimila operai all'anno'.

21 'Quando si scrive "domani, lunedì, riprende il lavoro nelle fabbriche" si scrive un falso. Un'altra versione linguistica dello stesso evento potrebbe essere: "Domani, lunedì, altri venti lavoratori saranno uccisi" '.

22 'se le Br sparano a qualcuno non ci piangiamo sopra. Muoiono 4 mila operai all'anno e nessuno piange.'

8

Social movements and cycles of contention: theoretical appendix

This book is a study of a cycle of contention, in which a gatekeeper to the political sphere interacted through framing transactions with a series of disorderly social movements. The purpose of this appendix is to define some of the key terms and concepts I've used, with a view to minimising unnecessary scholarly dispute.

Social movements and framing processes

Social movements can be defined as groups within society which combine three factors: an oppositional or reformist stance towards the political status quo; autonomy from the conventional political sphere; and a degree of ideological or cultural coherence, based on a shared set of fundamental concerns or values. Social groups which have two of these properties but lack the third are not social movements: examples include groups of hobbyists, parliamentary pressure groups or groups defined by an officially discouraged activity (e.g. cannabis smokers).

In this book, the interaction between social movements and political institutions is considered in terms of 'framing'. The concept draws on the work of Erving Goffman (Goffman 1974). A frame is 'an interpretive schemata that simplifies and condenses the "world out there" by selectively punctuating and encoding objects, situations, events, experiences, and sequences of actions' (Snow and Benford 1992: 137). In the social movement context, frames 'assign meaning to and interpret, relevant events and conditions in ways that are intended to mobilise potential adherents and constituents, to garner bystander support, and to demobilise antagonists' (Snow and Benford 1988: 198).

Frames, in other words, are combinations of values and reference points through which groups interpret their surroundings, manage their activity and present themselves to potential members. Social movements develop and sustain a distinctive ideological identity by putting forward new frames and modifying existing frames. Social movements' frames are liable to be challenged by their opponents: '[m]ovements and countermovements . . . are involved in framing contests attempting to persuade authorities and bystanders of the rightness of their cause' (Zald 1996: 269). This is particularly relevant to the establishment, assertion and contestation of social movement identities.

The framing processes carried out by groups within society are doubly embedded: on one hand, they are bound up with other attributes of the group within its social context, such as the influence it exerts over other groups; on the other, they are sustained through the group's activities within society. This analysis draws on the 'critical realist' model developed by Roy Bhaskar and others (e.g. Bhaskar 1979), which holds that 'social phenomena are *concept-dependent* . . . What the practices, institutions, rules, roles or relationships *are* depends on what they mean in society to its members' (Sayer 1984: 32; emphasis in original). Moreover, the production of meaning is itself a social activity: '[it is] not a question of knowledge developing autonomously first and then (perhaps) being applied in a practical context later: knowledge and practice are tied from the start' (Sayer 1984: 27). Framing is thus a practical activity, and one with potentially significant consequences. A challenge by one social actor to another's framing of its identity is likely to perceived, not as a philosophical dispute, but as a threat to the second group's capacity to pursue its own interests and wield influence. As Sassoon comments,

> the identity and image of a party is never entirely self-constructed. It requires the participation of the 'semiotic universe' within which the party operates, that is, it requires the accord of other parties, other forces, other agencies who have the power and the ability to validate this identity. This struggle is at the heart of all politics. (Sassoon 2003: 37)

Framing is also embedded more directly in practical activity. The constitution of frames of meaning by social groups is essentially an extension of the universal processes by which the world is interpreted and made meaningful. The selective and partisan quality of the frame reflects the inescapably partial nature of cognitive knowledge, as analysed by phenomenologists such as Alfred Schutz. For Schutz, knowledge is founded on types and on typification: '[t]he factual world of our experience . . . is experienced from the outset as a typical one. Objects are perceived as trees, animals, and the like . . . What is newly experienced is already known in the sense that it recalls similar or equal things formerly perceived' (Schutz 1962: 281). Moreover, the process of type-construction by which we structure experience is neither conscious nor disinterested, but a product of directed practical activity: 'Our practical interest alone, as it arises in a certain situation of our life . . . is the only relevant principle in the building up of the perspective structure in which our social world appears to us in daily life' (Schutz 1964: 72). Knowledge developed in this way is necessarily incomplete; however, there is no external standpoint from which it can be evaluated: 'There are everywhere gaps, intermissions, discontinuities. Apparently there is a kind of organisation by habits, rules and principles which we regularly apply with success. But the origin of our habits is almost beyond our control; the rules we apply are rules of thumb and their validity has never been verified' (Schutz 1964: 72–3). While we perceive social reality as comprehensively ordered, these typifications are themselves intrinsically fluid, provisional and intermingled with non-cognitive elements.

This perspective offers some useful correctives to Snow's somewhat abstract and rationalistic presentation of framing. Framing processes are involved with practical, non-cognitive activity, as with the underpinning of group identity through ceremonial and routine. Moreover, frames develop out of historical experience, group self-interest and collective activity rather than disinterested analysis: a successful frame is not a logically sound argument but a culturally and historically specific cluster of interrelated concerns and values. A related qualification is that framing processes will tend to be continual and provisional rather than discrete and definitive. Framing is embedded in social activity as a process, which continually produces and reproduces statements about how groups and individuals see the social world. It is also functionally embedded in social activity, structuring propositions which assist or hinder social actors in pursuing their interests.

In practical terms, the foregrounding of framing strategies suggests a particular approach to reading social history, sketched out in the analysis of historical material in this thesis. In this approach, texts produced by social actors are analysed for particular frames and combinations of frames. This approach can be called rhetorical or even literary, as it pays as much attention to distinctive epithets and turns of phrase as to sustained logical arguments; indeed, in some cases the ostensible argument of a text may effectively dissolve on examination, leaving only a distinctive articulation of frames. Having said that, this is a contribution to social and political history rather than to cultural studies. The rhetorical strategies identified by this method are analysed as the product of known social actors, interacting with other groups and individuals within a specific social context and for identifiable purposes. Indeed, the documents analysed are seen, not as a reflection or even a record of social interactions, but as interactions in their own right. To communicate a particular combination of frames may be in part an assertion of the interests of particular social actors, in their role as producers of meaning.

Political opportunities

In the social movement context, the setting for framing transactions can be seen as their political opportunity structure. Here McAdam (1996) identifies three key variables: whether a social movement can enter the political system in its own right; whether an organisation within the system will exert influence on its behalf, either as a committed ally or as an opportunistic sponsor; and the extent to which it will be able to continue to function if it chooses or is forced to remain outside the system.

The first of these variables is critical. As Kriesi points out, this is determined in part by the institutional structure of the state; 'weak' states offer opportunities in terms of 'input' (access to the political system by external contenders), while 'strong' states offer greater opportunities in terms of 'output' (the capacity to implement contentious policies). Institutional 'openness', associated by Kriesi with 'weak' states, can give social movements access to the political system (Kriesi 1995: 171). However, it is not necessarily the case that a state's strength in imposing its policies varies inversely with its openness. Nor does it necessarily follow that '[f]ragmentation, lack of internal coordination, and lack of professionalisation multiply the points of access' (Kriesi 1995: 171); these conditions would equally make it easier for a diffused bureaucracy to shield itself from systematic accountability. We can envisage a four-way typology of state openness and strength, as shown in table 8.1.

Kriesi's alternatives of the 'strong' and 'weak' state (the 'citadel' and the 'network') do not exhaust the available possibilities. The 'democratic centralist' structures adopted by Leninist parties and states are (at least in principle) an example of the 'machine' model, combining democratic openness with an unchallenged executive; similar claims have been advanced for the British parliamentary system, although in practice it may be a closer approximation to the 'citadel'. Conversely, the political system of post-war Italy exemplifies

Table 8.1 Types of state defined by 'input' and 'output' political opportunity structure

		Points of access to political system	
		Many	*Few*
Centres of political power	*Many*	Network — Multiple points of influence; no concentration of political power	Court — Multiple centres of political power; little accountability
	Few	Machine — Concentrated political power, open to influence from below	Citadel — Concentrated and unaccountable political power

the oligarchic 'court' model, combining an autocracy's closure to outside influence with the executive weakness of a polycentric system.

It is also worth emphasising that the assemblage of political opportunities and constraints is not simply given; opportunities and constraints develop over time as outcomes of actions taken by particular social actors, social movements included. Movement activity can promote either the expansion or the contraction of political opportunities for subsequent movements. 'Movements arise as the result of new or expanded opportunities; they signal the vulnerability of the state to collective action, thereby opening up opportunities for others; the process leads to state responses which, one way or another, produce a new opportunity structure' (Tarrow 1996: 61). This new opportunity structure is not necessarily more favourable to social movements: 'protesters' success may trigger reactions whose effects close off political opportunities: counter-mobilisation occurs, there is a backlash in public opinion, and the forces of order regroup as they adapt to new challenges' (Tarrow 1989: 23).

Tarrow and the repertoire of contention

With this background established, we can turn to Tarrow's model of the 'cycle of contention'. A key element of the model is Charles Tilly's concept of the 'repertoire'; this in turn is based on the assumption is that the actions taken by a group are related not only to the group's goals and resources but to the social context within which it operates. 'The repertoire is at once a structural and a cultural concept, involving not only what people *do* when they are engaged in conflict with others but what they *know how to do* and what others *expect* them to do' (Tarrow 1998: 30; emphasis in original).

Tarrow's analysis of the 'protest cycle' or 'cycle of contention' (Tarrow 1989: 8; 1998: 142) grounds the dynamics of social movements in repertoire innovation. In cycles of contention, Tarrow argues, social movements introduce new forms of action to society as a whole: 'Cycles of contention are the crucibles within which new cultural constructs born among critical communities are created, tested and refined' (Tarrow 1998: 145). Repertoire innovation promotes the assertion of new collective and the formation of a social movement. This can gain mass support if its tactical repertoire produces favourable results, altering the balance of political opportunities and constraints for the movement's constituency. The movement's organisations promote the diffusion of the new repertoire and its associated frames of meaning. The diffusion of its repertoire in turn promotes a reconfiguration of political opportunities in different geographical and social areas.

'It is the interaction among mass mobilisation, movement organisers, and traditional associations that produces a cycle of protest' (Tarrow 1989: 18). Existing organisations respond to the challenge of a successful repertoire by adopting it in a controlled form, functioning as gatekeeper to the political system. The social movements, or their surviving organisations, respond in turn by 'outbidding', offering ever more radical repertoires and frames. The protest cycle peaks with widespread diffusion and emulation, then declines as assimilation and neutralisation prevail; the outcome is the demobilisation of the new movements and the adoption of most of the new repertoire by existing organisations, creating 'a permanent expansion of the repertoire of democratic participation to include forms of action that were not present before' (Tarrow 1989: 67).

While the 'cycle of contention', driven by repertoire innovation, offers an encompassing framework for the study of social movement lifecycles, Tarrow presents it specifically as a means of analysing repertoire change: a cycle of contention is a point where new repertoires become available to society as a whole. As such, and despite occasional references to counter-mobilisation and repression, the model tends to assume that the outcome of a cycle of contention is positive: 'the new forms of collective action . . . become an enduring part of the repertoire of popular politics, surviving as a legacy of disorder for the next, and inevitable, cycle of protest' (Tarrow 1989: 348). Implicitly, the new repertoire and its supporting frames will have been successfully appropriated by a pre-existing organisation.

However, this is only one possible form of interaction between social movements and political institutions. Indeed, the apparent assumption that the new movement cannot enter the political system in its own right is questionable; Tarrow appears to assume a situation of relative political closure (a 'citadel' or 'court'), in which any political openings for a social movement are necessarily local and temporary, making the 'gatekeeper' role crucial. More importantly, even a movement met with relative political closure and a receptive 'gatekeeper' is likely to experience neither complete rejection nor complete acceptance. Rather, only some elements of the repertoire will be appropriated; others will be excluded by being framed as deviant or criminal. As noted earlier, Tilly shows a similar process taking place in the definition of the strike:

> during the nineteenth century workers, employers and governments engaged in a continuing struggle; its general outcome was not only the legalisation of some sort of strike activity but also the creation of shared understandings concerning the actions that *constituted* a strike. By no means all concerted withholding of labour qualified; the parties hammered out detailed rules excluding individual absenteeism, occupation of the premises, refusal to do particular jobs, and so forth. It is not simply that legislators made some forms of the strike legal and other forms of the strike illegal. That happened, too. But in the process the antagonists created – in practice as well as in theory – a sharper distinction between the strike and other forms of action with which it had previously often

been associated: sabotage, slowdown, absenteeism, the demonstration. A narrowed, contained strike entered the repertoire of workers' collective action. Pressure from the authorities shaped the particular contours of the nineteenth-century strike. (Tilly 1979: 134–5; emphasis in original)

Tarrow's model of a 'slow and patient' process of institutionalisation fails to register the conflictual quality of the process. Nor does he explore the possibility of unacceptable repertoire innovation: the emergence, through a cycle of contention, of a repertoire which is seen as beyond institutionalisation and is hence rejected outright by the movement's established interlocutors. The significance of this point is that the 'sharper distinction' described by Tilly cuts both ways: after the engagement between strikers and the authorities, some practices which had previously been associated with collective action were redefined as delinquency, disorder and violence. At the same time, crucially, the actions which had been legitimated were also redefined: irrespective of how they had originally been seen, these forms of action now ceased to be illegal. The key point here is that the classification of an action as criminal – or even as violent – is a Schutzian 'rule of thumb' resting on social consensus; and social consensus can and does change. Where new repertoires are met solely with rejection, however, repertoire innovation may seem to be no more than a transition from one form of delinquency to another, involving groups which were always doomed to criminality and marginalisation.

Contenders and gatekeepers: a model

In order to exploit the insights of Tarrow's model while avoiding these pitfalls, I propose a modified version of the cycle of contention. The starting point of the revised model is that episodes of contentious politics, and the social movements which are their most visible representative and result, arise within complex and differentiated societies: societies, in other words, in which multiple autonomous groups and institutions pursue their own interests while exerting different types and degrees of influence, both over individuals and over one another. This influence is mediated, and the social standing of these groups maintained, primarily through the values and meanings embedded in day-to-day practical activity, expressed in framing transactions.

There are four phases in a cycle of contention thus understood. In the phase of *innovation*, new forms of contentious politics appear. Contention develops when a group's structure of opportunity favours the development of a new contentious repertoire: a repertoire of action, in other words, which asserts the interests of the group in new and challenging ways. This repertoire becomes established as the group develops frames to support it; the first social movement organisations develop in this phase.

In the phase of *diffusion*, the new repertoire and its associated frames spread to different social and geographical areas through emulation and proselytisation. This phase may involve the extension of a single movement to multiple areas, the initiation of new but related movements, or a combination of both. Through the coexistence and competition of different variants of a set of frames, movement identities develop. This is also the phase in which movement organisations become established.

During this second phase the new movements gain influence within society; this inevitably runs counter to the influence of one or more established actor. The new movements attract support away from established organisations; their framings support oppositional identities; their repertoire discredits conventional repertoires. The influence exerted by the movements ultimately becomes incompatible with their exclusion from the political sphere. This is the peak of the cycle: the *engagement* between new movements and political society. In a relatively closed political system, the legitimacy of the movement is now at stake. Its key interlocutor is the 'gatekeeper': the organisation within the institutional sphere which represents the closest approximation to the values of a contentious movement. The gatekeeper's role is to stabilise the political system by neutralising external competitors. During the *engagement* phase, the gatekeeper recognises the movement as a potential antagonist and adopts a definite position with respect to its new repertoire.

This phase is conducted through framing processes, supporting the appropriation or rejection of different elements of the innovative repertoire. An inclusive gatekeeper responds to a contentious movement by appropriating its repertoire, in whole or in part, while realigning its own frames so as to occupy the movement's political space. This enables the movement's membership to gain most of the benefits of the new repertoire without the cost of rejecting the gatekeeper organisation. A hostile gatekeeper, by contrast, frames the new repertoire as politically inadmissible, realigning its own repertoire so as to remove any overlap with the movement. By raising the costs and jeopardising the benefits of the new repertoire, this makes the structure of opportunity of the movement's constituents unfavourable to the movement. In both cases the effect is to close down the tactical, ideological and organisational space available to the movement. The engagement phase is characterised by repeated assertions, rejections and reinterpretations of different elements of the movement's tactical repertoire, frames and membership. The framing and counter-framing process is iterative. In particular, the framing of a movement's membership as deviant or criminal will determine the counter-framing responses offered by the movement, forcing it either to challenge or to reinterpret the ascribed identity.

The final phase of the cycle is the *aftermath*. The nature of this phase depends on the outcome of the third phase. In a relatively open system, it is

marked by either the establishment or the marginalisation of the new movement, considered as a political force. The alternatives within a closed political
system are more stark. The movement's members may make a peaceful return
to the fold of conventional politics while the organisations of the political
sphere absorb the movement's repertoire. The result will be the decline of
the new movement, accompanied (as Tarrow argued) by an expansion of the
gatekeeper's own repertoire and political vocabulary. Less positively, the
defeat of the movement in the third phase will lead the movement's constituency not into newly legitimated versions of movement activism but into
enforced demobilisation. Meanwhile, a continuing commitment to the new
repertoire will ensure that a sizeable and determined minority remains committed to the movement; this group will ultimately be demobilised in turn,
possibly through direct repression. The result in this case is not only the loss
of the new repertoire of contention but a narrowing of the repertoire endorsed
by the gatekeeper, and hence of the repertoires available in the legitimate
political sphere.

It is worth stressing that these are extremes. In many cases the process
of engagement will be more ambiguous, combining areas of repertoire
expansion (and co-option of movement participants) and areas of repertoire
contraction (and repression). Moreover, there is a third possibility, in whch
the movement survives and retains its autonomy by lowering the level of
engagement and reframing its activities so as to avoid contested territory. Nor
is this final: when a new political opportunity structure arises, a previously
'self-limited' movement may spark a new round of engagement. Social
movements operating at lower levels of contention may go through repeated
phases of *diffusion* and *engagement*, with different elements of the movement's repertoire co-opted in successive *aftermath* phases.

This model of the cycle of contention has a number of features. Firstly, it
develops the concept of 'political opportunity structure' by situating it within
a model of society as composed of multiple sources of opportunity and constraint, political, economic and social. Secondly, the scope of repertoire
innovation is left open; the course of the 'engagement' phase remains to be
determined in individual cases, rather than being subject to prejudgments
associated with terms such as 'extreme' and 'violent'. Finally, this model
foregrounds the framing process. In a modification of Snow's original definition of framing as a discrete, explicit and conscious activity, framing is
understood to be a near-continual process, closely linked to practical activity
and material interests. The constitution of a movement with an internally
coherent identity and set of values is mediated through framing processes; so
too is the engagement between the movement and the gatekeeper organisation, which determines the subsequent course of the movement and the
ultimate expansion or otherwise of the mainstream political repertoire.

Thus redefined, framing processes are central to the cycle of contention, underpinning each of its other main elements. The cognitive challenge of a new tactical repertoire requires and in part generates its own supporting frames; on the other hand, innovative frames must be grounded in practical activity if they are not to become unsustainable. Opportunities for their part are doubly involved with framing processes. Firstly, social opportunities and constraints cannot be dissociated from the meanings and values through which they are articulated. The social relationships which constitute an actor's structure of opportunity are laden with meaning, and are built and maintained through framing processes. Secondly, opportunities must also be framed before they can be acted on: 'an opportunity unrecognised is no opportunity at all' (Gamson and Meyer 1996: 282). At both these levels, framing is a social process and hence potentially conflictual: 'Events are framed, but we frame events. The vulnerability of the framing process makes it a locus of potential struggle' (Gamson and Meyer 1996: 276).

In short, social movements develop through active, practically oriented, plural and conflictual processes of framing: framing is the process whereby movements formulate collective identities, validate mobilising structures, communicate repertoire innovation and recognise opportunities. As the growth of social movements leads a cycle of contention to enter the 'engagement' stage, an iterative exchange of framing transactions begins between the 'gatekeeper' organisation and the movement itself. Identities, structures and repertoires are modified and refined, defended or abandoned; meanwhile the gatekeeper modifies its own self-perception and self-presentation, promoting the expansion or contraction of its repertoire. An inclusive engagement will lead to political respectability and an expanded vocabulary of political participation; an exclusive engagement, like the one traced in this book, will lead only to criminalisation, repression and oblivion.

To end on a more hopeful note, this model of the interactions between social movements and the political sphere suggests two practical priorities for citizens of societies with relatively closed political systems (whether 'citadel' or 'court'). Firstly, institutional openness to influences from 'below' – or from outside the formal political sphere – is clearly a good in itself. A genuinely permeable system, whether 'machine' or 'network', will enable contentious social movements to sustain themselves and gain a political voice without depending on the changeable favours of an institutional gatekeeper. In a permeable system – a political arena without gatekeepers – the most outlandish ideology and the most radical gesture can coexist with programmes for the maintenance of the status quo, each free to gain whatever adherents they can attract. This is an ambitious but, I believe, an achievable goal. Secondly, in political systems which remain relatively impermeable, we should be alert to the power of the labelling mechanisms deployed by gatekeeper parties, in particular in the conditions of a negative engagement. We should be particularly wary of attempts to draw an authoritative dividing line between the 'moderate' and the 'extremist' elements of a social movement. A resolution passed by a national meeting of the 'movement of 1977' in April of that year concluded: 'The movement does not carry out excommunications and does not accept the criminalisation of any of its elements.' Neither should we.

References

Books and papers

Amyot, G. (1981), *The Italian Communist Party: the crisis of the Popular Front strategy*, London: Croom Helm

'Andrea' (1997), 'Intervista', in Del Bello (1997)

Asor Rosa, A. (1977a), *Le due società*, Turin: Einaudi

Balestrini, N. (1987), *Gli invisibili*, Milan: Bompiani

Balestrini, N. (1989), *L'editore*, Milan: Bompiani

Balestrini, N. and P. Moroni (1988), *L'orda d'oro*, Milan: SugarCo

Balestrini, N. and P. Moroni (1997), *L'orda d'oro* (revised edition), Milan: Feltrinelli

Becker, H. (1973), *Outsiders* (enlarged edition), New York: Free Press

Bhaskar, R. (1979), *The possibility of naturalism*, Brighton: Harvester

Biacchessi, D. (1998), 'Il caso Sofri: cronaca di un'inchiesta', online at www.sofri.org/biacchessi.html (accessed 30/1/2008)

Bobbio, L. (1988), *Lotta Continua* (second edition), Milan: Feltrinelli

Bonanno, A. (1979), *Del terrorismo, di alcuni imbecilli e di altre cose*, Catania: Edizioni di 'Anarchismo'

Caselli, G. C. and D. della Porta (1991), 'The history of the Red Brigades: organisational structures and strategies of action (1970–82)', in Catanzaro (1991a)

Catanzaro, R. (ed.) (1991a), *The Red Brigades and left-wing terrorism in Italy*, London: Pinter

Catanzaro, R. (1991b), 'Subjective experience and objective reality: an account of violence in the words of its protagonists', in Catanzaro (1991a)

Centro di Documentazione 'Fausto e Jaio' del centro sociale Leoncavallo (1995), 'Ipertesto sulle Brigate Rosse', www.ecn.org/leoncavallo/cdoc/br/index.htm, currently offline (accessed 30/4/2005)

Centro d'Iniziativa Luca Rossi (1998), 'Montaldi e l'esperienza proletaria', in L. Parente (ed.), *Danilo Montaldi e la cultura di sinistra del secondo dopoguerra*, Naples: Città del sole

Chaosmaleont (2001), 'Settantasette', online at http://web.tiscali.it/settanta7/ (accessed 30/1/2008)

Cohen, J. and A. Arato (1992), *Civil society and political theory*, London: MIT Press

Cossiga, F. (1997), 'Intervista', in Del Bello (1997)

Davis, H. and P. Walton (1983), 'Death of a premier: consensus and closure in international news', in Davis and Walton (eds), *Language, image, media*, Oxford: Blackwell

Deaglio, E. (1982), 'Intervista', online at www.xs4all.nl/~welschen/Archief/deaglio. html (accessed 30/1/2008)

Debray, R. (1967) (tr. B. Ortiz), *Revolution in the revolution?*, London: Pelican

Del Bello, C. (ed.) (1997), *Una sparatoria tranquilla: per una storia orale del '77*, Rome: Odradek

Della Porta, D. (1995), *Social movements, political violence and the state*, Cambridge: CUP

Echaurren, P. and C. Salaris (1999), *Controcultura in Italia 1967–1977*, Boringhieri: Turin

'Enne' (1977), 'Fare fight in Milan', *Zero* 4, December

Feltri, V. (1994), 'La religione antifascista', in F. Colombo and V. Feltri (1994), *Fascismo/Antifascismo*, Milan: Rizzoli

Feltrinelli, C. (2001) (tr. A. McEwen), *Senior Service*, London: Granta

Gamson, W. and D. Meyer (1996), 'Framing political opportunity', in McAdam, McCarthy and Zald (1996)

Giachetta, D. (1997), 'Il movimento del '77 e la violenza', *Per il Sessantotto* 11–12

Ginsborg, P. (1990), *A history of contemporary Italy*, London: Penguin

Goffman, E. (1974), *Frame analysis*, New York: Harper

Grandi, A. (2003), *La generazione degli anni perduti*, Turin: Einaudi

Grispigni, M. (1997), 'Elogio degli invisibili', in P. Virno et al., *Millenovecentosettantasette*, Rome: Manifestolibri

Hellman, S. (1988), *Italian Communism in transition*, Oxford: OUP

Istituto Carlo Cattaneo (2005), 'Serie storiche degli iscritti ai principali partiti politici italiani dal 1945 al 2004', online at www.cattaneo.org/italiano/archivi/iscritti/ Iscritti.xls (accessed 30/1/2008)

Jamieson, A. (1989), *The heart attacked: terrorism and conflict in the Italian state*, London: Marion Boyars

Kriesi, H. (1995), 'The political opportunity structure of new social movements: its impact on their mobilisation', in J.C. Jenkins and B. Klandermans (eds) (1995), *The politics of social protest*, London: UCL

Lumley, R. (1990), *States of emergency: cultures of revolt in Italy from 1968 to 1978*, London: Verso

Maccari, G. (2000), testimony to Commissione parlamentare d'inchiesta sul terrorismo in Italia e sulle cause della mancata individuazione dei responsabili delle stragi, 21/1/2000; online at www.parlamento.it/parlam/bicam/terror/stenografici/steno60a. htm (accessed 30/1/2008)

Malaspina, T. (1996), 'LC: sette anni di guai', *l'Espresso*, 5 September

Manconi, L. (1991), 'The political ideology of the Red Brigades', in Catanzaro (1991a)

Manfredi, G. (2003), 'Archivio anni '70', online at www.gianfrancomanfredi.com/anni70.html (accessed 30/1/2008)

Massari, R. (1979), *Marxismo e critica del terrorismo*, Rome: Newton Compton

McAdam, D. (1996), 'Conceptual origins, current problems, future directions', in McAdam, McCarthy and Zald (1996)

McAdam, D., J. McCarthy and M. Zald (eds.) (1996), *Comparative perspectives on social movements: political opportunities, mobilising structures, and cultural framings*, Cambridge: CUP

Mieli, P. (1984), '"Le Br non esistono", giurò la sinistra', *l'Espresso Archivio*, April

Miliucci, V. (1997), 'Intervista', in Del Bello (1997)

Monicelli, M. (1978), *L'ultrasinistra in Italia 1968–1978*, Rome: Laterza

Mordenti, R. (1997), 'Intervista', in Del Bello (1997)

Moroni, P. (1994), 'Origine dei centri sociali autogestiti a Milano', in Francesco Adinolfi et al., *Comunitá virtuali. I centri sociali in Italia*, Rome: Manifestolibri

Moroni, P. (1996), 'Un certo uso sociale dello spazio urbano', in Consorzio Aaster et al., *Centri sociali: geografie del desiderio*, Milan: Shake

Morucci, V. (1994), *A guerra finita: sei racconti*, Rome: Manifestolibri

Moss, D. (1989), *The politics of left-wing violence in Italy, 1969–85*, London: Macmillan

Napolitano, G., interviewed by E. Hobsbawm (1977), *The Italian road to socialism*, London: Journeyman

Negri, A. (1978), *Il dominio e il sabotaggio*, Milan: Feltrinelli

Novaro, C. (1991), 'Social networks and terrorism: the case of *Prima Linea*', in Catanzaro (1991a)

Piazza, G. (1987), 'Movimenti e sistema politico: il caso di Autonomia operaia' (thesis), Università degli studi di Catania

Piccioni, F. (1997), 'Intervista', in Del Bello (1997)

Pizzo, A. (1997), 'Il carcere e le mie tre vite' (interview with Pasquale Abatangelo), *Il Manifesto*, 20 April

Potere Operaio (1973), 'Primavalle: incendio a porte chiuse', formerly online at www.tmcrew.org/memoria/primavalle/ (site closed by Polizia Postale 27/5/2003; details at www.tmcrew.org/sequestro.html)

Progetto Memoria (1994), *La mappa perduta*, Milan: Sensibili alle foglie

Progetto Memoria (1996), *Le parole scritte*, Milan: Sensibili alle foglie

Rivera, A. (1997), 'Intervista', in Del Bello (1997)

Ruscoe, J. (1982), *The Italian Communist Party, 1976–81*, London: Macmillan

Salaris, C. (1997), 'Dada dappertutto', in *Derive Approdi* 15

Sassoon, D. (ed.) (1978), *The Italian Communists speak for themselves*, Nottingham: Spokesman

Sassoon, D. (1981), *The strategy of the Italian Communist Party*, London: Frances Pinter

Sassoon, D. (2003), 'Reflection on a death foretold: the life and times of the Italian Communist Party', in R. Leonardi and M. Fedele (eds) (2003), *Italy: politics and policy*, vol. 2, Aldershot: Ashgate

Sayer, A. (1984), *Method in social science: a realist approach*, London: Routledge
Schutz, A. (1962), *Collected Papers I: the problem of social reality*, The Hague: Martinus Nijhoff
Schutz, A. (1964), *Collected Papers II: studies in social theory*, The Hague: Martinus Nijhoff
Sciascia, L. (1987) (Italian publication 1978), 'The Moro affair', in L. Sciascia (tr. S. Rabinovitch), *The Moro affair and the mystery of Majorana*, Manchester: Carcanet
Shore, C. (1990), *Italian Communism: the escape from Leninism*, London: Pluto
Silj, A. (1977), *Mai più senza fucile!*, Florence: Vallecchi
Snow, D. and R. Benford (1988), 'Ideology, frame resonance, and participant mobilisation', in B. Klandermans, H. Kriesi and S. Tarrow (eds) (1988), *From structure to action*, London: JAI
Snow, D. and R. Benford (1992), 'Master frames and cycles of protest', in A. Morris and C.M. Mueller (eds), *Frontiers in social movement theory*, New Haven: Yale University Press
Tarrow, S. (1983), *Struggling to reform: social movements and policy change during cycles of protest*, Cornell University, Western Societies Paper no. 15
Tarrow, S. (1989), *Democracy and disorder: protest and politics in Italy 1965–1975*, Oxford: OUP
Tarrow, S. (1991), 'Violence and institutionalisation after the Italian protest cycle', in Catanzaro (1991a)
Tarrow, S. (1996), 'States and opportunities: the political structuring of social movements', in McAdam, McCarthy and Zald (1996)
Tarrow, S. (1998), *Power in movement* (second edition), Cambridge: CUP
Tilly, C. (1979), 'Repertoires of contention in America and Britain, 1750–1830', in M. Zald and J. McCarthy (eds) (1979), *The dynamics of social movements*, Cambridge, MA: Winthrop
Tronti, M. (1964), 'Lenin in Inghilterra', *Classe operaia* 1
Villoresi, L. (1997), 'Così andò quella mattina del 1977, quando Lama . . .', online at www.xs4all.nl/~welschen/Archief/lama.html (accessed 30/1/2008)
Vinciguerra, V. and M. Cipriani (1999), *Oppressione, repressione, rivolte: storia d'Italia dal 25 luglio 1943 ad oggi*, online at www.fondazionecipriani.it/Kronologia/introduzione.htm (accessed 30/1/2008)
Virno. P. (1997; originally published 1994), 'Do you remember counter-revolution?', in Balestrini and Moroni (1997)
Vite, F. (2002), '"Ma chi ha detto che non c'è". 1977: storie invisibili' (thesis), Università degli studi di Siena
Wright, S. (1996), 'Negri's class analysis: Italian autonomist theory in the seventies', *Reconstruction* 8
Wright, S. (1998), 'Missed opportunities – New Left readings of the Italian Resistance', in A. Davidson and S. Wright (eds) (1998), *'Never give in': the Italian Resistance and politics*, New York: Peter Lang
Wright, S. (2002), *Storming heaven: class composition and struggle in Italian autonomist Marxism*, London: Pluto

Zald, M. (1996), 'Culture, ideology and strategic framing', in McAdam, McCarthy and Zald (1996)

Newspapers

Anon. (1969a), 'ROMA IN PIAZZA MANIFESTA', *l'Unità*, 28 February, p1

Anon. (1969b), 'La politica del bastone', *l'Unità*, 28 February, p1

Anon. (1972a), 'Grave provocazione alla Sit-Siemens di Milano', *l'Unità*, 4 March, p2

Anon. (1972b), 'I sindacati condannano l'atto teppistico alla Siemens di Milano', *l'Unità*, 7 March, p4

Anon. (1972c), 'Nel momento più adatto', *l'Unità*, 17 March, p1

Anon. (1972d), 'La macchina della provocazione', *l'Unità*, 19 March, p1

Anon. (1972e), 'Aberranti posizioni di un gruppo estremista', *l'Unità*, 22 March, p6

Anon. (1973a), untitled picture caption, *l'Unità*, 24 March, p4

Anon. (1973b), 'Torino: bloccata dai 60 mila lavoratori la Fiat Mirafiori', *l'Unità* (Milan edition), 30 March, p4

Anon. (1973c), 'Un altro episodio della strategia della tensione/Una grava provocazione a Torino: sequestrato un dirigente della FIAT', *l'Unità*, 11 December, p1

Anon. (1973d), 'Nemici della classe operaia', *l'Unità*, 11 December, p7

Anon. (1973e), 'Una grande iniziativa del Comune democratico/Trasporti pubblici gratuiti da lunedì a Bologna', *l'Unità*, 29 March, p1

Anon. (1974a), 'Indegna gazzarra davanti a un negozio Coop', *l'Unità* (Milan edition), 13 October, p11

Anon. (1974b), 'Una trama evidente', *l'Unità*, 20 April, p1

Anon. (1974c), 'Sugli omicidi nella sede MSI puntuale la provocazione', *l'Unità*, 20 June, p1

Anon. (1974d), 'Il comunicato N. 8', *l'Unità*, 25 May, p5

Anon. (1975a), 'Assemblee, cortei, scioperi in tutto il Paese', *l'Unità*, 28 September, p2

Anon. (1975b), 'Il rischio delle mezze verità', *Corriere della Sera*, 9 July, p1

Anon. (1975c), 'Sulla base della versione fornita dalla polizia sull'uccisione di Anna Maria Mantini/Insufficienti e improvvisate le misure prese per catturare i "nappisti"', *l'Unità*, 10 July, p5

Anon. (1975d), 'Teppismo e provocazione', *l'Unità*, 29 September, p2

Anon. (1975e), 'Gli operai cacciano dall'Innocenti un gruppo di provocatori', *l'Unità*, 30 October, p16

Anon. (1976a), 'Un gesto criminale rivendicato per telefono dalle Brigate rosse/Reparto della Fiat-Mirafiori distrutto a Torino da un incendio', *l'Unità*, 4 April, p1

Anon. (1976b), 'Anche l'incendio alla FIAT Rivalta è parte di un piano provocatorio', *l'Unità*, 15 April, p1

Anon. (1976c), 'Gravissimo episodio dopo l'attacco di un commando all'ambasciata di Spagna/Roma: la polizia spara ed uccide un passante', *l'Unità*, 15 March, p1

Anon. (1976d), 'Chi era Francesco Coco', *l'Unità*, 9 June, p4

Anon. (1976e), 'Nessun alibi', *l'Unità*, 15 March, p1

Anon. (1976f), 'MANOVRE PROVOCATORIE PREORDINATE DA GRUPPI DI TEPPISTI/Degenera in violenze e vandalismi il festival di 'Re Nudo' al Parco Lambro', *l'Unità* (Milan edition), 29 June, p6

Anon. (1976g), 'Il comunicato della segreteria del PCI', *l'Unità*, 9 June, p1

Anon. (1976h), 'È evidente la mano di un'unica organizzazione terroristica/Stessa tecnica per tutti gli attentati', *l'Unità*, 15 April, p5

Anon. (1976i), 'Proposte iniziative unitarie di vigilanza', *l'Unità*, 15 April, p5

Anon. (1976j), 'Due giorni di collettivi e assemblee permanenti alla Statale occupata/ Molta confusione all'happening dei circoli giovanili milanesi', *l'Unità*, 29 November, p4

Anon. (1976k), '"RAID GASTRONOMICO" DI GIOVANI ESTREMISTI/Mangiano con l'autoriduzione in sette trattorie e pizzerie', *Corriere della Sera* (Milan edition), 28 June, p16

Anon. (1976l), 'Tensione in centro/"Espropriata" salumeria', *l'Unità* (Milan edition), 28 November, p11

Anon. (1976m), 'I sedicenti "Circoli giovanili", seminando caos e devastazioni, hanno perseguito fino all'ultimo il loro disegno provocatorio', *l'Unità* (Milan edition), 8 December, p10

Anon. (1976n), 'Il piano dei disordini studiato e preordinato a tavolino dai gruppi teppistici', *l'Unità* (Milan edition), 8 December, p10

Anon. (1976o), 'Il centro presidiato da migliaia di agenti e carabinieri/Provocazioni e gravi incidenti sconvolgono il centro di Milano per la "prima" alla Scala', *l'Unità*, 8 December, p1

Anon. (1977a), 'Cinismo e falsa pietà', *l'Unità*, 5 July, p1

Anon. (1977b), 'Milano: oggi al Lirico le conclusioni di Berlinguer', *l'Unità*, 30 January, p1

Anon. (1977c), 'Comunicato della Segreteria del PCI', *l'Unità*, 12 March, p1

Anon. (1977d), 'Gli "autonomi": una lunga storia di violenze squadristiche', *l'Unità*, 19 February, p5

Anon. (1977e), 'Roma sconvolta da gravi scontri/Uccisa una ragazza di 19 anni', *l'Unità*, 13 May, p1

Anon. (1977f), 'L'attacco alla manifestazione', *l'Unità*, 19 February, p5

Anon. (1977g), 'A cosa mirano le violenze degli "autonomi"/Le provocazioni a Torino contro studenti e operai', *l'Unità*, 5 March, p1

Anon. (1977h), 'Premeditazione', *l'Unità*, 22 April, p1

Anon. (1977i), 'Studenti aggrediti e feriti a Torino da squadristi "autonomi" armati', *l'Unità*, 3 March, p1

Anon. (1977j), 'Condannate a Torino le violenze provocate da bande teppistiche', *l'Unità*, 5 March, p6

Anon. (1977k), 'A Bologna 150 mila in piazza/Contro-corteo degli studenti', *Corriere della Sera*, 17 March, p1

Anon. (1977l) 'La discriminante democratica è decisiva', *l'Unità*, 18 March, p1

Anon. (1977m), 'La violenza non vincerà', *l'Unità*, 7 April, p1

Anon. (1977n), 'Chiarezza sulla posta in gioco', *l'Unità*, 28 July, p1

Anon. (1977o), 'Al servizio della reazione', *l'Unità*, 20 June, p1

Anon. (1977p), 'Il calcolo del terrorismo', *l'Unità*, 3 June, p1

Anon. (1977q), 'Come rispondere', *l'Unità*, 17 November, p1

Anon. (1977r), 'Lo stesso disegno', *l'Unità*, 30 November, p1

Anon. (1977s), 'Tensione e tafferugli tra gli autonomi isolati', *l'Unità*, 3 December, p6

Anon. (1977t) 'Il documento della Direzione', *l'Unità*, 20 February, p1

Anon. (1977u), 'I presunti "brigatisti rossi" sorpresi presso Verbania dai carabinieri', *l'Unità*, 30 April, p5

Asor Rosa, A. (1977b), 'Forme nuove di anticomunismo', *l'Unità*, 20 February, p3

Barbarisi, G. (1976), 'Tribuna Aperta/Che cosa rispondere all'autoriduzione', *Corriere della Sera* (Milan edition), 28 November, p15

Berlinguer, E. (1976), 'Il rapporto di Enrico Berlinguer al Comitato centrale e alla Commissione centrale di controllo', *l'Unità*, 19th October, p8

Berlinguer, E. (1977a), 'Chi sono i nuovi fascisti', *La Stampa*, 23 September, p1

Berlinguer, E. (1977b), 'Si agita l'anticomunismo per impedire il cambiamento', *l'Unità*, 19 September, p3

Berlinguer, E. (1977c), 'Con chi non è possibile dialogare', *l'Unità*, 23 September, p1

Biagi, E. (1977), 'Che guerra è la loro?', *Corriere della Sera*, 17 November, p1

Borgese, G. (1976), 'MILANO: DECLINO DI UN MITO GIOVANILE/Così muore il festival pop', *Corriere della Sera*, 29 June, p9

Botta, G. (1977) 'FERMA CONDANNA IN TUTTO IL PAESE/Dell'aggressione squadristica di Roma', *l'Unità*, 19 February, p1

Bufalini, P. (1977), 'Difesa dell'ordine democratico contro la violenza eversiva', *l'Unità*, 15 March, p1

Buozzi, G. (1977), 'Radio Alice: sequestrate tutte le apparecchiature', *l'Unità*, 14 March, p4

Cavallini, M. (1977a), 'Un convegno per tre giorni sul filo di precari equilibri', *l'Unità*, 26 September, p1

Cavallini, M. (1977b), 'IL CONVEGNO DI BOLOGNA GIRA A VUOTO', *l'Unità*, 25 September, p1

Cavallini, M. (1977c), 'Attacchi eversivi alle fabbriche/Come reagiscono gli operai', *l'Unità*, 21 June, p1

Criscuoli, S. (1977), 'Occorre un fermo impegno unitario contro ogni attacco antidemocratico/ROMA E BOLOGNA SCONVOLTE PER ORE DA ASSALTI DI GRUPPI TEPPISTICI ARMATI', *l'Unità*, 13 March, p1

d'Adda, G. (1974), 'La Procura: "Si indaga in ogni direzione"', *Corriere della Sera*, 8 October, p2

d'Adda, G. (1975), 'Innocenti: i sindacati prospettano l'occupazione dello stabilimento', *Corriere della Sera* (Milan edition), 30 October, p12

Enriotti, B. (1977a), 'In un clima sereno ma attento', *l'Unità*, 23 September, p1

Enriotti, B. (1977b), 'Indetta a Bologna per mercoledì una grande manifestazione unitaria', *l'Unità*, 14 March, p1

Enriotti, B. (1977c), 'Finito senza incidenti il raduno di Bologna/È prevalsa la forza della democrazia', *l'Unità*, 26 September, p1

Fasola, A. (1975), 'Non "prendere" ma conquistare', *l'Unità*, 29 October, p2

'R. Ga' (1972), 'Gli squadristi alla conquista d'un posto nei circoli "rossi"', *l'Unità*, 5 March, p7

Ghiara, M. (1977), 'Non basta far tacere le P.38', *l'Unità*, 20 May, p1

Irdi, L. (1976), 'Assalto ultrà alla'ambasciata di Spagna/La polizia spara, un passante rimane ucciso', *Corriere della Sera*, 15 March, p1

Lama, L. (1973), 'Una dichiarazione di Lama', *l'Unità*, 11 December, p7

Lama, L. (1977), 'Il discorso di Luciano Lama', *l'Unità*, 19 February, p4

'm. m.' (1977), 'SI APRE QUESTA MATTINA A ROMA/Oggi l'assemblea nazionale delle Facoltà in lotta', *L'Unità*, 26 February, p1

Madeo, A. (1969), 'DIMOSTRAZIONI DI STUDENTI E ATTIVISTI COMUNISTI', *Corriere della Sera*, 28 February, p1

Maldonado, T. (1977), 'In quale altra città del mondo?', *l'Unità*, 27 September, p2

Marrocco, M. (1977), 'Due uomini di coraggio', *Corriere della Sera*, 3 July, p1

Marzullo, K. (1969), 'ROMA IN STATO D'ASSEDIO', *l'Unità*, 28 February, p2

Marzullo, K. (1977), 'Nel capoluogo emiliano vigorosa risposta popolare alle provocazioni', *l'Unità*, 13 March, p1

Moncalvo, G. (1977), '"Anche il fascismo cominciò con la marcia su Bologna"', *Corriere della Sera*, 20 September, p1

Monti, V. (1974), 'Erano ultrà i due banditi ammazzati durante l'assalto in banca a Firenze', *Corriere della Sera*, 31 October, p11

Monti, V. (1977), 'Ancora incidenti nel capoluogo emiliano', *Corriere della Sera*, 14 March, p1

Napolitano, G. (1972), 'Responsabilità DC', *l'Unità*, 21 May, p1

Nava, M. (1976) 'CHI SONO E COSA VOGLIONO I PROTAGONISTI DEL RADUNO/Parlano come pellirossa i giovani arrabbiati alla Statale', *Corriere della Sera* (Milan edition), 28 November, p16

Padellaro, A. (1977), 'Cossiga preannuncia una legge per chiudere i covi del terrorismo', *Corriere della Sera*, 8 February, p1 [bylined 'A. Pa.']

Palumbo, A. (1977), 'Tritolo a Milano sui binari del metrò/Fallita l'azione degli autonomi a Roma', *l'Unità*, 20 May, p1

Paolucci, I. (1977a), 'Una spirale di sanguinosi provocazioni', *l'Unità*, 20 September, p1

Paolucci, I. (1977b), 'Terrorismo e paura', *l'Unità*, 5 May, p1

Passanisi, E. (1976), 'Chi vuole turbare la stagione dei contratti', *Corriere della Sera*, 4 April, p1

Pecchioli, U. (1977), 'Unità contro gli attacchi eversivi', *l'Unità*, 14 March, p1

Petruccioli, C. (1977a), 'Ricomporre il mosaico', *l'Unità*, 15 May, p1

Petruccioli, C. (1977b), 'Far vivere una democrazia di massa e andare alle radici della protesta giovanile/GLI INSEGNAMENTI DI BOLOGNA', *l'Unità*, 27 September, p1

Potere Operaio (1972a), 'Un rivoluzionario è caduto', in *Potere Operaio del lunedì*, 26 Marcha

Potere Operaio (1972b), 'Morte di un poliziotto', in *Potere Operaio del lunedì*, 28 May

Rivolta, C. (1977), '"I Lama nel Tibet", il leader in fuga', in *La Repubblica*, 19 February

Savioli, A. (1977a), 'Centinaia di migliaia di metalmeccanici e di cittadini alla manifestazione di Roma/UNA FORZA OPERAIA IMMENSA/reclama una svolta politica, economica, morale/e si erge a sicuro baluardo della democrazia', *l'Unità*, 3 December, p1

Savioli, A. (1977b), 'Conoscere il terrorismo per poterlo sconfiggere' (interview with Ugo Pecchioli), *l'Unità*, 14 December, p1

Scagliarini, A. (1977a), 'La città sconvolta per ore dalle violenze', *l'Unità*, 12 March, p1 [bylined 'a. s.']

Scagliarini, A. (1977b), 'Le indagini confermano: era un piano preordinato', *l'Unità*, 18 March, p5 [bylined 'a. s.']

Scagliarini, A. (1977c), 'Necessaria l'unità delle forze democratiche contro la spirale delle violenze e delle provocazioni/Gravissimi scontri a Bologna', *l'Unità*, 12 March, p1

Scagliarini, A. (1977d), 'Bologna: violenze già preordinate dai centri propagandistici eversivi', *l'Unità*, 19 March, p1 [bylined 'a. s.']

Scagliarini, A. (1977e), 'Ancora scontri ieri sera: 50 arresti', *l'Unità*, 14 March, p4

Sposito, L. (1973), 'Fanatici della guerriglia urbana', *Corriere della Sera*, 11 December, p10

Tornabuoni, L. (1977), 'Si sposta sul piano politico la polemica per la guerriglia contro Lama all'università/Il segretario della CGIL: "È nuovo fascismo"', *Corriere della Sera*, 19 February, p1

Tortorella, A. (1972), 'La destra e i sui alibi', *l'Unità*, 19 May, p1

Tortorella, A. (1977a), 'Saper vedere il pericolo', *l'Unità*, 19 February, p1

Tortorella, A. (1977b), 'Lavoro intellettuale e metodo della libertà', *l'Unità*, 31 July, p1

Veca, S. (1977), 'Qualcosa di nuovo è in marcia', *l'Unità*, 27 September, p2

Index